TAKING HUMOUR SERIOUSLY

When do we laugh? Why do we laugh? What makes us stop? What does 'humour' consist of? Listen to any everyday conversation: it is full of the constant interruptions and detours of humour. Look at the TV schedules for any evening – how many of the programmes are comedies or contain a degree of humour? Humour and comedy invite our pleasure at every step we take – they are absolutely integral to any culture. In *Taking Humour Seriously*, Jerry Palmer argues that we must take humour seriously (as well as humorously) or fail to understand a fundamental part of culture.

Taking Humour Seriously unravels the reasons why humour is a challenge for every different theoretical approach. It is multi-dimensional, it is part of personality and part of our cognitive and emotional processes; it is subject to social rules governing appropriate behaviour on different occasions. It is part of literary and audio-visual narrative; it is subject to moral and aesthetic judgment, and it is a rhetorical instrument. Palmer argues that it is only through investigating those separate dimensions that we can begin to understand the phenomenon of humour.

Taking Humour Seriously examines the role humour and comedy play in many different types of society. It also looks at the many different approaches to its study – from Freud to anthropology, from literary criticism to biology. Finally it considers its limits – the things that prevent humour and comedy from delivering their usual pleasures – and explores the aesthetic value of those pleasures.

Jerry Palmer is Professor of Communications at London Guildhall University and the author of numerous studies of popular culture, fiction, film and comedy. His books include *The Logic of the Absurd: On Film and TV Comedy* and *Potboilers: Concepts, Methods and Case Studies in Popular Fiction*.

TAKING HUMOUR SERIOUSLY

Jerry Palmer

London and New York

First published 1994
by Routledge
11 New Fetter Lane, London EC4P 4EE

Simultaneously published in the USA and Canada
by Routledge
29 West 35th Street, New York, NY 10001

Typeset in 10/12pt Times by
Ponting–Green Publishing Services, Chesham, Bucks
Printed in Great Britain by
T.J. Press (Padstow) Ltd, Cornwall
Printed on acid free paper

British Library Cataloguing in Publication Data
A catalogue record for this book is available from
the British Library

Library of Congress Cataloging in Publication Data
Palmer, Jerry.
Taking humour seriously/Jerry Palmer.
p.   cm.
Includes bibliographical references (p.) and index.
1. Wit and humour–History and criticism.
2. Comedy–History and criticism.
I. Title.
PN6147.P7   1994
306.4'81–dc20   93–15323

ISBN 0–415–10266–9 (hbk)
ISBN 0–415–10267–7 (pbk)

Some years ago I was told about a documentary on Danish television, about a South American tribe who had embraced Christianity, but with some reservations. As a result, members of this tribe wore a thin cord round their necks so that if they went to Heaven and didn't like it, they could say to God: 'Look, I killed myself.'

This book is dedicated to the anonymous joker who thought that one up, for his or her exemplary combination of risk-taking and intelligence.

CONTENTS

INTRODUCTION

Taking humour seriously: the paradox is striking.[1] Why take humour seriously at all? The comedian Ken Dodd is reputed to have said that the difference between himself and Freud was that Freud had never had to do a performance at the Glasgow Palais on a wet Monday night. The implication is that amateurs should keep their mouths shut, and perhaps that learned writing on the subject of jokes is simply a waste of everybody's time. And yet Ken Dodd is also reputed to have read Freud, and to have a substantial library of eminently serious books about humour – which he himself takes very seriously. No doubt humour is a serious subject for a comedian because that's how he or she earns his or her living. It is a serious subject for others because it is an element of most human communication: listen to any conversation and it is full of jokes, puns, humorous allusions, word play for the sake of it, etc. Moreover, humanity is the only species with a sense of humour, zoologists tell us, confirming Aristotle's insight that laughter is a distinguishing feature of our species. Perhaps one day a software house will create a computer programme that invents original jokes; but the computer will not be a fully human entity until it enjoys them (if then).

The paradox also points to another dimension of this essay, the question of aesthetic discrimination: to argue that some comedy is art is to take it very seriously indeed. More exactly, aesthetic judgment is a dimension of debates about humour and comedy which is constantly on the sidelines of what I am writing, and occasionally central to it. In its traditional form its effect is to exclude most of what I am concerned with here, on the grounds that it is worthless, for humour and comedy are in part distinguished from each other by discrimination. In general, in the twentieth century, aesthetic judgment is held to be worthwhile because refinement of taste makes for a better sort of person, and culture 'improves' a society. But taste is also a feature of all acts of consumption, including the consumption of services such as humorous performance, and in this sense taste has little in common with what aesthetic refinement is traditionally held to be. Nonetheless, taste is an integral part of culture in the sociological sense of the word, the set of norms and values which regulate behaviour in a society; or more generally, that society's 'way

1

of life'. In aesthetic terms, there is perhaps little point in taking most humour seriously; but in cultural terms there is every point: what people laugh at, how and when they laugh is absolutely central to their culture, and it is not necessary to be able to show some putative effects of the act of laughing at such-and-such – for instance, lack of respect for the object of derision – to make this case. In any event, that is why I take humour seriously. But the question of pleasure and seriousness does not stop there. Aesthetic value is not just a question of cognition, but of affect as well: beauty gives pleasure, even if not everything that gives pleasure is usually thought of as beauty.

In an article about humour and comedy in ancient Greece and Rome, Russell (1991) asserts that people laughed at much the same kind of things then as they do now: in a cab in the USA he was told a story about a current event that reproduced a story in Homer, and similar jokes about lovers and cuckolds are to be found in Homer, in the medieval French *fabliaux* and current comedy. Certainly these examples illustrate the thesis; yet another example Russell gives fits less easily. At the state funeral of the Emperor Vespasian (who was renowned for his meanness) the actor who was playing Vespasian asked how much the procession was costing; when the senators told him the cost was ten million sesterces, he said 'Give me a hundred thousand and throw me in the Tiber!' (1991: 99–100). Certainly jokes about meanness (not to mention indignity) abound nowadays, and no doubt have been commonplace in the two millennia separating us from Vespasian. But something else is jarring in this joke: the occasion. Is it possible to imagine that at the State funeral of – say – Queen Elizabeth II someone among the officials would perpetrate such a joke? By the standards of our culture this is very disrespectful humour on an occasion when we would demand high seriousness. Even if the theme of the joke is continuous across two millennia, the occasion certainly is not.

What is at stake in Russell's argument is well known: do meaning and value derive from the self-contained systems of cultures, each of which is the only possible source of judgment about such meanings and values? Or is there some overarching logic to history – for instance, 'progress' or 'human nature' – which makes judgment across the boundaries of cultures possible? Clearly, insofar as humour and comedy are concerned Russell is on the anti-relativist side: the apparent permanence of jokes about cuckolds and meanness suggests the validity of anti-relativism. But the theme of a joke is only one of its dimensions: the occasion on which it is told and the identity of the teller and the audience constitute another dimension, and in this instance it would seem as though there is a significant difference between ancient Rome and our times. Now the argument about universalism and relativism in culture is not one to be settled in a few words, nor even in a single book; but it will become clear in the course of this essay that neither of the traditional answers make much sense in the light of what we can learn from the study of humour and comedy. We will return to the implications in the Conclusion, but we can already see that distinguishing between different dimensions of a joke is one way of going beyond the simple either/or of relativism and universalism: perhaps there are universal joke themes; or even if there are no universal themes perhaps there is a single psychological or semiotic mechanism to be found everywhere, in all humour and comedy. But regardless of whether this is true or not, the occasions on which particular types of joking are appropriate may well vary considerably between different societies. We will see that there are several such considerations.

By 'humour' I mean everything that is actually or potentially funny, and the processes by which this 'funniness' occurs. Just saying this immediately raises two obvious problems: first, there is the question of how to identify the object of study; second, the scope of an essay with this pretension: how can anyone, no matter how arrogant – not to say megalomaniac – pretend to analyse everything that is actually or potentially funny? The very claim is hilarious.

Of course I am not making such a claim. When I define 'humour' as anything actually or potentially funny, I do not mean I am going to discuss everything that has been, or might have been, found funny by someone; I mean that I am not in principle, in advance, excluding any such phenomenon from discussion – as I might do if I was only interested in jokes and the unconscious, as Freud was, or if I was only interested in literary comedy, as many critical and historical texts are. Beyond that I am asserting a possibility: that all such phenomena may have something in common, their funniness, and that this is a legitimate object of study. 'Humour' is the label I have chosen for this unitary quality – largely because 'funniness' is such a clumsy word, and the original noun form of 'funny' ('fun') has too wide a meaning to be any use here.

My purpose is the ambition of much work in cultural studies: to see how particular cultural phenomena exist in several dimensions at once, and how an account of those dimensions enhances our knowledge. Humour and comedy are studied in most human science or humanities disciplines: there is an anthropology of humour, a sociology and a psychology of it, theorising it is basic to modern Freudianism, and to film and literary criticism its study is as central as the study of tragedy or realist narrative. In each of these fields there is an abundant literature on the subject – for anyone approaching the subject (seriously!) for the first time, a real *embarras de richesses*. Yet, as one reads the material, something very striking emerges: until roughly ten years ago, remarkably few of these specialists in their own disciplines bothered to read material deriving from any of the others: the psychology of humour rarely said anything about its features that derive from the social structure, sociologists often ignored anthropological discoveries, neither showed the least interest in the discoveries about the nature of comic narrative made by the aesthetic disciplines and the latter proceeded, on the whole, in equally bland ignorance of behavioural and social scientific considerations. The rare exceptions to this generalisation were all the more striking for their rarity.

Yet it is easy to show how conceptual problems that arise within single-discipline treatments of the subject could be resolved by the removal of the blinkers. For example: psychologists have often observed that humour is apt to fail when it is directed at something which is strongly approved of by the audience – an obvious example is jokes about some community leader who is well-liked. Yet it is well known that professional comedians can get laughs from people about exactly such topics. One resolution of this paradox is probably that psychology experiments tend to be conducted using single jokes in isolation, whereas professional comedians are extremely careful about placing their jokes in sequence so that each has the maximum impact, and audiences are well 'warmed up' before any controversial material is introduced: even slight acquaintance with the structure of narrative would reveal the pertinence of such considerations. Another possible resolution of the paradox is that professional comedians perform on occasions which are defined as comic in advance, by the nature of the occasion; psychology experiments do not benefit from this predisposing circumstance, under which there may be an increased licence to mock what is otherwise approved of. Perhaps it is simply that the majority of psychological experiments into humour are done in the USA, and the professional comedians I have in mind are British: the 1987 cancellation of the British satirical programme *Spitting Image* on American TV suggests that either American humour or its public regulation may be different in this respect from British.

Over the last ten years a large body of studies has emerged which is at least in part interdisciplinary. Anthropologists and film critics use Freud, psychologists refer to historical studies, literary critics take account of social frameworks, etc. No doubt a fair proportion of the readers of this essay will have considerable knowledge of this new tradition, without which I could not have written these pages. Much of the writing during this period has been concerned with what is clearly the most central problem that any such study must address: *what is* humour (or laughter, or comedy, or a joke)? It seems clear that the turn to interdisciplinarity is largely motivated by the recognition that this fundamental question cannot be answered without it. Yet once one makes this jump out of discipline confines, one is struck by the conceptual difficulties that arise: each discipline starts from a different set of preconceptions. Those disciplines based on textual commentary – literary criticism or film studies, for example – tend to proceed on the basis that there is some feature of texts which is responsible for humour. Psychologists look for mental processes involved in the production or reception of humour. Sociologists and anthropologists look at the social processes within which it occurs.

However, threading their way through these different concerns is a set of questions which between them invite analysis of everything that is important about humour. Those questions are:

– When do we find something funny?
– Why do we we find something funny?
– What makes us find something funny?
– What prevents us from finding something funny?

No doubt, put in this abrupt form, these questions are not readily comprehensible. The question 'when' refers to the notion that finding something funny is in part a product of the occasion on which the something happens: finding something funny is much more likely under socially appropriate circumstances than under socially inappropriate ones, and knowledge of this distinction seems to be part of everyday culture. Part I explores the ramifications of this idea, and especially the various ways – across historical and anthropological change and difference – in which social occasions act as cues to participants to find something funny.

The question 'why' refers to the notion that mirth and laughter have a function in the human scheme of things, that we can explain what is happening by seeing how it is functionally related to our behaviour in general. For example, it is possible that at least in modern Western societies men and women have different 'senses of humour'; if so, this may be because humour is functionally related to gender. Part II analyses the evidence of functions.

The question 'what makes us' (which is not readily distinguishable in common-sense terms from the question 'why') is about the structure of humour: what is going on, either in the mind or in the thing that we find funny, which provokes us to find it funny. Texts are at least in part responsible for laughter by the way they place it within narrative, and different classes of texts place it very differently. Part III deals with various approaches to the analysis of the structure of humour.

The last question is perhaps the easiest to understand, although it is the least debated: humour is a very fragile thing, and every professional comedian knows about the fear of dead silence, the joke that has dismally failed; Part IV suggests that understanding comic failure is as important as understanding its success. Here I try to systematise our information about the limits to humorousness.

I make no pretence to have answered these questions, at least not in any thorough fashion; what I have tried to do is to show what answers have been given, to explore the pitfalls hidden in them and to show what is at stake in answering each of them. In the end, therefore, I am not trying to answer the question 'What is humour?' because I do not think it *is* any one thing: it appears to exist in a series of different dimensions, and it is only by analysing each of them, in its own right, that we can approach the subject sensibly.

These considerations refer to the scope of what I am dealing with. The question of the identity of what is being studied revolves around whether there is indeed a unitary quality to which the label 'funniness' can legitimately be applied. Here language is scarcely reassuring. The problem of what word to use when referring to particular funny events in the world is well known. What is the difference between 'joke' and 'jest', between 'funny' and 'comic', between 'mirth' and 'jocularity', between 'wit' and 'satire'? Out of curiosity I started making a list of words which are all labels for funniness, and came up with the following in short order: laughter, mirth, joke, jest, witticism, wit, comedy, satire, parody, farce, clowning, buffoonery, jollity. ... At this point I realised that I was in for a long trek and turned to Roget's *Thesaurus*: 'funny' in the index refers the reader to 'witty 839 adj' and 'funny 849 adj' (plus some other senses that are not relevant here). Paragraph 839 contains some 250 words or expressions that in one way or another refer to the phenomenon of funniness, and refers the reader to roughly another twenty paragraphs in the *Thesaurus*; at this point I gave up on this approach, since the point was already obvious: too many words, most of them overlapping with another at some point. And this is only within English: as soon as one tries to translate, the problems multiply. Probably the best known example is the translator's note in the *Standard Edition* of Freud's book on jokes (Freud, 1960). The German title uses the word *Witz*, translated throughout the book as 'joke' even though the English term 'wit' is another obvious candidate:

> In ordinary English usage 'wit' and 'witty' have a highly restricted meaning and are applied only to the most refined and intellectual kind of jokes. The briefest inspection of the examples in these pages will show that 'Witz' and 'witzig' have a far wider connotation. 'Joke' on the other hand seems itself to be far too wide and to cover the German 'Scherz' as well.
>
> (Freud, 1976: 35)

This is a problem because Freud regularly uses the word *Scherz* (which the *Standard Edition* translates as 'jest') to mean something fundamentally different from *Witz*. *Witz* also means 'ingenuity', 'wit' in the older English sense of sharp perception pithily but unfunnily expressed, and colloquially can even mean 'sense' or 'purpose'. On several counts 'Witz' and 'joke' are not really equivalents because German and English semantics do not impose sense upon phenomena in the same way (whether they *create* phenomena in the same moment – e.g. in the process of *différance* – is a debate I prefer to avoid). The French translation (Freud, 1930) translates *Witz* sometimes as *mot d'esprit* (which would usually be regarded as the equivalent of the English 'wit'), sometimes as *esprit* by itself, which means 'mind' as well as 'wit', and when it means 'wit' refers to the mental quality rather than its product in the form of 'witticisms'.

Lurking behind translators' notes lies a fundamental problem: how do we know that something is a joke? For instance, the story I quoted as an epigraph to this book, and which I interpreted as a joke: I cannot be sure that it was intended as such, though I would like to think it was. No doubt we have all had the chastening experience of being told we have missed a joke, and of finding things unintentionally funny. If we cannot be sure that we recognise the dividing line between humour and non-humour we cannot have any idea whether there are an enormous number of phenomena in the world that we haven't even started to analyse because we have failed to notice their existence. Profusion reveals the perfusion of signs, and readily breeds confusion: every decoding is another encoding, to use the deconstructionist slogan. It is impossible to explore the meanings of all the labels that refer to the many possible varieties of experience that some evidence suggests has been found funny by somebody, sometime. What I have tried to do is to analyse the mechanisms that underlie these varieties of funniness, mechanisms which are variously social, psychological and semiotic. For example, the term 'satire' either refers to a particular genre at times in history when there really was such a thing as a system of genres, or it refers more generally to humour that criticises or victimises someone or something; I have not analysed satire, but I have given accounts both of elements of genre systems as they apply to comic texts, and of the role of the butt in humour: the role of the butt and the role of genre systems are fundamental, the changing meanings of the word 'satire' are arguably a surface indication of these deeper processes. The only long-term consistent distinction within the realm of the funny that I have constructed is the distinction between comic texts, formalised either in recorded textuality or in performance (or both), and more or less unscripted humour in everyday life: for the former I have reserved the term 'comedy'. Even here I readily admit that the distinction is far from watertight: the 'standardised' joke ('Have you heard the one about ...?'; 'There was this bloke ...') as told in everyday situations is in fact a kind of script, and its delivery has something in common with performance even though its performers rarely enjoy the privilege of the performance space of the stage. Despite this inconsistency, it seems worth preserving the distinction on the grounds that the phenomenology of the two situations is different: the existence of the performance space, or of textuality, creates a different relationship between what is said and the participants in the exchange, to what obtains in interactions structured only by the framework of 'ordinary everyday life'. Since I have reserved the term 'comedy' for texts and performances, and am using the term 'humour' for a unitary quality that includes both everyday life and formalised texts and performances, it's clear that one of my central assumptions is that everyday culture supplies texts and performances with one of their central categories, funniness.

But I cannot by definition have any certainty that the things I am analysing are in fact typical of some unitary quality called 'funniness', and we shall see that there are good reasons for imagining that there is in fact no such thing.

Part I

OCCASIONS FOR HUMOUR

1

JOKING RELATIONSHIPS

Consider this situation: it is the day of your grandfather's funeral, you are in the service, with all your relatives and your grandparents' friends. Suddenly you are seized with the overwhelming urge to tell a joke. Standing on one side of you is your brother, on the other your aunt; do you tell the joke? And if so, to which of the two? Let us also assume, for the sake of argument, that you are young and male, and the joke you want to tell is a 'dirty' joke. Assuming a minimal degree of sociality on your part, and an averagely reticent relationship with your aunt, the answer is likely to be either neither of them, or your brother; there is a place, a time and a list of normal interlocutors for 'dirty' jokes in our culture, and neither family funerals nor most family members figure on the list.

The situation is of course caricatural: an extreme version of circumstances where this levity is considered inappropriate. Other such circumstances might include church services in general, military parades, job interviews (though there would probably be exceptions here), being interrogated by the police, first meetings with strangers anywhere other than a pub or a party. And we may note that although a joke about sex was specified, in order to make the outcome obvious, it is largely the case that any joke, regardless of its theme or manner of delivery, would be similarly taboo in any of the social circumstances listed here. Such knowledge is part of the common sense of our culture, part of the set of rules for polite conduct which we all learn in the ordinary course of growing up, without any special, institutionalised form of instruction being necessary. No doubt the details vary from region to region, from social class to social class, and to some extent from person to person or family to family. Even more, it is equally clear that deviation from these rules occurs: people do tell jokes under inappropriate circumstances, sometimes no doubt through inadequate awareness of the rules governing the occasion – i.e. the rules observed by the majority of those present – sometimes no doubt in order to subvert the nature of the occasion: say, the dignity of a religious or military ceremony. But we should note that for the subversion to take a form satisfactory to the subverter it is likely that the joke would have to be shared: that is why, in all likelihood, if you did tell a joke at your grandfather's funeral it would be more likely that your brother was chosen as audience rather than your aunt.

This example implies various principles involved in humour. It indicates that the social identity of the occasion is problematic, that the identity of the participants (including the relationships between them) is problematic, and that the theme of the joke may be problematically related to these sociological dimensions. More generally, it indicates a principle fundamental to humour, and long ago formulated by Douglas: that a joke must not only be *recognised* as such, but also *permitted* (1968: 366). We shall see in Part IV that the question of permission is less simple than first sight suggests, but for the moment we may content ourselves with the observation that permissibility is indeed an integral dimension of humour.

Part I of this book is concerned with the extent to which the social identity of occasions and participants determines the existence of humour. The caricatural opening example indicated a thoroughgoing prohibition on humour which is relatively rare in our culture: of all the situations that make up the normal course of everyday life, there are relatively few where jokes are really out of the question – although no doubt rather more where certain categories of joke are outlawed: anti-Semitic jokes at a bar-mitzvah, jokes in favour of cowardice at a regimental dinner. Similarly, there are few if any categories of person with whom joking is out of the question – even if you cannot tell your aunt a dirty joke during a funeral, it is certainly well within the bounds of normality to joke with her on other occasions. Now let us think of the opposite possibility: are there any situations where jokes are *obligatory* in our culture? Clearly it would be very strange if a professional comedian said or did nothing funny during the course of a performance and if you are at a party or in the pub with a group who are all telling jokes or making funny remarks, total abstinence from humour might be regarded as anti-social; otherwise it is rare to find circumstances where joking behaviour is obligatory, let alone to find a type of relationship where the partners are obliged to joke with each other (see Sykes, 1966).

Assuming this brief outline sketch of the social circumstances of joking in our culture is approximately correct, let us make a comparison with another form of social organisation where the circumstances surrounding joking are very different. In many tribal societies joking occurs predominantly within the framework of 'joking relationships': that is to say, the list of people with whom one may indulge in joking behaviour is regulated, and therefore the occasions on which such behaviour is possible are regulated by the occasions on which one meets these people. In this form of social organisation of humour we see very clearly revealed something which is much more difficult to perceive on the basis of an examination of our own society alone: that the *occasions for* humour may be analytically independent of the contents or structure or psychological function of humour. Without prejudging whether this is universally so or not, we may use the literature on 'joking relationships' in tribal society to clarify what could be meant by a dimension of humour based solely on the occasions on which it is permissible; thereafter we may ask ourselves whether this dimension of humour is to be found elsewhere as well, or whether it is a feature of tribal society only.

In the first summary analysis of joking relationships, Radcliffe-Brown (1952) suggests they have several basic features. In the first instance, they are relationships in which 'one is by custom permitted, and in some instances required, to tease or make fun of the other, who in turn is required to take no offence' (1952: 90). This stresses what is by far the most important aspect of the relationships in question: that they are non-optional, or prescriptive, that it is not up to the individual to choose whether joking is appropriate or not under these circumstances, with two exceptions. First, any individual has potential joking relationships with a very large number of others, of which only a small number may in fact be realised due to lack of opportunity. Second, if neither partner (on any given occasion) initiates joking behaviour the relationship of joking partner may nonetheless continue without any hiatus or suggestion of failure. The second feature of these relationships is that they are based in the kinship pattern or some other objective feature of the social structure in question. Although there is wide variation between societies in this respect, the commonest joking relationships appear to be between siblings-in-law and between grandparents and grandchildren; they are also reported between categories of relation such as cross-cousins (i.e. cousin by marriage), uncle and nephew/aunt and niece, and even between vaguer kin such as all those with a common ancestor at the distance of great-grandparents or beyond, for instance the 'duuse' relationship reported by Barley (1983: 92f.). Joking relationships are also to be found between entire clans or tribes, between villages, between groups of men who were all circumcised at the same time or groups of women all of whom started menstruating at the same time. We shall see that place in kinship patterns is central to Radcliffe-Brown's explanation of joking relations.

The third element in Radcliffe-Brown's theory is the observation that the forms of behaviour expected of joking partners are such 'that in any other social context it would express and arouse hostility', and that it is the context of the fixed joking relation which ensures that offence is neither given nor taken. Although much joking behaviour between joking relatives consists essentially of witticisms or teasing, it is frequently the case that it goes far beyond these limits: Dogon joking partners exchange the grossest insults and commonly talk about each other's parents' sexual organs when meeting; the Kaguru 'think it witty to throw excrement at certain cousins' and the Lodagaba dance grotesquely at joking partners' funerals; at Tarahumara funerals the deceased's joking partner will 'dance up to a simulated corpse made of old clothing and kick at it while making lewd jokes and gestures', and Luguru joking partners will even lie down in the grave, demanding payment before allowing the funeral to proceed and will make sexual

13

advances to women mourners. Tarahumara grandfathers will chase their granddaughters with a corncob simulating a penis and pretend to rape them, and the girls retaliate in kind, pretending to grope under the old man's loincloth; parallel behaviour is observed between grandson and grandmother, although usually in a more restrained version (Douglas, 1968: 364–5; Kennedy, 1970: 41f.; Christensen, 1963: 1317f.). Under all of these circumstances no member of the relevant culture would dream of finding the proceedings anything but hilarious. These few examples indicate the extent to which the behaviour normal within joking relations would be deemed totally unsuitable under any other circumstances, for in none of these societies would such behaviour be tolerated except in this context. Clearly, also, such behaviour would not be tolerated in modern Western society, regardless of setting and regardless of whether the intention was humorous or not; the level of transgression acceptable in tribal societies' joking relationships is clearly – insofar as these examples are typical – far beyond what is acceptable in the industrial world. However, this should not lead us to imagine that *any* form of behaviour would be possible in joking relationships: although the ethnographic literature has little to say on this subject, it is known that in some circumstances only certain parts of the body may be touched in obscene horseplay, but not others (see Sharman, 1969; Apte, 1985: 32).

Three other features of the behaviour theorised by Radcliffe-Brown demand comment; although he himself does not refer to them, it is clear from the literature he summarises that they are common. First, the tendency for joking behaviour to be aggressive and/or obscene is often held to indicate that the primary source of joking relations is sexual. Brant (1948), for example, argues on the basis of a survey of some 220 societies that joking relations arise most frequently, although not exclusively, between those who are potential sexual partners. Second, such behaviour is public behaviour, both in the sense that it is not in any sense furtive, and in the more important sense that there is usually an audience (Kennedy, 1970: 52) – this feature underlines how fully integrated into the social structure such behaviour is. Third, as Apte points out (1985: ch. 2), there is considerable dissymmetry between male and female in these relationships. Although joking relationships are extremely common between men and men, and between men and women, they are rare between women and women in tribal societies, although more frequent in peasant societies, where female modesty prevents joking when men are present but allows it when men are absent. Clearly this refers us to the dimension of power in humorous situations (see Part IV).

Radcliffe-Brown's theory aims to explain this behaviour by assigning it a function – specifically, a latent function, since (as we shall see) the function in question is often denied by participants. What should be stressed in this context is how closely related function is to the identity of the participants. In brief outline, his theory is that joking relations are a form of 'permitted disrespect' which enters the social structure at points of stress, points where some aspect of the relationship involves both 'disjunction and conjunction' between the participants – for example marriage, where the wife's family and the husband's family have different interests *vis-à-vis* their offspring, and where relationships that demand respect (for example, the relation of younger to elder) may run counter to relationships where discord – e.g. economic competition – would be likely. Joking relationships, he argues, arise at such ambivalent points in the social system, and their nature, the ambiguous relationship between friendship and hostility that is intrinsic to joking – or at any rate to the forms observed here – both expresses and contains the ambivalence that derives from the positions that participants occupy in the social structure. The functional aspects of this theory will be discussed in the pages devoted to the 'functions' of humour (Part II); what should be stressed in the present context are two features of his theory:

1 This theory of joking makes no reference at all to the contents of jokes, and no explicit reference to the form, or process of humour (although it is clear that Radcliffe-Brown is assuming a common-sense model of it).
2 Humour is explained entirely on the basis of the social relationships between the participants. That is to say, it is clear that for Radcliffe-Brown humour functions psycho-socially: it performs its *social* function through its *psychological* function, through the way in which it affects the mind – it relieves specific forms of tension; yet this tension is assumed to arise entirely from the nature of the social relationships between people, with no individual variation. And indeed this is necessarily so, for the whole point about joking relations is precisely the fact that they are largely non-optional – not just in Radcliffe-Brown's theory, but according to an enormous body of empirical research. Assuming the accuracy of the empirical research, this would suggest that the occasions on which humour occurs, as well as the sociological relationships between the participants, are a matter which is largely independent of either the structure or the function of humour.

The adequacy of Radcliffe-Brown's model has frequently been challenged, primarily on grounds related to its functionalism (see Part II). However, one criticism commonly made in recent comments refers directly to the relevance of the notion of occasions for humour. It is based on Radcliffe-Brown's assumption that he is able to recognise what a joke is. It is axiomatic that laughter does not necessarily mark the place of a joke – it might mark embarrassment, for instance. Radcliffe-Brown assumes that non-offence at something potentially offensive combined with laughter necessarily indicates a joke; in this he is making an assumption that would probably be valid in our society, but it is perhaps a piece of ethnocentrism. Only if we could be sure that there was some universal feature to jokes that made them clearly recognisable could we be sure that our assignment of a given event to the category 'joke' was correct. For example, the story about the recent Christians quoted as an epigraph to these pages: there it is interpreted as a joke, but it is difficult to know whether it was intended as such, or as a serious device. It is a commonplace of studies of joking relationships to assert that when x insults y and no offence is taken, what has occurred is a joke – that is to say, it is asserted that the insult is the phenomenal form of a relationship whose essence is that it is a joking relationship; but perhaps – some anthropologists argue – it is really in essence an insulting relationship, whose phenomenal form is that of a joke: the point is that in Western society we would be right in interpreting the relationships between the two categories of action in these terms, but in another social structure there can be no certainty that such an interpretation is correct (Apte, 1985: 34ff.). What this criticism points to is the necessity of working out the relationship between occasions for joking and the structure of humour; we shall return to this point.

Radcliffe-Brown's theory of joking relationships was based largely on studies of tribal social structures and was probably not intended to have any application outside of this framework. Clearly the feature of the social structure responsible for this exclusive focus is the fact that joking relationships are institutionalised – or 'ritualised' – for this is a feature that is not to be found in modern Western industrial societies. Now this focus produced both the theory's main strength and a considerable weakness. The strength is that, despite the criticisms of detail that have been offered, the empirical evidence clearly reveals that we are indeed in the presence of a set of institutionalised relationships which provide a framework for humour; its existence suggests that the psychological and/or semantic structure of humour is not – as is often supposed – the most fundamental layer of humour, for here we are in the presence of an independent variable in the humour equation, its setting or occasion; this directs our attention to the question of the role that setting, or occasion, or social relationships between participants may play in the overall nature of humour, not only in tribal society, but in other forms of society as well. The concomitant weakness is that the exclusive focus on the institutional setting for humour blinded Radcliffe-Brown to the question of the *form* of the joke, i.e. its semantic and/or psychological structure, and this produced two further problems, both analysed in Douglas' (1968) 'The Social Control of Cognition'. The first of these is that Radcliffe-Brown is forced to ignore the content of the jokes that he refers to, in the sense that even if he notes them, the contents are practically irrelevant to the functional account of joking relationships (except in the mimimum common-sense manner referred to above); the result – which constitutes the second problem – is that the jokes in question become well-nigh incomprehensible, and have to be referred to cultural relativism for an explanation: if *we* (Westerners) cannot understand them, this is because we are not members of the appropriate culture, and we re-enter the problem of whether we are right in assigning any given action to the category 'joke' or not.

The critical observation that Douglas makes of Radcliffe-Brown's theory is the starting point for her own theory. The form of the joke, she holds, is universal, and she hopes that by finding a relationship between this universal form and the occasions on which joking is a permitted, or even obligatory activity, it will be possible to ascribe a universal function to joking. Her definition of joke form is conventional: 'It brings into relation disparate elements in such a way that one accepted pattern is challenged by the appearance of another which in some way was hidden in the first' (1968: 365).

This challenge is simultaneously ascribed a psychological modality: it is the relaxation of conscious control in favour of some pressure or other from the subconscious, a conception derived from Freud (see Part II). But this universal form and function must be related, Douglas insists, to the joking occasion: jokes occur – i.e. are permitted as well as attempted – at points in the social structure where something in the social relationship in question has the same form as the joke form. Thus, if the bishop gets stuck in the lift, suddenly the mildest sally becomes hilarious, because the social situation mirrors exactly the joke form – the subversion of one pattern by another which was hidden in it. Another example is taken from observation of the relationships normal on Norwegian fishing boats, where the net boss, who supervises the actual fish catching process, has an area of authority which is entirely distinct from that of the captain: the captain commands until the nets are lowered, the net boss commands once they are down. While the captain is in command the net boss constantly makes jokes, but once he is in command the joking stops; the technicalities of fishing and the division of expertise that goes with them are such that a pattern of partially subverted authority is normal, and the joke form mirrors this, therefore joking is possible; once the situation is changed, it no longer is.

In this context it is possible to give ritual or prescriptive joking a new meaning: the combination of the joke form and the kind of occasion when it is possible affirms something Douglas regards as a feature of all social structures: the sense of community, as opposed to the sense of structure. By structure she means the formal skeleton of any society: its laws, fixed customs, kinship system, etc.; community refers instead to the entirely informal network constituted by fellow-feeling, and joking is especially apt to express this since it both mirrors the subversion of established patterns and is based in pleasure, specifically the pleasure that derives from the relaxation of conscious control in favour of the unconscious: 'Laughter and jokes, since they attack classification and hierarchy, are obviously apt symbols for expressing community in this sense of unhierarchised, undifferentiated social relations' (1968: 370). The strength of Douglas' theory derives from the manner in which she brings together joke form – the semantic structure of jokes – jokes' psychological function and jokes' place in the social structure. Concomitantly, problems seem to arise from the very scope which is the argument's strength. In the first place, it seems questionable whether joking always does in fact mirror specific social situations: apt though her examples

17

are, and easy though it is to find similar examples oneself, especially in the world of work, they are subject to counterfactual examples which undermine their typicality. For example, one common setting for joking in industrial society is a group of friends sitting around doing nothing much else – maybe drinking or eating. In what sense does this situation have a structure that is isomorphic with that of the joke (the subversion of an accepted pattern)? It is difficult to find such a structure here, unless one regards the sheer fact of 'doing nothing much' as undermining some feature of social structure; but 'leisure' is a thoroughly institutionalised feature of modern society (see Mulkay, 1988: 170–3). Similarly with joking considered as a form of professional entertainment: although it is quite true that much professional joking is satirical, and thus does in fact tend to undermine established patterns of respect ('hierarchical classification', in Douglas' terms), the actual social situation – paid entertainment – does not seem to do so: it is a normal part of the division of labour in a highly differentiated society. It seems likely, on the basis of these considerations, that the rigid division between the world of leisure and the world of work, so typical of industrial society and so untypical of tribal society, may undermine the universality of the patterns which Douglas sets out to establish. Second, we have already seen the difficulties that beset assigning events to the category 'joke'; if it was in fact the case that joke structure has universal features, then Douglas' case would be strong; however, such an assertion could only be validated on the assumption that the anthropologist was in fact successfully recognising as jokes all events that were so classified by participants, and not including unsuitable events in the classification. But it is very difficult to do this because by definition counterfactual examples would be invisible.

These comments have been aimed at an analysis of forms of joking behaviour which are premised largely, or even entirely – it is not clear which of these is the case – upon the relationship between the individuals concerned, and the evidence considered has been drawn largely from the study of tribal societies. At this stage we can ask the question: what relevance, if any, does such a model have for the study of other social structures, and especially industrial society?

The concept of joking relationships has been used by sociologists and anthropologists in the study of various sub-groups in industrial society. In general, the drift of such studies has been to explore whether particular social frameworks allow forms of joking behaviour which might not be allowed in other circumstances, and/or to assign a social function to joking behaviour. Here it must be stressed that it is easy to confuse these two emphases: it is a commonplace of studies of humour in modern society that the form of the joke allows topics to be broached that might otherwise remain condemned to silence; this is a question of the social function of joking, not of the occasion for joking, since clearly it is the form of the joke that is determinant here, not the nature of the occasion on which the joking behaviour occurs. Of these two foci, it is the former which is closer to the concern of the present chapter, and the second will be considered under the heading of the function of humour (Part II).

In a large Glasgow printworks this pattern of joking relationships was found (Sykes, 1966): men of all ages joked together, routinely, in a thoroughly obscene fashion, as did old men and old women (the young/old divide occurred at around 25, or at marriage); young men and old women would engage in mildly obscene banter but only if the exchange was initiated by the women; old men would routinely engage in highly obscene banter with young women, and 'were permitted a great deal of licence in publicly touching, kissing and petting the young women', which caused no resentment on the part of the women (1966: 190). Between young men and young women, however, the situation was significantly different, for although *suggestive* banter was normal, gross obscenity was not, and any form of public bodily contact was discouraged – although of course the same young people were known to be 'petting' in private in various parts of the factory. Correlatively, although public sexual horseplay was normal between old men and young women, any attempts at *private* bodily contact between them, initiated by the men, was heavily disapproved of by all.

Two conclusions may be drawn from this study. The first is that this implies a different conception of the relationship between joking and sexuality than the one commonly accepted in earlier ethnographic studies of tribal societies, where it was found that joking was normal between potential sexual partners (Christensen, 1963; Brant, 1948): the Glasgow study shows that joking is more prevalent between those who are not potential sexual partners – this is why public sexual contact and gross obscenity is permitted between old men and young women, but private contact forbidden, and the obverse is true of young women and young men. More exactly, perhaps, we should say that the nature of the joking relationships in question is related to the type of humour that is possible under various circumstances, since Sykes' study refers to one brand of humour only, sexual humour. The second conclusion is that despite differences of detail between this study and earlier ethnographic studies, an essential point is agreed: that joking – or at least joking about sex – is indeed a matter of occasion, defined by the relationships between the participants, and indeed by the setting, for it seems intuitively likely that what is tolerated at work might well not be tolerated at home, or even on other public social occasions; this conclusion is supported by a study of joking between longshoremen in Portland, Oregon, which found that the types of obscene joking, insults and nicknames which were all considered normal in the work environment were considered grossly offensive elsewhere (Apte, 1985: 54). Intuitively it seems likely that this principle is extendable outside the immediate contexts observed here: writing in *Woman's Own* magazine in 1982, Agony Aunt Claire Rayner berates feminists who refuse to accept that joking about sexuality is anything other than chauvinism, if not sexual harassment; this suggests that contexts in which sexual joking is acceptable are reasonably widespread in our culture, and that within these contexts refusal to accept a joke as a joke is considered an inappropriate response. But it seems unlikely that the principle of occasion controlling joking behaviour could be extended to cover non-sexual joking in an industrial population with the same degree of clarity as is revealed in Sykes' study. It is also questionable whether the broad humour described would be acceptable in other social settings in industrial society, for in both cases we are talking about local working-class sub-cultures. (For a consideration of the question of power in these situations, see Part IV.)

Coser (1960) discusses the position of joking in staff meetings in a psychiatric hospital. Here the nature of the humour is inseparable from the hierarchical positions of the participants. Senior members of the hierarchy make humorous remarks at the expense of their juniors, and these are taken as a form of mild reproof, thus negotiating the potentially awkward boundary between the status of colleague and the status of subordination; junior members of the hierarchy make self-deprecating jokes and outside consultants make jokes at the expense of the patients; ancillary staff do not joke, but laugh at others' jokes. Seniors are more likely to engage in humour than the others. Both the frequency and the direction of the humour indicate that position in the hierarchy exerts a high degree of control over the nature of the humorous exchanges involved, and thus in general that the identity of the participants is integral.

Handelman and Kapferer (1972) distinguish between two possible co-ordinates for joking situations, one of which corresponds approximately with the traditional conception of joking relationships – which they call 'category-routinised' joking – and the other of which implies a new conception of them: 'setting-specific' joking. In the former circumstance, some feature or other of the relationship between the individuals involved in the joking activity indicates to all concerned that forms of behaviour that would otherwise be offensive are to be taken as a joke. One such relational feature would be the joking relationships studied by Radcliffe-Brown among others, but it would not be the only possible feature. A joking sequence between two workers in a Zambian copper mine is explained in terms of the tribal relationship between them, which is traditionally a joking one, but another sequence involves a group in a workshop in Jerusalem, where an insult is accepted as a joke not because the general nature of the social relationship between the participants includes the notion of a joking relationship, good for all occasions and all topics, but because it has become conventional among the group in question to regard this particular insult as a joke – it has effectively become a comic ritual, or game. In the second circumstance – 'setting-specific' joking – the acceptance that a given piece of behaviour is to be considered a joke has to be negotiated on each and every occasion, for there is nothing in the relationship between the participants which indicates that it is to be considered such. Such indications must therefore be found in the structure of the behaviour itself, and must be interpreted as such before it can be commonly agreed that what has just occurred is indeed a joke: otherwise it may be interpreted as stupidity or offensiveness.

In either of the frameworks Handelman and Kapferer establish it is clear that there has to be a cue that a joke is occurring, even if there is a prescriptive relationship between joking partners, as is the case among the Zambian mineworkers. And it is clear from the details of the event as reported why this has to be so: the men in question, who are traditionally joking partners, are also workmates, and under these circumstances it is out of the question that all activity between them should consist of joking; in this framework, therefore, it is essential that some cue should indicate that there is a transition – in intent at least – from seriousness to joking. Now this point is heavy with implications for the traditional theory of joking relationships, for either in the societies studied all activity between joking partners was joking, or there must have been some cue to indicate the transition from one activity to the other. Radcliffe-Brown indicates that the former is not the case, since joking relationships do not lapse through non-activation; thus cues must be normal. From this follow two further points:

1 given that a cue is proffered, is it possible for the recipient of the cue to then refuse to accept that what subsequently occurs is a joke?
2 what is the nature of the cue? Is it necessarily humorous itself, or is it some other feature of the situation in question?

In the context of a prescriptive relationship, it ought to be impossible for the cue recipient to refuse an invitation to joke: the non-optional nature of the relationship ought to ensure a uniform response. However, in practice there are well-attested details of such refusals. A British Colonial Office official reported an instance where a woman brought a case of assault against a man who publicly and without permission manhandled her; the man's defence was that they were joking partners, and on many previous occasions had joked together. It was easily established that they belonged to tribes that were traditionally in a joking relationship, and that they had in fact joked together previously. However, the woman insisted that she perceived the incident as an assault, and the magistrate found the man guilty, with the joking relationship admitted as a mitigating circumstance (Pedler, 1940). Is it possible to reduce this ambiguity? Pedler suggests that her reaction might be comprehensible in terms of fear that people might think the joking partner was her lover, and studies of joking relationships sometimes suggest that whereas in the past such relationships gave licence for sexual liaisons, the cumulative impact of Christianity and Western colonial norms of behaviour had reduced this licence (Christensen, 1963: 1319). Possibly, then, the ambiguity recorded in this example refers to the ambiguous impact of Westernisation.

What is the nature of the cue? *Ex hypothesi*, the cue must indicate that what is about to occur is humorous. It would seem that there are two basic ways in which a cue could be constructed, on the basis of either the situation in which the humour is to occur, or some feature or other of the statement or actions which constitute the humour. In the former case, it is possible that joking relationships are only activated on specified occasions: for example, Kennedy's (1970) study of the Tarahumara Indians suggests that joking only occurred during beer parties and at funerals, and this model might be more generally applicable; unfortunately, however, most studies of joking relationships do not consider this possibility. If this was the case, the combination of a prescriptive joking relationship and a prescriptive or permissive joking context would serve as a cue for humour. Clearly neither of the cases referred to above fit this description. In the second case, it would be some feature of the actions or statements involved which would identify them as humorous. In the incident which Handelman and Kapferer discuss (1972: 498ff.), the mineworker enters a room in the plant, which is not part of his work-station, swinging a dead bird in his hand in such a way as to call attention to it; it is a bird which members of one tribe employed there regard as carrion, but others regard as edible. It is the incongruity of the bird in the work setting, combined with the man's intrusion into another room, which defines the episode as potentially humorous. At the most general level, therefore, it seems likely that the cue must contain some element that is itself related to humour: the cue, in other words, must have a structure which is logically and analytically distinct from the nature of the occasion which is defined as humorous. If this is not the case, then we must ask in what sense the cue is a cue to humour, and we would risk infinite regression, in which the cue would be identified as a cue to humour because what followed was humour, but where the progression into humour would only be comprehensible on the basis that the cue to humour was recognised as such by participants: a severe tautology. The key element in the cue would appear to be some form of transgression of whatever is recognised as normality in the context in question; Mulkay suggests that markers such as body language, tone of voice, the use of an inappropriate discursive mode (e.g. excessive seriousness or a fake accent) would be typical of this process (1988: 47f.). We shall return to this question when we consider the structure of humour in Part III.

To these formal studies we can add the informal observation that two types of relationship in our society seem particularly apt for joking: grandparent/grandchild and friendship in general. Of course, neither relationship prescribes joking, but in both cases joking seems to arise very naturally and spontaneously. In the case of friendship we may guess that this is because friendship is the only relationship in our society which is entirely optional and reciprocal, and is thus free of the constraints imposed by any formal framework such as family, workplace, etc. In the case of grandparents, it is likely that the absence of the parental duty of discipline combines with the closeness of family ties to provide a very particular setting. In addition, certain settings are especially apt: weddings, parties, single-sex gatherings of colleagues or neighbours, pubs or bars, etc. In each case – with the exception of the wedding – alcohol and informality promote the same forms of behaviour: relaxation of the purposiveness of work and some of the inhibitions of hierarchy; partial disregard for calculations about the effects of actions; all combine to produce a certain easiness. In the case of weddings, it is the purpose of the ceremony and perhaps especially the traditional legitimation of sexual pleasure (even if now largely superfluous in this respect) which produces this mood. No doubt these points are obvious: their importance is that they underline the autonomy of the dimension of occasion, for it is the setting as much as the structure of humour that explains what happens here.

At this point the notion of prescriptive frames for joking has delivered as much as it is capable of. We have acquired the following information:

1 It is empirically established that prescriptive frames for joking do exist, for despite all the caveats concerning the viability of early research on the subject, this has never been seriously questioned.
2 These relationships certainly exist on a wide scale in tribal society, even if it is uncertain exactly what their meaning is, or exactly how they are imbricated with other elements in the social structure.
3 It appears that there are analogous relationships, or situations, in industrial society, although it is far from clear how widespread they are and to what extent they are non-optional.
4 It seems likely that the existence of prescriptive relationships is not in itself a sufficient explanation of the structure of humorous occasions, unless we accept the unlikely additional hypothesis that all behaviour between joking partners is joking behaviour; indeed, it is clear from empirical studies that joking partners are also involved in a series of other activities – e.g. ritual exchange of gifts, responsibility for marriage arrangements (Labouret, 1929; Barley, 1983: 83).
5 It follows from this that some sort of cue mechanism is essential. The cue mechanism may be a, marker of the type that Mulkay suggests, it may be the stipulation that what is about to occur is a joke, or it may be the semantic structure of the activity in question. At the same time it is also clear that the cue mechanism by itself is by no means necessarily sufficient to mark the occasion as humorous: the sociological dimension is integral to the achievement of humour, but is not in itself sufficient.

The next two chapters will be devoted to one way in which the sociological nature of an occasion can constitute such a cue mechanism: ceremonies or similar occasions where it is stipulated in advance that what will happen is humorous.

2

CLOWNS AND RELIGION

In the previous chapter we have seen how the occasion on which humour is achievable may be defined by the relationship between the participants. We have also seen certain problems connected with the notion that the relationship between participants could be the sole defining factor in settling that the occasion was appropriate for humour, problems centring around the cue properties of relationships and statements or actions. Now in a sense, of course, it is inevitable that any definition of an occasion as appropriate for any sort of activity will be made on the basis of the relationships between the participants, since any such definition is necessarily a social act and all social phenomena are relational in character. However, the defining characteristic of the relationships examined in the previous chapter is that they were reciprocal: in any joking partnership what is sauce for the goose is also sauce for the gander; if A can make a joke with B, then by definition B can make a joke with A. Thus any occasion for humour defined as such on this basis is one in which all participants may act in the same way. (Such an analysis omits the crucial question of power: see Part IV, below.)

In this chapter another form of defining an occasion as suitable for humour will be explored: a definition based not on a reciprocal relationship between participants, but one based on the identity of one group of the participants, in other words a situation in which while there is certainly a relationship between the participants – since this is a priori true of all social situations – the relationship is non-reciprocal, based on two groups within the participants engaging in different activities. This form of definition of the situation or occasion consists of a comic *performance* by one or more members of the participating group, watched or listened to by the others – the audience. If this seems an unnecessarily complex way of introducing the notion of comic performance or 'entertainment' (a notion commonsensical to the point of obviousness in our culture), it should be said that the point of discussing it in this context is precisely in order to problematise it, and that in two ways:

1 In relation to cultural contexts in which the notion of comic performance is not normal or not the same as ours (we shall see that what constitutes comic

performance has evolved through history, fundamentally changing its relationship to the wider social context in the process).

2 In relation precisely to the notion of occasions for humour in general: the whole point of a comic *performance* is that it is defined as a social occasion on which humour is not only permissible but desirable. This definition is set up in advance of the performance by the identity of the performer, and sometimes the nature of the occasion, in a way analogous to the role of the joking relationship in tribal societies.

In other words a comic performance is endowed with cue properties by its social nature; it is because it is defined (in advance of any particular performance) as being an occasion appropriate for humour that it is capable of acting as a cue for participants to define the activities they witness as being humorous and not of some other nature (offensive, childish, brutal, etc.).

An example will show the value of these considerations. From the earliest records of history until the late Renaissance in Europe the domestic fool – or court jester, as (s)he is also known – was a standard figure. It is recorded that the Fifth Dynasty Pharaoh Dadkeri-Assi kept a court fool, and that ancient Chinese emperors kept them, as did Haroun-al-Rashid and Tamburlaine; in Imperial Rome there was a fool market, akin to the slave market (Towson, 1976: 21ff.). They were well known throughout medieval Europe, and continued in existence until later than is often realised: Pepys noted in his diary (1919: 353) that Charles II instated a court fool in 1668 and the last recorded domestic fool in Britain was at Hilton Castle in County Durham in 1746 (Doran, 1858: 218). Edward IV had a court fool called Scogan, whose exploits are well known from a written record of them – although how accurate the record is has been called in doubt, since the same jests are also attributed to other fools. On one occasion Scogan so annoyed Edward with one of his pranks that he was banished and forbidden upon pain of death ever to set foot on English soil again. He duly set out for France, but was soon back in England and at court. When charged with disobeying the king's express prohibition he took off his shoes – they were full of French soil! He was pardoned and reinstated, presumably amidst great mirth. One of the French kings kept a fool called Marot; one day when they were walking together, the king told Marot to walk on his left, as he could not abide having a fool on his right; 'Is that so?' replied Marot, moving across to the king's left. 'I can bear it very well' (Towson, 1976: 21ff.). These stories – and many like them – are apocryphal, of course, since records of such things are notoriously unreliable, and are especially to be mistrusted when the only source for them dates from a time when traditional humorous institutions such as the fool were under attack: for such stories romanticise the role of the fool. However, unless all the stories are untrue it seems very likely that court fools enjoyed a degree of licence in their public discourse with their masters and other social superiors which was significantly different from the servility with which the latter were commonly surrounded, and certainly far in excess of what would have been allowed any but the king's closest familiars in private. In other words, such actions are an example precisely of an occasion defined as suitable for comedy on the basis of the identity of one of the participants: because the witty riposte comes from the fool, it is defined as funny and not as offensive.[1] No doubt this appears an extreme example, in this sense: if the identity of the fool did not define the incident as funny, there can be no doubt that it would be something very different, in the circumstances in question – for anybody else to publicly behave towards an absolute monarch in this way could have been *lèse-majesté*, a crime punishable with great severity. By contrast, a joke told by a comedian on television today would still be recognised as a joke if told by somebody else in a bar, or any of the many other occasions which are recognised, in our culture, as appropriate. However, it is only in relation to the norms of our culture that it seems an extreme example, for we shall see that the range of behaviour permitted to comic performers in other societies is considerably greater than that which they are allowed in our own, and the occasions on which they are allowed to do it include many which we would find utterly unsuitable (it should be stressed that this statement implies no value judgment for or against either culture: assuming reports are accurate, the divergence is a fact).

The range of activities recognised as 'comic performance' is indeed immensely variable, and the range of social circumstances which are recognised as appropriate for them is extended, so much so that the English language has no terminology which is capable of embracing all of them under a single heading. I have chosen to use the word 'clowns' as an 'umbrella' category, for this reason: most of the activities to be described contain, prominently, the types of activity still conventionally associated with the word – funniness, costume appropriate only for the circumstances in question, exaggerated gestures involving considerable acrobatic skill, etc. That the activities also involve many things not nowadays conventionally associated with clowning will become obvious; nonetheless, for our purposes the word 'clown' should be taken to refer to any or all types of comic performance.

A convenient starting-point is the sacred clowns of Amerindian tribes. It is a well-established feature of the anthropology of these tribes that clowning plays a significant role in their cultures.[2] By this is meant that in these cultures there are individuals or groups of individuals among whose social roles is the one of undertaking actions, on specified occasions, which arouse mirth on the part of other members of those cultures. To call them clowns, or sacred clowns, or ceremonial buffoons, is of course an act of ethnocentricity on the part of those who apply the labels in question, since the labels given by participants seem to be very different, and there does not even appear to be a single one that is used throughout Amerindian civilisations. Such an act of labelling is particularly problematic in this context since – as we shall see –

it is clear that many of their activities do not, and are not intended to, arouse mirth; thus to call them 'clowns' etc. is to select one part of their role as the one that is most significant. It seems likely that this was originally done, by the travellers who first came in contact with these tribes and witnessed the ceremonies in question, because this was the aspect of the role that was most striking to them, for they were in the vast majority educated white Europeans – at least, those who left reports of their visits were such – and to them it was the clowning role that was most discordant with their own preconceived ideas of appropriate behaviour.[3] Nonetheless, insofar as it is permissible to conceive of 'humour' as a distinctive entity, capable of analysis as such, it is permissible to stress this aspect of their roles since it is this that is in question in the present context; this is an important restriction, for we shall see that one of the implications of the study of the history of clowning is that the separation of humour from other phenomena – its conceivability as something distinct, as an entity in its own right with its own specificity – is something which may be culturally distinctive and which may need to be explained in itself.

The identity of the clown as the defining feature in humorous occasions is especially relevant in the case of the Amerindian sacred clowns because their behaviour involves such extremes of transgression – transgression, it should be added, not primarily of the norms of our culture (though it certainly is such), but of the norms of the cultures in question. Thus (to take an often quoted example) Pueblo clowns engage in extremes of obscenity – grabbing each others' genitals, pretending to masturbate each other, simulating intercourse with members of the audience, etc. – and this in a society where

> casual bodily contacts are uncommon, where people are timid about gossiping, and where sexual expression in public is very restrained. . . .
> The appeal to sexual emotion made by the clowns . . . [is] a deliberate intention to give as outright a representation of sex as possible, *for fun.*
> (Parsons and Beales, 1934: 499f.; emphasis in the original)

Very commonly Pueblo clowns among their other activities eat dung and drink urine (ibid.: 493); they will even do such things as bite the heads off live mice, disembowel live dogs and pretend to quarrel over which is to eat the 'tastiest' bit of the intestines (Charles, 1945: 30f.). The Kwakiutl Fool Dancers 'when excited by their possessing spirits, ran about with lances, knives or clubs, hitting people, or in serious cases even stabbing and killing them. Disliking clean and beautiful things, they attempted to break, destroy and soil them' (Steward, 1931: 192). Less dramatically, the Cahuilla clowns annoy people by throwing water over them and dropping live coals down their backs, and Huichol clowns torment people with 'botherations', and prevent them sleeping by shaking rattles in their ears and tugging their clothing (ibid.).

Even stranger – to a modern Western way of thinking – such activities are done during the tribes' most sacred ceremonies, and are part of a wider set of behaviour in which the clowns consistently burlesque the ceremonies while they are going on; thus, as sacred dances and songs are being performed, the clowns will – alongside the singers and dancers – give a deliberately clumsy, off-key, loutish 'imitation' of the sacred original, which is greeted with gales of laughter by the audience, who are also participating in the sacred ceremony at the same time. On these occasions the clowns wear special costumes and masks, which certainly look grotesque to a contemporary Westerner, though it is questionable whether they look ridiculous to participants, since they appear to have a religious significance.[4] Also a commonplace among Amerindian clowns is 'contrary behaviour', in other words doing the exact inverse of what is normal: speaking backwards, doing the opposite of what is requested, 'mistaking' light for heavy, hot for cold and vice versa. In warfare, 'contrary clowns' will ride their ponies backwards into battle, shooting their bows and arrows over their shoulders; they have to be told not to attack the enemy (Ray, 1945).

This raises a point, mentioned already, of considerable theoretical importance: are these activities considered funny by participants (including their original audience in this category, even if calling the non-'contrary' members of a war party an audience is stretching terminology somewhat)? The answer appears to be both yes and no. The activities of the Pueblo clowns are clearly found hilarious by all, but the contrary activities of other tribes are not always such. In the societies studied by Ray (1945), clowning is a part of a wider set of ceremonies which involve some members of the tribe assuming the character of a mythological creature, the Bluejay, and behaving in a completely unnatural fashion for the duration of the ceremonies (which is two months a year): eating only pitch, wearing no clothes despite normally sub-zero temperatures, sleeping in trees, never speaking or only speaking backwards, etc. Ray points out that many of these activities are not considered at all funny; for instance, the Bluejay can cure ills and find objects hidden under the snow, however far away they may be; but in other tribes, ceremonies and assumed characters which to the outsider appear not very different lead to great hilarity, although even here the same character, wearing the same 'ludicrous' costume may on one occasion be hilarious and on another profoundly serious (Ray, 1945: 75, 84). The Pueblo clowns too have other social functions – such as healing – which are not the source of mirth for their fellows; the Koyemshi clowns of the Zuni tribe are involved in ceremonies intended to bring rain, and participate in the annual 'Advent of the Gods' ceremony where they undergo 'exacting privations of speech, sleep and food'. They are thought to have supernatural powers and are held in awe: 'They are *the most feared* and the most beloved of all Zuni impersonators' (Parsons and Beales, 1934: 494; emphasis added).

These comments have referred exclusively to Amerindian societies, but it is clear from Apte's summary of anthropological studies of the religious functions of humour that such traits are to be found in many other parts of the world too.[5]

What can we learn from this material? In the first place, clearly, that insofar as these occasions are 'humorous' in some sense of the word at least analogous to modern usage, they are so because of the identity of the clowns, perhaps in conjunction with the identity of the occasion: the sexual and scatological actions, if performed by anybody else in these societies, would be profoundly repulsive to all, but because they are performed by the clowns they are hilarious instead; what participants would make of the contrary behaviour actions if performed by anybody else is not the subject of comment in anthropological literature. And yet it is also clear that many of the clowns' actions are not considered funny, and therefore it cannot be their identity alone that is responsible for funniness: the cue properties must derive from something else too. Clearly the occasion on which they perform the acts is one possible cue: we may hypothesise that the mixture of the clowns' identity and such-and-such a specified occasion would between them act as a cue. But we would then need to ask: would any conceivable action, undertaken by the clown on that occasion be seen as funny? Or would only specified actions? If the latter is the case, would other acts be seen as offensive, or merely as non-funny? Clearly the actions the clowns perform are seen by participants/spectators as transgressions of some norm or other; if some forms of transgression were offensive while others were not, then we would be led to suppose that the clowns' funny actions were of a conventional nature, of unknown origin; if some were funny and others non-funny, then we would have to suppose that there was something in the nature of the actions in themselves which served as a cue to their humorous properties: the actions themselves would serve as markers through their structure.

Second, the place that clowns occupy in the social structures of these societies is instructive. Such societies are in general marked by a relatively low degree of the division of labour, and professional clowns seem rather rare: Steward refers to one case of hereditary clowns (1931: 200), but in general clowns are either members of the 'societies' which are a basic sub-division of Amerindian tribes, and which have many other social functions, or they are elected – as in the case of the Koyemshi clowns studied by Parsons and Beales – for a limited period, or they may be self-selecting, as in the case of the contrary clowns studied by Ray, on the basis of an appropriate supernatural experience, for instance a dream. In none of these cases do the clowns apparently 'earn their living' from clowning. In all cases they have a very high social status, to the extent that there is one recorded case where if a clown criticises a chief, the chief has to be replaced (Levine, 1961: 73). It is not unknown in our societies for humorists to play a part in the downfall of public figures: it seems likely that Senator Gary Hart's retreat from presidential nomination was at least helped by the spate of jokes that followed the revelation of his relationship with actress Donna Rice in 1987 (*Observer*,

23.8.87); similarly, in 1992 the British Government Minister David Mellor was publicly revealed to have been pursuing a liaison with a young actress, and it is likely that some of the more ridiculous aspects of the situation sufficiently compromised his dignity to make resignation necessary. But despite incidents such as these, it is unthinkable that such a situation would be institutionalised in the modern industrial West. The high social status enjoyed by sacred clowns no doubt derives from the fact that they are a part of the religious institutions of that society, and we are returned to the paradox mentioned above: that the clowns' activities form part of the most sacred ceremonies of the societies in question, that they can be both feared and loved (note that this cannot be because of some property of the individuals in question: Koyemshi clowns are elected for a year – it is the attributes of the role that produce these emotions). Let us consider this from a totally ethnocentric point of view for a moment. Although in our society it is perfectly possible both to mock something and to believe in it as well, it is (1) the more difficult the more profoundly it is believed in; (2) it is difficult to do both simultaneously; (3) it is difficult to imagine an institutionalised ceremony in which seriousness and mockery of the ceremony itself would both figure simultaneously. Clearly the role of the sacred clowns in tribal society transcends this division.

Third, we should notice the range of activities that are considered funny when performed by the clowns, for it includes many actions which are unlikely to be considered funny in our society under any conceivable circumstances – biting the heads off live mice, for instance (on the assumption that the clowns' own audience in fact found this funny). The fact that their activities include things which our culture is highly unlikely to find funny apparently strengthens the sociological argument that humour is not a property of actions or statements, but a property of the social circumstances in question; that nothing, in short, is naturally funny. However, we shall see when we come to consider the immanent, semantic structure of humour in a subsequent chapter that this conclusion does not necessarily follow. On the other hand, we should note the apparent correlation between the type of occasion on which Amerindian clowns perform, their status and the range of activities which are appropriate for humour in their cultures: if such things are unthinkable in our world, it is perhaps because humour for us is 'mere entertainment', whereas for the Amerindian tribes it is much more: the delight that the clowns arouse has a series of values attached to it that far transcends the notion of entertainment as it applies in modern Western industrial civilisation.

Thus the identity of comic performers, and perhaps of the occasion of performance, defines humour as an appropriate response to a range of activities that might not otherwise be seen as funny. How do participants know that performers and occasions have relevant identities? Clearly the answer is tradition, custom, etc. How do such traditions and customs arise?

Of course it is basic to the notion of tradition that it should appear to exist 'from time immemorial': the idea that it might have an origin is inconsistent with the purpose of tradition, which implicitly asserts that 'it has always been so'. Moreover, the origins of many traditions are simply lost in time. But the question is still worth asking, because traditions do have origins, and when they are traceable they tell us a lot about the place that such activities occupy in a society. In the case of comic performance in Europe, it is possible to give a partial answer to this question by referring to the origins of comedy in ancient Greece, and to the re-emergence of comic performance in the Middle Ages.

There is general agreement that there is a close link between the origin of the Greek theatre and the religious rites associated with Dionysus – but less agreement about the details of the connection.[6] Comedy, like tragedy, became institutionalised in ancient Greece through the competitions that were a part of various civic festivals of which the best known were held in Athens. The official annual comedy competition was instituted in or around 486 BC in Athens, and formed part of the City Dionysia festival; comedies were also performed at another Athenian Dionysiac festival, the Lenaea. However, it is as near certain as makes no difference that both comedy and tragedy developed from some earlier representational or ritual form, and what this form might have been has been the subject of speculation from Aristotle onwards. This question is important because what is under examination is the process by which a 'performance space' came to be created, the process by which a civilisation accepted that people (actors) could impersonate other people and imitate fictitious actions in a space set aside for the purpose, where the public gathered in order to witness this special category of event. In short, it is here that we can see the category of 'comic performance' coming into existence. More exactly, we could see it if evidence was available; as it is, our knowledge is built up from deductions backwards from later records, with some frag-mentary evidence from an earlier period, and all the deductions in question appear to be subject to controversy among specialists. We can best understand the process by reviewing what is a matter of consensus and what is disputed.

There is certainly consensus over the location of comedy in the Dionysia. The City Dionysia was a civic festival, held in the presence of all the active population – i.e. the adult male citizens of the city – and perhaps attended by their dependants too: women, children and slaves; foreigners would also be present in limited numbers. The drama competitions were only a part of the festival, which included ceremonial processions, military displays, singing and dancing and banquets. Thus the comic performance of the earliest Athenian comedy (Old Comedy – Aristophanes, for example) was an event of a type different from modern theatrical performance:

> This place, which was the scene of the collective festival, provided a
> proper home not only for the dramatic contest but also for other
> celebrations which were no less strictly tied to the civic system: at the

City Dionysia, honors were voted to citizens, the tribute from Athens'
allies was exhibited in the theater, the orphans of war who had been
raised at the city's expense were paraded in the theater in full panoply
in the year in which they reached majority. . . . The community of the
plays' spectators, arranged in the auditorium according to tribal order
(no different from what happened on the field of battle or in the burial
of the war dead) was not distinct from the community of citizens.

(Longo, 1990: 15)

In short, the audience is structured not by its consumer choice of the artefact
in question, but by the nature of the festival and each individual's place in the
civic order. For example, the auditorium was divided into 'wedges' of seats,
and each wedge was for one tribe; women (if they attended) were seated
separately (Winkler, 1990: 39n.).

The festival was in honour of Dionysus, whose cult had become part of
state religion. What kind of God was Dionysus? What was the meaning of his
cult? Unfortunately there is no clear answer to these questions. It seems likely
that the Dionysiac cult originated outside Greece, possibly in Thrace or
Phrygia, and that as it was introduced into Greece it was modified to fit in
better with other, long-established Greek religious views, notably those
distinguishing between Gods and (wo)men on the grounds of human mortality.
The core of the original ritual may have been a frenzied orgy by women
devotees which consisted of running amok in the wilderness at night,
probably drunk, and – perhaps – ripping apart a live animal and devouring it
raw; this may have replaced an earlier human sacrifice (Guthrie, 1950:
172ff.). Between the original ritual, perhaps involving communion (in the
fullest sense of the word) with a supernatural being of terrifying power and
only ambiguous benevolence towards humanity, and the later civic ceremonies that included comedy performances, lie a series of rural ceremonies
known primarily from their representation in Aristophanes' *Acharnaians*: a
procession, an offering to the god and a phallic song to Phales, the personified
symbol of fertility and the nocturnal companion of Dionysus in his revels.
They are also commonly held to have included a lot of obscene humour, often
insulting, and a lot of drunkenness. The one clear feature of Dionysus is his
ambiguity: he is associated both with fertility and pleasure, but also with stark
terror; a recent study concludes that Dionysus is 'another way of thinking'
(quoted Goldhill, 1990: 126).

Certainly the procession in honour of Dionysus which opened the City
Dionysia carried phalluses, and comic actors wore a leather phallus which
protruded below their tunics, as well as grotesquely padded stomach and
buttocks. Certainly Old Comedy was obscene: for example, a central scene in
Aristophanes' *Acharnaians* involves a Megaran coming to the market in
Athens to sell his daughters, but because of the impoverishment caused by
war he is convinced he won't be able to sell them as such, and disguises them

32

(completely unsuccessfully) as pigs. The point of the scene is that in Aristophanes' Greek the word for pig (*choiros*) was also the slang word for vagina (Henderson, 1991: 123, 131). Certainly the Dionysiac festivities involved drunkenness as well as obscenity: 'All phallephoric ceremonies appear to take place in an atmosphere of unbridled gaiety. There appears to be attached to them, indissolubly – along with an obscenity that gives rise to coarse, hearty laughter – the disordered rhythm of singing and dancing' (Ghiron-Bistagne, 1976: 208). The prominent phallus, obscene humour, drunkenness: these are the factually-based links between the original Dionysiac rituals and comedy, and they have given rise to many theories about the nature of comic performance in ancient Greece. Clearly some theorising is necessary, for various reasons:

1 the close relationship between theatrical performance and the place of festivals in the civic order clearly indicates that the performances were not just entertainment, or 'culture' in the modern, individualistic, elitist, 'improving' sense;
2 the origin of the performance space is problematic, since it is likely that the original Dionysiac ritual did not distinguish between performers and participants (Longo, 1991: 16); it can even be argued that Old Comedy did not depend upon spectators' identification of the space of the theatre as mimetic (Slater, 1987);
3 sexual display was contrary to the central Greek value of modesty (not guilt), and the obscenity of Old Comedy is clearly transgressive (Henderson, 1991: 13–17, 32).

For a long time it was said that comedy in general, and especially Athenian Old Comedy, was an assertion of some essential human sense of vitality, which was not directly represented but which was evoked in the sense of well-being that the pleasures of humour produced (Cornford, 1914 is the origin of this school of thought). Central to this argument was the supposition that Athenian Old Comedy was in some way related to the Dionysiac cults and that the obscenity was of ritual significance, probably connected to fertility (Gurewitch, 1975: 34ff.). This view derived from a conception of ancient religion, myth and theatre in general, in which everything derived from an original, pre-historic core of ritual magic. The rituals linked to the cult of Dionysus were said to incorporate both the terror of death and the joy of rebirth, and they subsequently became the distinctive formal rhythms of tragedy and comedy. This analysis, deriving ultimately from Nietzsche's *Birth of Tragedy* and Frazer's *Golden Bough*, influenced an entire tradition of studies of the theatre; beneath severe disagreements of detail, these studies 'all share the basic rhythm of the alternation of death and life; they show the same fundamental pattern embodying the same message: that death is the necessary prelude to renewed and invigorated life' (Friedrich, 1983: 171).

Well-known studies of Shakespeare's comedies (e.g. Barber, 1959) pursued

33

the same line of argument. In general, the comic performances were seen as an incarnation of holiday, ritual, sacred time or carnival, in which a reversal of norms and a release from usual obligations was the basis of the event (Henderson, 1991: 285; see Stallybrass and White, 1986: 7–26 for an overview of this tradition). Here we see something like a universal function of comic performance, akin to Douglas' 'sense of community', and the origin of Athenian comedy is central to the argument. However, more recent debates cast doubt on the usefulness of Old Comedy for these purposes.

First, the question of obscenity and its possible ritual significance. The 'carnival' thesis essentially asserts that in this instance the obscenity was a form of sympathetic magic, intended to attract the benevolence of the gods:

> Tragedy seems to have crystallised all the apotropaic [i.e. avoidance-oriented] aspects of the ancient agrarian rites, satyr plays and comedy having developed the propitiatory side of the festival: the benevolence of the gods who protect nature must be obtained through laughter.
> (Ghiron-Bistagne, 1976: 293; cf. Goldhill, 1990: 126ff.)

But Henderson argues that because obscenity for the Greeks was the opposite of modesty, it always functions primarily as a form of ritual strife and ritual degradation of the other; the fact that religious cults also featured high levels of obscenity and scatology should not lead us to assume they performed the same functions in the two cases, since by the time of Old Comedy the theatrical competitions were largely independent of the cults in question (though not of civic festivals in general); also, Athenian comedy ceased to be obscene towards the end of the fifth century, whereas the cults continued their obscenity and scatology for some centuries (1991: 17, 32). Moreover, the occasion on which this theatrical obscenity was manifest was not one in which every norm was inverted, but one which was highly structured and regulated by the strictly enforced rules of the Festival and the competition (1991: 285f.).

Second, the question of the phallus-bearing actors. According to Aristotle, comedy derives from those who led the phallic songs, and the etymology of 'comedy' derives from 'komos', the phallus-bearing procession (Giangrande, 1963); that is to say, the comic actor derives from the leader of the songs, who slowly acquires a separate role. The problem with this line of argument is that the actors' costume was not the costume of the attendants of Dionysus in Attica (which includes Athens) but in the Peloponnese; in Attica the attendants are always portrayed as Sileni, i.e. satyrs, with horses' tails and ears. The argument advanced by Giangrande proposes a solution which also suggests that as theatrical impersonation developed out of religious ritual, the activities in question changed their meaning by being modified. The phallus-wearing actor was not imported into Attica from the Peloponnese, but was a survival of an earlier fertility cult/dance in both regions. But in Attic comedy the chorus is not padded, nor does it wear the phallus. The fertility cult consisted of dances, and the Attic chorus was similarly a lyric, non-mimetic performance. However, the cult phallus-bearers are not only singing but also giving a sacred representation, yet they are not actors, since they do not impersonate; also there is no changeable plot as there came to be in plays. That is to say, the fertility cult procession already contains some elements that are proto-theatrical. In the Peloponnese, the fertility dance gets secularised; in Attica, Dionysiac religion is grafted on, which conserves the ritual element of the cult. Somehow, the dramatic potential of these different elements was realised.

If Giangrande's conclusion is somewhat lame in comparison with the sophistication of his argument, the implication of his approach is nonetheless important: it is that the separation of the actor from the chorus, and of both from the audience, shows that however the development from pre-theatrical cults to theatre occurred, the meaning of the various components in it changed on the way: the chorus is not simply the celebrants of Dionysiac ritual, but represent the citizens of Athens confronting events which have such-and-such a meaning, which is no doubt related in some way to Dionysus.

Lastly, there is disagreement over a question which is rather more important from our point of view: the relationship between Athenian Old Comedy and other forms of clowning in ancient Greece. It is known that as well as the comic form developed in Athens there was another tradition, of uncertain provenance, which seems to have more closely resembled what we would call farce or clowning. It appears to have flourished around Sparta, perhaps in Megara and in the Greek colonies in Sicily. The actors in this form were also padded and phallus-bearing, and one of the names given to this farce, *phlyakes*, appears to relate it to the prehistoric fertility cult already mentioned, of which it could be a secularised descendant (Giangrande, 1963: 1ff.). For many years it was held that this farce tradition was at the origins of Athenian Old Comedy (Nicoll, 1931: 21–7; Ghiron-Bistagne, 1976: 138, 151; Easterling and Knox, 1985: 366n.). Recent commentators argue against this line of development, suggesting that the individuals identified on inscriptions were not real poets or actors but legendary characters or stock dramatic types, and that there is no proof of such farce existing before the Athenian competitions; Megaran jokes – notably in Aristophanes – are not taken from farce, but are simply jokes about the boorishness of Megarans in general (Henderson, 1991: Appendix).

The significance of this point is that this farce was one of the ways in which Greek comedy was taken over by the Romans, and it was the Roman adaptations which ensured the survival of the form into the Christian era, and ultimately into the modern world. The Roman adoption of Greek comedy also took the form of imitation of Athenian New Comedy, which flourished a century later than the Old Comedy; this was the form self-consciously imitated by European playwrights of the Renaissance – Shakespeare's *Comedy of Errors*, for instance, is clearly modelled on an antique original –

to the extent that it became the dominant model for comedy throughout the neo-classical period. It is at least arguable that the best-known Roman comic author, Plautus, deliberately injected increased elements of farce into the Greek sources he imitated, presumably to bring them more into line with Roman popular tastes (Castellani, 1988).

By common consent, this tradition (often known as mime) forms a link between the popular culture of ancient Greece and the culture of the Roman Empire (Duckworth, 1952: ch. 2). The Sicilian farces were exported to the mainland of Italy where they became known eventually in Latin as *fabulae Atellanae*, from the name of the town where they were first performed. This style of performance then became the basis for popular comedy in Rome and throughout the Empire. That it was considered distinctly different from comedy as developed in the Athenian competitions is suggested by the terminology used by Latin authors to describe the mimes: they were called *planipedes*, i.e. flatfoot or barefoot, as they performed wearing neither the *cothurnus*, the platform boot or buskin worn by tragic actors, nor the *soccus*, the light flat shoe worn by comic actors; it is likely that they performed barefoot because dance and acrobatics of various sorts were a normal part of their repertoire. (These distinctions in costume date from after the period of Athenian Old Comedy.) On the other hand, many Latin authors refer to comedy, mimes and *fabulae Atellanae* as if they were all the same thing; others distinguish mime on the grounds of its 'base things and worthless characters', and its indecency (Nicoll, 1931: 81ff.); no doubt such distinctions tell us as much about the authors as about the mimes, since the written word was largely a prerogative of the upper classes in Rome.

Two final points need to be made about the comic performances of the ancient Mediterranean empires: first, their physical location; second, the social identity of the performers.

Greek comedy was performed originally in the market place (Longo, 1990: 16n.), subsequently in the municipal theatres created for their part in the Dionysiac festivals. The first permanent, stone-built theatre in Athens dates from the late fourth century BC, but it is known that it was preceded by substantial timber structures there and elsewhere (Easterling and Knox, 1985: 263, 266; see Bieber, 1961: ch. 5, for more detail). In the earliest days Roman mime was performed in the circuses and at festivals on temporary stages with some rough scenery and some props – as indeed was all Roman theatre until the first permanent theatre was built (by Pompey) in 55 BC; there were earlier permanent theatres in Sicily and elsewhere in southern Italy, which dated from the period of Greek influence (Bieber, 1961: ch. 13). Subsequently, the mimes were performed in the permanent theatres built in many parts of the Empire, where they served as interludes and at the end of tragedies. As with the Dionysia, the festivals were religious occasions that were part of the official calendar of the Republic, and were preceded by several days of entertainment such as races and boxing matches. According to Nicoll, most mime performances were during the games and other festivals, which suggests that the link between religion and comedy was not entirely lost, at least in the early stages of Roman history. However, festivals were often repeated (nominally for religious reasons, such as a fault in the ritual) and it has been suggested that the popularity of a particular theatrical performance, such as certain of Plautus' comedies, may have been a motive in itself for such repetition (Duckworth, 1952: 78).

In the earliest days of the Greek theatre, performers were volunteers, recruited and paid by the poet or by the chorus-organiser. The chorus appears to have been chosen from among the *ephebes*, the young men who had just come of age and were undergoing military and civic training (Winkler, 1990). Towards the end of the fifth century BC the state regulated the recruitment of actors; in the fourth century there was a surge in recruitment into the profession, and some actors became 'international stars'; the Macedonian court under Phillip and Alexander the Great became the focus for theatre but after the latter's death in 323 BC the actors were left in disarray, and from this probably derive the first professional associations. Despite an element of secularisation, the associations were primarily religious organisations, and the annually elected president had the title and functions of a priest (Ghiron-Bistagne, 1976: 136, 171). Eventually, performance became partially detached from religion:

> Any pretext is sufficient for their performances, the whims of patrons as much as religious festivals. The taste of illustrious protectors and the generosity of rich private citizens promoted this 'secularisation' of their profession for a while. . . . Laughter (in the New Comedy) loses the ritual character that it drew from the obscenity of the ancient *komoi*.
>
> (Ghiron-Bistagne, 1976: 136, 205)

In Rome too playwrights and actors were organised into a guild in 207 BC, but although the association was nominally religious – a cult devoted to Minerva/ Athena, the goddess of skills – none of the festivals at which performances were normal were in honour of Minerva, and therefore 'the association was superficial and the secularisation of the profession all but complete' (Kenney and Clausen, 1982: 84).

The social status of theatre personnel in early Rome was low: initially playwriting was in the hands of slaves and freedmen, and literature in general was not considered an appropriate activity for members of the ruling class until the second century BC; even thereafter, the small group of nobles who dominated Roman literature tended to disdain the theatre, and the little theatre that they did write – e.g. Seneca's tragedies – was not performed in public. Actors appear to have been excluded from military service: Livy distinguishes between amateur performance of the *fabulae Atellanae* in the earliest stages of Roman theatre, whose performers 'retained membership in their tribes and served in the army' and those professional perfomers who did not (Duckworth, 1952: 6). In general actors suffered under a series of legal disabilities in Rome: they had no civil rights under the Republic (this was relaxed in the Empire, but subsequently reinstituted), they could not appoint attorneys in the courts, or appear as such, and they could not bring criminal actions in the courts; no member of the nobility could marry an actor or actress. So undignified was acting felt to be that nobles were not allowed to act; if they did, they lost their civil status. Nero obliged nobles to appear on the stage, and Julius Caesar forced the noble playwright Laberius to act in his own mime in revenge for a series of public jokes at his expense (Chambers, 1909: vol. I, 8f.; Nicoll, 1931: 96ff.; Kenney and Clausen, 1982: 293f.). However, in the late Empire this situation changed. The most popular mimes became literal stars, undertaking very well-paid pan-Empire tours; despite legal disabilities, mimes were befriended by the powerful and acquired respectable positions in society – the most famous instance is Theodora, who despite a reputation for promiscuity, became Justinian's mistress and subsequently his Empress, ruling in her own right after his death (Nicoll, 1931: 93ff.). As this example implies, mime companies included actresses, whereas tragedy and comedy were performed exclusively by men.

Under the emperors the games and the theatres increasingly became a means of keeping the population happy, and at the end of the Empire, under the Gothic emperors of the late fifth century AD, it is known that at least certain provinces of the Empire appointed a *tribunus voluptatum*, an official charged with supplying and regulating the public provision of 'pleasures', including stage performances, taking over a function previously the lot of the praetors and quaestors, or magistrates, who were also responsible for public funds (Chambers, 1909: vol. II, Appendix A; Nicoll, 1931: 98, 141f.). This suggests that by the end of the Empire, the provision of public spectacles was both important enough to merit a permanent official, and also sufficiently distinct from other public activities to be the subject of separate administrative measures; in its turn this suggests a separation between such activities and religious functions, in other words the existence of something that could be called 'entertainment' alone. It is also clear that the mimes frequently performed in private houses, the more opulent of which sometimes had their own theatres; comic performances also occurred at private votive or funeral games (Kenney and Clausen, 1982: 81).

These few pages have surveyed ten centuries of the history of European comedy. Of course, they do not amount to a history of that form during the period – they merely present a brief analytic account of the relevance of this history to some of the issues that concern us. Here we focus on the social category of comic performance as a way of defining an occasion as appropriate for mirth and we can see clearly in the history of ancient comedy that by a process that is only approximately understood a religious rite in which mirth played a part became a secular occasion on which a performance inherited the right to arouse mirth. Sometimes this history is used to ground an analysis of comedy in which it serves a universal function, as part of 'sacred time', or carnival. We have seen that recent analyses raise objections to this idea, and it does not seem likely that such a universal function can be based on these examples. More modestly, we can look at the relationship between prescriptive occasions for mirth and permissive occasions. The religious nature of the occasions that lie at the origin of ancient comedy – like the joking relations of African societies – act as a very strong encouragement, if not a direct insistence, for the spectator to find transgression funny; perhaps not all transgressions, but a certain range of them, and this occurs in societies where the behaviour that is found funny during these ceremonies is very transgressive by the standards of those societies themselves. In modern industrial societies, it seems clear that there is a far lower degree of prescription of humour. We do not have formalised joking relationships, even if certain relationships – e.g. young friends, grandparents and grandchildren – are commonly held more suitable than others, and even though comic performance is prescriptive in the sense that the performer must try to be funny, and we are likely to want him or her to make us laugh, this is a process that is subject to consumer choice: the identity of the performer and the occasion, the relationship to the audience, all are filtered through the choices made by the consumer. Does this change the nature of laughter in our societies? We shall return to this question.

3

MEDIEVAL COMEDY: FOOLS AND FOLLY

Mimes and the theatres fell foul, ultimately, of two enemies who proved more implacable than the Roman nobility: the conquering Goths and the Christian Church, both of whom despised the theatres and their performers. St Augustine, writing in the fifth century, records that the theatres were closing everywhere: many cities were sacked by the Goths, and in the others public revenues were inadequate to maintain the theatres; the Goths nonetheless continued for some considerable time to allow the provision of them for their new subject peoples. The attitudes of the early Church were entirely negative, for the Fathers largely regarded the theatre and everything to do with it as the works of the devil. Actors were not allowed to join the Church unless they repented, priests were forbidden all attendance at the theatre and laymen were forbidden attendance on Sundays and other holy days – a blanket prohibition on laymen was often suggested but never applied as it would certainly only have been honoured in the breach. Between them, Gothic disdain and Church condemnation closed the theatres, eventually: Isidore of Seville, writing in the seventh century, uses only the past tense when speaking of the theatre. But despite the closing of the theatres, neither the texts of classical plays nor the performance skills of the mimes disappeared. Perhaps because the preservation of manuscripts was an end in itself, perhaps because of the status of the ancient languages, even such theologically dubious texts as dramatic ones were kept: Plautus' and Terence's comedies were highly regarded during the Middle Ages, and even imitated. However, all such imitations appear to have emanated from a single circle of monks, and were clearly not intended for performance. Indeed, they did not realise that Terence and Plautus had ever had theatrical performance in the antique – and modern – sense; they thought they were narrated by a single individual and simultaneously played by mimes (Faivre, 1988: 35). The mimes themselves seem to have continued their performances elsewhere, for Church condemnations of their activities continue throughout the Dark Ages (Chambers, 1909: vol. I, 10–22; Nicoll, 1931: 135–50). But it is questionable whether their performances involved impersonation, or 'acting' in the modern sense (Faivre, 1988: 33–40).

There is general agreement that the medieval theatre – at least in Britain and France – had its origin in Church ritual (Faivre, 1988: 16–30; cf. Evans, 1976: 134–9). In the tenth century, elements of the Bible such as the opening of the tomb and the Resurrection are given a kind of dramatic representation: monks dressed as women come to a place in the Church designated as the tomb, and another one dressed as the angel tells them Christ is risen. This dramatisation is separate from the liturgy proper – e.g. the mass. Subsequently the liturgy becomes centred on the officiating priest, instead of consisting of mass participation of the faithful – it becomes a spectacle. In some places these spectacles rapidly become more highly developed – more events are portrayed, with more roles; in others change is slow, and in many places there is ecclesiastical resistance to using theatricality and impersonation for religious purposes. Increasingly, the theatrical element becomes charged with emotion, where the skill of the 'players' provokes reaction on the part of the congregation/audience. Theatrical time is introduced – for example, the discontinuity between episodes in a Bible story has to be perceived by the spectator as a narrative element. The same is true of space – Jerusalem and Damascus are side by side in representations of the conversion of St Paul. It is commonly held that these dramatisations gave rise to more extended mimetic performances outside Church premises – the 'Mystery' plays – whose basic design was closely modelled on Church precursors. For example, the theatrical space was modelled on the distinction between those places which had a sacred significance – e.g. the crib in Bethlehem – and the 'indifferent' space which separated the others and which could be used for any dramatic purpose (King, 1987).

Performance in the Middle Ages was not restricted to the Church spectacles and the plays that derived from them. Singing, tumbling and the recital of poetry were the province of what modern English commonly calls the minstrel. It has been argued that the minstrels were the mimes of antiquity under a new name, but so little is known about the culture of the Dark Ages that any provenance is speculative (Nicoll, 1931: ch. 3, pt 2; Faivre, 1988: 33–40). From the point of view of the Church, the minstrel was at best an ambiguous figure, as is clear from an often-commented passage from Thomas de Chabham's *Penitential* which distinguishes between those 'histriones', as he calls them, who may be tolerated, and those who may not on the grounds of the type of performance they give:

There are three kinds of *histriones*. Some transform and transfigure their bodies with indecent dances and gestures, now indecently unclothing themselves, now putting on horrible masks. There are besides those who have no definite profession, but act as vagabonds, not having any certain domicile; these frequent the courts of the great and say scandalous and shameful things concerning those who are not present so as to delight the rest. . . . There is yet a third class of *histriones* who play musical instruments for the delectation of men, and of these there are

41

two types. Some frequent public drinking places and lascivious gatherings, and there sings stanzas to move men to lasciviousness. . . . Besides these there are others, who are called *joculatores*, who sing of the gestes of princes and the lives of the saints . . . they do not perform innumerable indecencies like male and female dancers do, and those who play by means of indecent images.

(Quoted Nicoll, 1931: 152; Petit de Julleville, 1968: 20f.)

De Chabham's purpose is to distinguish between those sorts of *histriones* who are utterly to be condemned, and those who are to be tolerated: only the ones he calls *joculatores* are acceptable, but whether his use of the term reflects a genuine division of labour among the performers is uncertain. Indeed, the terminology which is used in medieval documents to refer to performers of all sorts is complicated and inconsistent (Chambers, 1909: vol. II, Appendix B).

Since virtually all literature was recited in the Middle Ages, it is arguable that the distinction between the minstrel and the actor makes little sense, at least in France (Faivre, 1988: 33–40). (We should note that this thesis implies that the distinction between recitation and impersonation is of little importance.) While many texts were clearly meant to be performed by minstrels, others are dialogues interspersed with narrative poetry, including the earliest texts of the Passion plays. Often characters narrate what they are doing or what they have seen. These texts are thus a mixture of narrative and theatre. Perhaps what happened was this: the minstrel disappears because of the crisis caused by the Hundred Years' War; the remaining ones tend to settle down in one court, or just provide music for dances; minstrels' texts then became adapted for representation. This may have happened because gradually the Mystery plays came to be performed by secular organisations, originally volunteers from the urban guilds of merchants and artisans, subsequently by paid professional actors; the volunteer performances were free, but the later ones involved an entrance fee (Konigson, 1979). These partly secularised performances were put on at events which were not only dictated by the religious calendar, but by the civic calendar too, and Aubailly (1975) argues that the early history of the secular theatre in France is best understood as part of the growing independence of the urban guild organisations from both feudal and Church control.

These considerations help us to make sense of the reinvention of theatrical performance in the Middle Ages; but they say nothing about comic performance. Before we turn to this subject we must consider another central category of medieval civilisation, the fool, for it is through this category that medieval culture – or at least the official culture of the Church – analysed comedy and humour. The court jester, for instance, is a form of fool.[1]

Much of the discussion of folly by medieval writers is not in fact a discussion of humour at all, for folly – especially in the hands of Church writers – was a much broader category; indeed it is not susceptible of a single definition, for it has a series of disparate, even antithetical senses.[2] In the first place, it had negative meanings, referring either to stupidity, i.e. the opposite of whatever common sense dictates, or to sinfulness, the opposite of what God dictates. The difference between the two lay in the importance of the objective that folly hindered: if it only hindered things to do with this world then it was condonable, if stupid; if it hindered virtue, and thus the growth of the City of God, it was non-condonable; in this sense, folly became more or less synonymous with vice, or at least closely associated with it. But in the second place, folly had a meaning that was always potentially antithetical to the first: since everything to do with this world was vanity (death inevitably triumphs in the end), wise precepts concerned with sensible conduct were ultimately useless, and therefore folly was justified, in a sense. For instance, the long-standing medieval favourite of the verbal jousts between King Solomon and the 'hairy, obscene fool' Marcolf, in which Marcolf consistently reveals that his folly is the equal of the king's wisdom, demonstrates that the terms are effectively reversed: it is Marcolf who is the wise man, because he knows he is a fool, and Solomon who is the real fool because he thinks he is wise (Swain, 1932: 30–6; Jones, 1991). In this second sense, folly could also mean naively living according to an ideal, thus losing worldly advantages; in a sense such conduct was stupid, but it was better than arrant worldliness, which was considered intrinsically sinful; folly in the second sense could be considered a path to salvation. Whence the irony of the Mysteries, in which Christ is reviled as a fool by his persecutors, who consider their wisdom superior to his, thus unintentionally revealing their own folly (Billington, 1984: 18ff.). It is this ambiguity in the definition of folly which allows it to be the source of irony in many of the central documents of medieval and early Renaissance thought, of which the most famous is Erasmus' *Praise of Folly*; in folly nothing is what it appears to be, and it becomes a flexible tool for comment on a variety of aspects of human existence.

Further, Church writers distinguished between 'artificial' and 'natural' fools. Natural fools were those who were in some way mentally deficient, or just plain stupid, whereas artificial fools were those who counterfeited this state in order to amuse others: minstrels who imitated drunken behaviour or sang bawdy songs, and all the participants in fool festivals (see below) and other entertainments involving deliberate foolish behaviour – in short, all clowns. The positive senses of folly all derive from the concept of the natural fool: a natural fool could be a holy innocent, or could inadvertently reveal the folly of the apparently wise, but the artificial fool was, for the Church, not to be condoned – although he does not use this terminology, the first two of de Chabham's varieties of condemnable *histriones* are also artificial fools. The analysis of folly could be summarised diagrammatically, thus:

	Artificial fool	Natural fool
Negative	Clowning Fool activities	Stupidity Vice
Positive	None	Holy innocence

In practice, of course, there was a convergence between the definition of the artificial fool and the definition of folly as stupidity and vice: some men were naturally stupid and/or vicious, others did wrong by pretending to be stupid.

Thus those most directly concerned with the production of humour were condemned by the Church. Indeed, the Church had had considerable difficulty in coming to terms with laughter in general, for it was confronted by two contradictory pieces of evidence on the subject. On the one hand, Aristotle – who was respected almost as much as the Scriptures – claimed that laughter was one of humanity's most fundamentally distinctive features; on the other hand, the Bible does not mention Christ ever having laughed, and Christ was held to be the incarnate model of humanity. The question was never resolved, and both views were held to be orthodox. The Church initially condemned all laughter, but subsequently moved in the direction of regulating it, of distinguishing between good and bad laughter. In the earliest monastic regulations (in the fifth century) laughter is condemned as the grossest breach of the rule of silence, and later it is considered as a breach of the rule of humility; it is also considered the greatest dirtying of the mouth, which should act as a filter for good and evil to enter and leave the body; therefore it must be prevented. From the fourth to the tenth centuries attempts were made to suppress laughter, but it is clear that it was in fact commonplace in the Church, since manuscripts refer to a category of humour called the *joca monacorum*, the kind of jokes told in monasteries. Subsequently it was admitted that some forms of laughter were legitimate: the smile was held to be not only acceptable, but even proof of good character, and having a happy mien (*visage joyeux*, *vultus hilaris*) was a sign of saintliness; indeed it is clear from Church writings that occasionally monks drew excessive conclusions from this principle, such as asserting that collapsing helpless with laughter (the French expression *le fou rire* catches this phenomenon) was a religious experience (Le Goff, 1989: 4–8, 12–13). From the thirteenth century onwards the mendicant friars self-consciously used jokes in sermons aimed at the laity to catch their attention, to make them well-disposed towards listening to sermons and sometimes to make theological or moral points (Horowitz and Menache, 1992).

Of course, this should not be taken to mean that humorists were condemned by others: in fact the number and tenor of Church condemnations is usually taken as an indication of the tenacity with which fool/humorous institutions withstood the onslaught of Church criticism. Thomas de Chabham, in another passage, candidly admits the strength of what he is condemning:

It is known that until now there has been the perverse custom in many places, where on any holy feast day wanton women and youthful fools gather together and sing wanton and diabolical songs the whole night through in the Churchyards and in the Church to which they lead their ring dances and practise many other shameful games. All such activity is to be prohibited with the greatest diligence, if it is possible. However, it is encouraged in many places for many men would not otherwise come to such feasts if they could not play games.

(Quoted Billington, 1984: 2)

And hundreds of years later, in 1535 or '36, a nobleman out 'talent-spotting' for the king writes to Thomas Cromwell – who administered the birth of the Church of England – in terms whose ambiguity leaves us in no doubt that both the condemnation and the popularity continued:

You know the King's grace has one old fool: Sexton, as good as might be which because of age is unlikely to continue. I have spied one young fool at Croland which in my opinion shall be much more pleasant than ever Sexton was . . . and he is not past fifteen years old. Which is every day new to the hearer . . . albeit I myself have but small delectation in follies.

(Quoted Billington, 1984: 33; spelling modernised)

Here the writer is plainly divided between his obvious knowledge of and (presumably) taste for clowning, and respect for Church opinions.

What sorts of activities came under the heading of 'artificial folly'? In the first place, references to 'wanton dances' and 'indecent nakedness' in de Chabham clearly point to popular feasts: the evidence of medieval manuscript illustration shows that until c. 1350 fool festivities involved naked dancing (Billington, 1984: 4ff.). In the second place, we shall see shortly that early farce theatre was clearly linked with the concept of folly. Third, there was a series of occasions and activities which were explicitly devoted to the enacting of 'folly'; of these the most important – or at least the most discussed – was The Feast of Fools.

This was an ecclesiastical festival that took place annually between Christmas and Twelfth Night.[3] It consisted of a series of Church services in which certain of the normal ecclesiastical roles were reversed and included many elements that were direct parodies of central elements of Church ritual. For four hundred years there are regular records of attempts to regulate and suppress it (which are in fact our main source of information). A description of the elements of the ceremony found obnoxious by the Church hierarchy is to be found in a letter from the Faculty of Theology in Paris to the Bishops of France, dated 12 March 1445:

> Priests and clerks may be seen wearing masks and monstrous visages at the hours of office. They dance in the choir dressed as women, panders or minstrels. They sing wanton songs. They eat black puddings at the horn of the altar while the celebrant is saying mass. They play at dice there. They cense with stinking smoke from the soles of old shoes. They run and leap through the Church, without a blush at their own shame. Finally they drive about the town and its theatres in shabby traps and carts; and rouse the laughter of their fellows and the bystanders in infamous performances, with indecent gestures and verses scurrilous and unchaste.
>
> (Quoted Chambers, 1909: vol. I, 294)

The Feast of Fools was practised in many parts of Europe. It was certainly celebrated in English churches because there are records of objections to it; it was traditionally held to have been extirpated at the end of the fourteenth century, but although it seems to have been driven out of the Churches, it now seems likely to have continued on a secular basis for some time longer (Billington, 1984: ch. 1). Also, Church condemnations during the Middle Ages should always be seen in a wider context: the Feast was a Church festival, not something imported into it by the laity – all performers were Churchmen, lay people only an audience; second, condemnations were usually on an individualistic basis and did not reflect wider Church policy (Faivre, 1988: 27). Lucotte du Tilliot, writing in the mid-eighteenth century, records instances of the feast in sixteen French towns, and later histories such as Chambers list many more. In France and Flanders, where it seems to have been most deeply rooted, the litany of protests and condemnations continues until 1668 – although it seems to have become increasingly rare after the mid-sixteenth century. Moreover, it is clear that it was only part of a network of such activity, both in Britain and on the Continent. As the Feast of Fools declined under increasing clerical attacks, its functions were in some respects taken over (in France) by the *sociétés joyeuses*, of which the most famous (because longest lived) was the Mère Folle of Dijon.[4] These *sociétés joyeuses* were entirely secular, and seem to have had their roots (sociologically) in professional organisations of a proto-Trades Union type, such as the Basoches (organisations of law clerks in France), which also held seasonal festivities of various kinds. The *sociétés joyeuses* held marches through the streets in which they shouted comments about anything that had happened in the locality which could give rise to often slanderous wit, and occasionally paraded people who had earned their displeasure in the procession in a thoroughly undignified fashion – a *chevauchée* or *charivari*. Such activities were part of the 'moral economy' of the Middle Ages. The *sociétés joyeuses* were also involved in the Miracle plays and in other early theatre, such as farces and fool plays (*sotties*); these activities were held at seasonal festivals such as Christmas and the pre-Lent carnival, at national triumphs and royal or noble entry ceremonies into the town; they were also held for the admission of new members. Although there do not appear to have been formal organisations of fool behaviour in Britain on the French model, it is well known that certain occcasions were held appropriate for organised fool behaviour, as witness the long records of 'mummings' in royal and municipal account books, and the ample records of Christmas and New Year festivities led by a 'Lord of Misrule' (Chambers, 1909: vol. I, chs 16 and 17).

These various occasions, in short, in their different ways, create a situation in which it is possible to define behaviour as being comic and/or as entertainment. In what ways does this relate to the development of a comic performance in the modern sense? This is the subject of extended comment by J-C. Aubailly (1975: chs 2–4); while there is no reason to suppose that the process that occurred in France was replicated elsewhere, it may serve as an example of how this transition was possible.

It is well known that the French minstrels' (*jongleurs* or de Chabham's 'joculatores') repertoire included comedy, whether in the form of brief farcical performances (an early medieval French poem refers to them imitating drunks and fools: Aubailly, 1975: 35) or reciting the short comic poems called *fabliaux*. It has always been agreed that the *fabliaux* have essentially the same content as the farces that are a standard part of the later theatrical repertoire. The *fabliau* disappears during the early fourteenth century, farce appears at its end in theatrical form; thus it is likely that comic texts undergo a similar progression to Mysteries and Passion plays. After the Hundred Years' War the minstrels disappeared from France, for their main patrons – the landed aristocracy – were ruined by the war. The theatre as it existed before the war was largely a bourgeois phenomenon: the main occasions for dramatic performance were the Saint's Day festivals of the patron saints of the municipal literary societies; these too tended to abandon their earlier practices under the pressure of the war. This period saw the rise of the *sociétés joyeuses*, taking over the functions of the Feast of Fools and other similar popular festivals: another form of popular activity now became dominated by middle-class urban organisations. In these developments the social basis of comic theatre is created. The earliest theatrical comedies are parodies of various elements of religious life, as are the traditional festivals; the pleasure of both derives from permitted transgression. Common forms of such parodies were burlesque sermons at marriages and public festivals and parodies of official documents such as treaties and royal ordinances: perhaps, speculates Aubailly, the *jongleur* or other clown walked behind the herald, parodying him as he performed his task; the parodies played upon traditional comic themes: sexuality (usually in the form of misogyny), drunkenness and gluttony replacing the noble behaviour appropriate for what was being

47

parodied. These parodies of occasions and functions become elements in the construction of comic character in the full dramatic sense. Two examples show this development. First, a social function can be parodied by showing it being performed by someone who is inadequate to the function in question – say, a gluttonous or lecherous priest; this involves some minimal delineation of the character of the person in question, which easily develops into a character portrayal in a fuller sense. Second, much comedy of this period is based on parodies of known and established literary genres – for example, an epic about a tournament between gluttony and Lent. Such parodies were highly political in that the genres parodied were conventionally associated with the aristocracy. Originally given in the form of recited monologues, they easily developed into dialogues, with two reciters/actors taking a part each.

From these forms, Aubailly argues, developed the two secular theatrical forms that dominated the drama of late medieval France: the farce and the *sottie* (or fool play). The farces were conventionalised portraits of everyday situations, with the emphasis clearly on its ridiculous aspects; the *sotties* were more extended allegorical commentaries on the social order as a whole, using the traditional liberty of the fool to attack various aspects of the social order; that is to say, because the voice of the fool was the voice of unreason (but an unreason which might always have within it the seeds of a higher reason, a reason only partially accessible to human reason), the fool had the role of speaking the unspeakable, of revealing through his/her folly the folly that afflicts all humankind.

In the late Middle Ages this licence became a justification for satirical attacks upon various aspects of the social structure, whether the personal actions of individuals or more general comments on the 'ills of the times'. Thus the *sottie* in general can be seen to have a political dimension: 'fools know . . . that it's under normal circumstances that the world is upside down, and therefore to set it arse-about-head is putting it back the right way up' (Faivre, 1988: 59).

In part this was possible because the fool societies were corporations with all the privileges that medieval French law invested in them; the complexity of rival jurisdictions, each of them a jealously guarded privilege, helped to create a rare level of impunity for such satire, despite occasional exemplary punishments (Petit de Julleville, 1968: chs 5–7). The continuity in this respect between the *sotties* and the traditional concept of folly is well summarised by Swain:

> in the early sixteenth century the range of ideas connected with the concept of folly gave [the *sotties*], in its personification, a peculiarly supple instrument both for entertainment and for satire.
>
> The *sottie* found its fullest use in providing a vehicle for criticism . . . but the censorship soon suppressed it, and its other functions as pure entertainment and as general analysis of human nature were more

acceptably embodied in the new comedy and tragedy developing under
the inspiration of the classical revival.

(Swain, 1932: 112)

It is worth noting, in passing, the manifold ambiguities hidden by this
'acceptably': why should it have been more 'acceptable' for these functions
to be embodied in the new imitations of classical antiquity? We shall see,
when we turn to the structure of humour in Part III, that this question demands
an extended answer, and one that is heavy with implications for an understanding of the modern practice and theory of comedy.

Finally, these considerations should be placed in a wider context, the
medieval notion of carnival in general. In a strict sense, 'carnival' was the
period of celebration that preceded Lent (often starting around the New
Year), a period of play and disorder – sometimes riotous – and sensual self-
indulgence. In a more general sense, it is nowadays usually taken to refer to
all those elements of medieval popular culture based upon similar sorts of
behaviour, which appeared whenever occasions such as festivals, Saint's
Days or fairs allowed it (Bakhtin, 1970; Stallybrass and White, 1986: 1–43).
In the limited sense, carnival was more common in Mediterranean countries
than in Northern Europe, but the activities associated with it seem to have
been universal in Europe. Such activities were public, taking place in the
streets and squares, but often moving into private houses as well. It was a time
of enormous eating and drinking, a time of 'such boiling and broiling, such
roasting and toasting, such stewing and brewing, such baking, frying,
mincing, cutting, carving, devouring, and gorbellied gourmandising, that a
man would think people did take in two months' provision at once into their
paunches', according to a contemporary English observer (quoted Burke,
1978: 183). In the streets these well-fed and watered citizens danced, sang,
made music, dressed in bizarre costumes and acted out the parts of their
costumes, threw water and flour over each other, dressed as fools and ran
around hitting each other with pigs' bladders on sticks, insulting each other
and singing satirical verses. In short, it was a time when the forbidden was
normal. More formalised activities included performances of various sorts,
organised by groups such as the *sociétés joyeuses* or the Lords of Misrule.
The performances were a mixture of improvisation and tradition, not exactly
serious but not exactly pure entertainment either. They usually included a
costumed procession with floats (or a *charivari*), a competition such as
racing, football matches or tug-of-war and a play – usually a farce – or mock
sermons, mock weddings or the French fake tournament between Carnival (a
fat man on barrel, with hams hung round his neck) and Lent (a thin old woman
seated on a chair, hung with fish) (Burke, 1978: 182–5).

In short, the Middle Ages knew a mass of activities and occasions on which
what we would call entertainment, some of it comic, would occur. But it is
important to distinguish what was occurring then from the anachronistic

'entertainment'. Stallybrass and White (1986: 8–9) make the important point that in the context of carnival laughter is not an individual reaction to an isolated (comic) event, but an entire context of perception. That is to say, on such an occasion participants see the world around them in a different light, which indicates to them the presence of a logic other than the one which regulates the official order of the Church and the polity. In the official order everything is ordered around a hierarchy in which God, law and authority are superordinate, where everything that is right and noble is given precedence. But in carnival everything is upside down: what is valued is the low, the self-indulgent, the grotesque, good-fellowship for its own sake; in particular, it is the body that is valued rather than the soul and honour, and it is the body in all its corporeality, the 'grotesque body' as Bakhtin calls it. Here the stress is laid upon those features of the body which link it directly with the outside world – the various apertures through which the outside world passes into us, especially in the form of food and drink; and the corresponding exit apertures. With this goes emphasis upon those parts of the body which most emphasise fleshliness – the belly and the buttocks, for example. What Bakhtin calls 'grotesque realism' – as found in Rabelais, for example – consists of representations which lay stress upon these features of humanity. For him, grotesque realism has three functions in a pre-capitalist society: it is the image-ideal of the popular community as a heterogeneous and boundless totality; it is an imaginary repertoire of festive and comic elements, to be used on appropriate occasions; it is a materialist metaphysics where the grotesque 'bodies forth the cosmos' (Stallybrass and White, 1986: 10–11).

Modern critics have tended to see medieval comedy – as most medieval literature – as crude and unsophisticated, and to study it primarily as a stage on the way towards the 'proper' literature of the Renaissance and after. Of course, by the standards developed after the Renaissance to apply to the then new literature, such judgments are correct. But they miss the point. For the medieval mind, the ultimate guarantee of meaning was not referentiality, the capacity to mirror the real, to show the visible reality of the world around us; it was Divine Providence and custom that gave meaning to human discourse, that were – to use modern terminology – the 'ultimate signifiers' that anchored the flux of semiosis. Nowhere is this seen more clearly than in medieval comic performance, the purpose of which was less to reveal something new about the nature of the visible world around us than to participate in customary activities and occasions in order to produce a sense of well-being and to confirm traditional views of the ultimate order of the cosmos.

CONCLUSION TO PART I

What have we learnt from the preceding discussion? What matters are undecided? What elements from this material cast light on topics to be discussed later?

First, it is clear that the occasion on which humour is achievable is indeed an independent variable in humour. We have seen that occasion can be constructed in either of two ways: it is permissive (it allows humour) or it is prescriptive (it demands humour). Certainly the notion of prescription is not without value; we have seen that many different categories of occasion have prescriptive elements in them: humorous activity by a partner in a joking relationship must be accepted as such; the fool cannot give offence in medieval Europe because (s)he is a fool; what is advertised as a humorous entertainment must contain humour; the Feast of Fools centrally involved the injection of levity into otherwise serious matters; and so forth. However, we have also seen that it is difficult to conceive of occasions as entirely prescriptive: even the occasions which are largely prescriptive must allow the possibility of non-humorous behaviour: joking partners do many things together which are non-humorous; the fool is allowed the licence traditionally accorded because folly in medieval Europe is far from exclusively humorous; a humorous entertainment may fail to amuse precisely insofar as there is no obligation to be amused under these circumstances.

Thus it is probably better to think of occasion as permissive, with prescriptive elements; this raises the second topic to be noted: can occasion act as a cue to humour? We have seen that in many clowning ceremonies and reciprocal joking relationships activities are performed which under other circumstances would be grossly offensive; here there can be little doubt that it is the social circumstances of the performance which are responsible for activities being accorded the status of humour, and therefore the occasion acts as a cue. But the principle extends beyond the distinction between humour and offence, since it potentially offers a solution to a difficult problem in traditional definitions of humorous structure: that all definitions seem to be either partial or excessively general, either not allowing for activities that common sense would allow as humorous, or allowing other activities that clearly are not to be considered such. If we accept that the nature of the occasion may be intrinsic to the definition of an act as humorous, it is clear that any given activity or utterance may be either humorous or non-humorous, depending upon the nature of the occasion. Thus it is not surprising that attempts to create immanent definitions of humour are commonly either under- or over-predictive. On the other hand, we have seen that occasion cannot by itself distinguish between the humorous and the non-humorous; therefore the notion of the structure of humour cannot simply be evacuated; we shall return to these questions in Part III.

Third, we have seen that under various circumstances, humour is directly linked to forms of ceremonial, that there are indeed comic ceremonies – Dionysiac ritual, clowning ceremonies, the Feast of Fools, etc. We also know that according to one theory, all comedy is an incarnation of a basic 'festive sense' originally incarnated in ritual. Recent scholarship has questioned whether this theory can claim the authority it derived from studies of Greek Old Comedy, and whether there is any genuine universality involved. However, the study of 'carnival' in the medieval and Renaissance period suggests that at least in this culture the space of festivity was integral. If the older 'universalising' theory now seems jejune, it is nonetheless clear that in many civilisations there is indeed an elective affinity between the form of humour, transgression and religious ceremony. While we cannot assume that the relationship is in any sense constant, we may at least observe that there appears to be a relationship. However, even this modest conclusion must be tempered by a warning about ethnocentricity: how can we know that what we think is comedy is in fact such? Why should we not regard it as basically something else, for instance social criticism? Certainly in our society transgression, laughter and pleasure add up to comedy or humour; but perhaps that mixture is specific to us.

Fourth, we must consider an element of the sociological dimension of humour which has been lacking in these analyses. The examples taken have been largely socially homogeneous, in the sense that there has been little or no differentiation between the various participants in terms of the distribution of power between them within the comic act. We saw that in Coser's analysis opportunities for various humorous forms were distributed according to power differences, and it is clear that in medieval society permission to achieve humour was central to the processes described: to that extent we have seen examples of humour where the distribution of power was integral. But the forms of analysis pursued have not explored this dimension of those circumstances, and power has been relegated to the level of consensus, where the power to grant permission was treated as a right. We shall see in Part IV that this is inadequate.

Lastly, the question of historical and sociological relativism, mentioned in the Introduction. It should be clear from the examples in the preceding pages that there are many forms of humour which it would be difficult to import into our culture. Nonetheless, it is also clear that at least within European history, there are long continuities of humour: for example, Aristophanes' *Lysistrata* is still performed with great success nowadays. But there are two caveats to bear in mind before proceeding to an argument in favour of humorous universals: first, we are talking about a culture which has been partially homogeneous across a long period of history because of self-conscious imitation of the past. Second, the nature of the occasions on which comedy and humour were created has varied so greatly across European history that we must ask whether the jokes in question would mean the same thing even if they were literally word-for-word repeated. To take again the example of *Lysistrata*: when we laugh at it in the twentieth century, does our laughter have the same meaning as the laughter which greeted it in Aristophanes' time, when ribald obscenity may have had a religious significance?

Part II

THE FUNCTIONS OF HUMOUR

4

FUNCTION AND
FUNCTIONALISM

It has often been commented, from Aristotle onwards, that the human species is the only species that laughs. One implication of this observation is the question: why should it be that we have this privilege? What purpose is there in humour and laughter? What function does it fulfil in the scheme of things of which we are a part? Some such question inevitably arises as soon as we step outside the confines of remarks about when we laugh or what makes us laugh: after answering them we are still left with the question: why is there laughter? Why should it be that we (alone) have this capacity?

In the twentieth century answers are usually cast in terms of social, psychological or biological functions; in other words, humour is seen as part of our collective adaptation to our situation. But in the past speculation was by no means so limited: as we have seen, the medieval Church was much exercised by this question, in the sense that when it confronted the contra-dictory evidence of the Bible and Aristotle on the question of whether laughter was one of the defining characteristics of humanity it was essentially trying to decide what the purpose of laughter was.[1]

Modern answers have often seen humour as part of our species' adaptation to its environment. For instance, the English polymath Jonathan Miller (doctor, theatre producer, humorist) has argued that 'if there is so much pleasure associated with it, like sex, there must be a biological payoff. Pleasure doesn't get locked onto an activity unless there's a payoff for the species' (Miller, n.d.a). The payoff that he sees is one that derives from the nature of humour, its basis in discrepancy or incongruity (see Part III): it has

> something to do with the exercise of some sort of perception which enables us to see things for the first time, to reconsider our categories and therefore to be a little bit more flexible and versatile when we come to dealing with the world in future . . . it has to do with what I've called a cognitive rehearsal of some sort. . . . The more we laugh the more we see the point of things, the better we are, the cleverer we are at reconsidering what the world is like. [We use] the experience of humour as sabbatical leave from the binding categories that we use as rules of

thumb to allow us to conduct our way around the world. This is why humour plays such an important part in our social arrangements.

(Miller, n.d.a and b)

In a similar vein Bjørn Ekmann argues that biological and psychological determinations of behaviour are the most basic, and social and artistic forms are inflections of them. Humour is seen in a framework that marries Darwin and Freud: the economy of psychic expenditure that Freud argues is the basis of jokes (see below, Chapter 6) is part of our species' fitness for survival. It produces spiritual equipoise for the individual and thus helps group cohesion, for this equipoise is a form of management of psychological and instinctual forces that threaten equilibrium. It is thus a form of ethological integration, and aids social bonding. It also serves this function through the creation and preservation of group identity: because joking is a rule-bound activity, it has the characteristics of ritual, the common acceptance of which is a means of forming group identity (Ekmann, 1981: 8–12).

In such theories laughter is seen as a universal feature of the human species. That is to say, it is supposed that beneath all the differences in what people laugh at, or the circumstances under which they permit laughter, there is some universal feature: a purpose. However, it is not essential to believe in a universal purpose of humour in order to define it functionally, and many analyses find particular functions for humour in particular social circumstances, or even particular functions for specific types of humour, or humorous themes. A brief instance is to be found in Obrdlik (1941), about the role of 'gallows humour' ('black humour' is an approximate English equivalent of this German expression) in Czechoslovakia under the Nazi occupation. He defines gallows humour as any humour in a precarious situation (cf. Freud, 1928), and argues that in Czechoslovakia it served to bolster morale by compensating for fear. Here no attempt is made to arrive at a universal theory of how humour relates to the human species' situation in the world in general, the focus is a particular style of humour under particular social circumstances and a functional description results.

A commonplace observation among recent psychological analyses of humour has been that it has the capacity to reduce anxiety. As a result it has started to take its place among therapeutic measures. On the other hand, there is some evidence that humour is only successful in alleviating anxiety if the level of anxiety in question is relatively low; in cases of high anxiety it may even have the opposite effect, increasing it (Ziv, 1992).

Powell (1983) sees humour as a form of the social control of deviance. Starting from the observation that people who do unpopular things readily become the butt of jokes criticising their 'deviant' activity, he constructs a hierarchy of acts of increasing deviance and a hierarchy of sanctions against them. Minimal deviance – say, a slight breach of manners, or mildly eccentric behaviour – will attract no sanction at all, or only the mildest and most informal of sanctions. Somewhat more anomalous behaviour will be perceived as 'funny' and laughed at. Further up the scale of anomaly or deviance, an act will be seen as 'crazy', and more formal sanctions are applied: disciplinary sanctions within institutions such as schools or factories, medical or legal sanctions perhaps in the wider social sphere. Beyond this level of deviance, actions are likely to be classified as evil, and the full force of the law applied.

Studies of jokes in various professional and industrial settings define humour in terms of the social functions that the activity serves within the particular setting in question.

Coser (1959; 1960) studied various functions of laughter in the setting of a hospital. Where laughter among patients was concerned, she noted that the themes of joking made it serve three clear functions: to ward off danger (this argument is essentially the same as in the analysis of gallows humour), to rebel against authority and as a relief from mechanical routine (1959: 175). But beyond the functions given by the themes of the humour lay a further function: all of the humour was a way of expressing various gripes, but whereas a gripe expressed in a straightforward assertion is an expression of a purely individual experience, jocularity makes it a collective expression by that of 'transforming a personal experience into one that can be shared' (1959: 176). Laughter among colleagues is structured in a different way (1960). There she finds that most humour is generated by senior members of medical staff and is frequently used as a mild reproof for their juniors; when junior staff members initiate humour, it tends to be self-deprecating. Coser concludes that such humour functions to ease tensions caused by the contradiction between hierarchy and collegiality: how is it possible to maintain a relationship in which mutual trust and acceptance is essential and yet where the fact of hierarchy means that one party to the agreement can give orders that another is bound to obey? Humour is one answer.

Bradney's study of the functions of humour among a large department store staff comes to similar conclusions. The nature of the tasks involved constantly creates mild friction, as people have to co-operate with each other in ways that are only partially organised in the formal administrative structure of the firm. At times when small favours have to be asked, or where one person's work routine inevitably creates small difficulties for another, jocularity intervenes to oil the wheels. Sales assistants are paid partly on a commission basis, and therefore anything which gets in the way of achieving a sale is grounds for some anxiety; joking is a way of defusing the tension that occurs under such circumstances. Joking most readily occurs between people with the same status in the organisation, but occasionally across hierarchical divides. The nature of the store creates

a divergence of interests among sales assistants, i.e. 'social disjunction', as a result of their formal relationship. . . . Yet it is essential . . . that the relationship between assistants should not become strained. The 'social conjunction' between the assistants . . . makes essential the avoidance of strife in the department, and it is at the point where conflict is most likely to arise that the joking occurs.

(Bradney, 1957: 183)

A function that is commonly ascribed to humour is that it allows the mention of taboo subjects. A brief version of this thesis is to be found in remarks by the English film producer Michael Balcon. Speaking of his film *Kind Hearts and Coronets*, in which the hero murders his way to a ducal title and marriage to a woman he has recently widowed, he comments that such subject matter is only representable in the form of comedy, because here it is possible to act out in safety the basest urges that are common to us all (Richards and Aldgate, 1983: 102–4; cf. Ellis, 1975: 114–17). The observation of a relationship between taboo subjects and humour can produce two different theories. On the one hand, it gives rise to a traditional theory of humour as a 'safety valve' for anti-social impulses. Orwell's essay on MacGill's 'saucy' postcards makes essentially this point: these mildly obscene or scatological cartoons only make sense within a society which regulates sexual expression in a fairly strict way; every society must regulate sexual expression in some way, and Orwell thinks that a fairly strict regulation such as was usual in Britain in the first half of this century is in fact the norm for 'civilised' societies. Under these circumstances, laughter at 'sauciness' is a temporary release from the inhibitions involved, a safety valve which in no way challenges the inhibitions, but allows us to return to them as it were refreshed by a brief holiday absence (Orwell, 1961).

Another thesis is to be found in Emerson (1969). She too observes that jokes are used to introduce taboo subjects, but so far from acting as safety valves she sees them as stages in a negotiation about how to introduce these taboo subjects into everyday discourse and deal with them in a serious vein. Her examples are taken from conversations in a hospital, a setting where it is commonplace for certain topics to be excluded from conversation between medical staff and patients. That is to say, there are 'institutional guidelines' in force controlling what can be talked about and what cannot. But these guidelines may be set aside, by mutual agreement following negotiation, and a common way of organising this is to introduce the banned topic via a joke, and then to follow it up seriously. Naturally, there is a risk involved: the other party may refuse to recognise the joker's right either to make a joke about this subject, or to transpose the topic to the serious mode; such negotiations are open-ended, in the sense that the outcome is never predetermined, and frequently involve retroactive definitions of whether such-and-such a remark was a joke or an act of offensiveness:

In staff–patient encounters, prohibitions against discussing certain matters clash with practical necessities or strong concerns about death, indignities, and staff competence. It is in situations where pressures for discussion and prohibitions exist simultaneously that negotiations to ignore the prohibitions are most likely to arise. When parties succeed in negotiating such agreements, they establish a presumption of trust. Not only can they trust each other in routine matters, but they share complicity for rule violations which potentially can be extended.

(1969: 180)

In the 'safety-valve' thesis the observation of a relationship between taboo and humour leads to the conclusion that humour operates to release the pressure of inhibition without affecting the application of the inhibition in non-comic circumstances. But the detailed observations in Emerson's study lead to the opposite conclusion: that it is perfectly possible – though by no means a foregone conclusion – that humour can be used to directly subvert well-established rules of behaviour by raising taboo topics that can remain on the agenda. The divergence in the conclusions is probably to be explained by the difference in the social processes under study. In the Orwell case, he is looking at consumer items whose function is established in advance as entertainment; nothing is said about how they are actually received by the individuals using them, but it is likely that Orwell is right, simply because of the social function of the objects concerned: it is written into their social use that buying them implies no ideological commitment. On the other hand, it is clear that in the long run, over a period of roughly a century, the frank admission of hedonism that they imply has certainly been part of a general change in the regulation of sexual expression, and one where the period in question (World War II) is often seen as a turning point. Perhaps therefore, even in this case, Emerson's thesis has the greater plausibility: the humorous introduction of a taboo topic can readily lead to its serious inclusion on an agenda. This thesis is readily verified in the type of everyday interactions that she observes, less readily so in interactions where one participant is an artefact and not a person.

In a detailed study of ethnic jokes, where the overt butt is some group in the population, Davies traces a link between the theme of the jokes and a particular social function (1982). These jokes, told throughout the Western world, conventionally link the butt with the character traits of stupidity or stinginess. With stupidity jokes, in the United States the butt is Poles, in the United Kingdom it is the Irish, in France it is the Belgians; in each of these instances, the fact of 'foreign-ness' is clearly paramount, even where a passport is shared. But in other instances the identity of the butt is more problematic: in Italy, it is the police; in Denmark it is 'men from Aarhus', an industrial and university town in the north of the country whose inhabitants do not seem to suffer from any other discrimination. With stinginess jokes, the butt is the Scots in England, inhabitants of the Auvergne in France, the Jews in most Western countries. In Eastern Europe and the former USSR, such jokes were traditionally told about the police and communist apparatchiks. What these different identities establish is that any group will do as the butt, provided it can plausibly be regarded as outside the 'mainstream' of the culture in question – although whether this can be said of the inhabitants of Aarhus is dubious. In any event, Davies argues, such jokes are not primarily about ethnicity, or prejudice against the group in question, but about the normative structure of our society. Modern industrial society places a premium upon two features of personality, which are potentially contradictory: upon rational pursuit of advantage, and upon the capacity to enjoy the fruits of such success. Jokes about stupidity presuppose the centrality of critical, rational intelligence, the capacity to act flexibly in response to new situations.[2] Jokes about stinginess refer to the presupposition that the purpose of wealth is enjoyment. Thus the jokes in question operate at points of great sensitivity in the collective consciousness of modern society, especially one which is bolstered by many of its central institutions: one's place in the social structure depends in large measure upon command of this form of intelligence, since educational performance and progression in job opportunities are inseparable from it, and level of consumption – or 'taste' – is a prime indicator of social identity. Thus jokes about stupidity, in which the stupidity is always someone else's, speak to a central experience of our civilisation, of modernity; they speak to it, says Davies, in such a way as to alleviate anxieties about one's own performance in this respect: at least for the duration of the joke, inadequate performance is a property of the other, and our own laughter is a 'proof' that we are not implicated. In general, whatever their themes, jokes about mean or stupid 'outsiders' project character traits which are the obverse of a central feature of our value system onto some marginal group, thus acting to alleviate anxiety about personal position for the joker.

The previous pages have given a brief overview of some functions that have been ascribed to humour, or to particular forms of humour or to particular jokes. No doubt there are many other functional descriptions of humour, but it is already clear that certain themes recur: relief from tension, anxiety or fear; breach of inhibitions; celebration of consociality. In the theories we have examined differences arise when these functions are given a location in the social structure: in the first place, we should distinguish between the argument that all humour has a function – deriving from some universal feature of humour as a form of activity – and the argument that particular forms of humour may have various functions. In the second place, we should distinguish between the argument that humour, or forms of humour, may have some function or other in any conceivable set of circumstances, and the argument that it will only operate under specific circumstances. 'Function' as a concept may refer to any or all of these, and we need to specify more clearly what a 'functional' explanation or description consists of.

We can start with an example, the notion of the 'joking relationship' as elaborated by Radcliffe-Brown (see Part I). Radcliffe-Brown's theory aims to explain this behaviour by assigning it a function – specifically, a latent function, since (as we shall see) the function in question is often not perceived by participants. This function derives from the nature of the other social relationships – primarily kinship relationships – that link the participants. Joking relations are a form of permitted disrespect which enters the social structure at points of stress, points where another dimension of the social relationship between joking partners involves both 'disjunction and con-junction' between the participants – for example marriage, where the wife's family and the husband's family have different interests *vis-à-vis* their offspring, and where a dimension of a relationship that demands respect (for example, the relation of younger to elder) may run counter to a dimension where discord – e.g. economic competition – would be likely. Joking relationships, he argues, arise at such ambivalent points in the social system, and their nature, the ambiguous relationship between friendship and hostility that is intrinsic to joking – or at any rate to the forms observed here – both expresses and contains the ambivalence that derives from the positions that participants occupy in the social structure.

Joking relationships are functional equivalents of 'avoidance relation-ships', situations where partners are obliged to avoid each other's presence. These Radcliffe-Brown attributes to the need to prevent the stress and tension which might arise from non-avoidance: for example, the transmission of the collective inheritance and thus of continuity demands respect for the ascend-ing generation; this respect – where it conflicts with the stresses of disjunctive relationships such as marriage – is expressed in the form of avoidance, and thus – typically – sons avoid their mothers-in-law out of respect. At the same time, the stresses that result from conflicting demands (disjunction) also produce the countervailing licensed disrespect of joking relationships, which are displaced onto another zone of the kinship pattern where respect is not demanded but the same set of conflicting demands are made. Sons avoid their mothers-in-law but joke with their siblings-in-law: marriage produces ten-sions in both sets of relationships, but in the one case the necessity of respect produces avoidance, in the other the non-necessity of respect allows the licensed disrespect of ritual joking. That is to say, the existence of avoidance relationships is strong evidence for the nature of joking relationships – both are designed to prevent unnecessary, dysfunctional stress and tension, and are therefore to be understood as functional equivalents since both perform the same function.

Thus the conflicting demands made upon the partners in marriage arouse what Radcliffe-Brown calls social disjunction, and it is clear that such stresses can easily arise and that joking relations between siblings-in-law could plausibly play a role in stress reduction under these circumstances. But another common location of joking relationships is grandparents/children. In this case it is less clear how joking relations could play such a role: what is the source of potential disjunction in this case? It is, according to Radcliffe-Brown, that the grandparents' generation is in the process of quitting social life whereas the grandchildrens' generation is entering it; whether there is here any potential source of tension and conflict seems uncertain, and it seems difficult to argue that such disjunction would be comparable either in kind or degree with the types of disjunction that obtain in the case of marriage. Of course, if joking relationships between grandparents and grandchildren were significantly different in kind from joking relations between siblings-in-law, then perhaps this would not be significant, but both are capable of being equally rumbustious and even obscene.

Even more difficult to reconcile with the Radcliffe-Brown model is the evidence of joking relations between whole clans and/or tribes, or even between groups defined on the basis of locality: Paulme (1939) describes joking relationships between whole villages, and Rigby (1968) describes joking relationships between whole clans and tribes. Such explanation as Radcliffe-Brown offers of these relationships is contained in the assertion that the relationship of exteriority between members of one clan/tribe and another necessarily 'involves possible or actual hostility'; therefore any fixed relationships between them – such as a joking relationship – must be based on a recognition of this separation, but must also recognise the reality of 'the social conjunction of friendliness and mutual aid' which is also present (he asserts) in the relationship between clans and tribes (1952: 94). Thus the relationship between clans and tribes, he asserts, presents a combination of conjunction and disjunction which is similar to the combination present in marital and alternate generation relations, and the joking relationship between clans and tribes consists of 'real friendliness and mutual aid combined with an appearance of hostility'. Clearly the adequacy of this explanation must turn upon empirical evidence concerning the conjunction and disjunction of clans and tribes (if such a thing is possible); in the absence of any one can only conclude that this is a model-saving assertion. Moreover, if such empirical evidence is available, it seems somewhat unlikely that relationships of conjunction and disjunction would be uniform, and very questionable whether they would be likely to coincide with inter-tribal or inter-clan joking relationships: in other words, *ex hypothesi*, the relationships of conjunction and disjunction between clans and tribes must apply to all tribes and clans (at any rate in the absence of other superordinate relationships), but it is empirically clear that joking relationships only exist between certain tribes and clans. Indeed, Rigby's study of Gogo joking relationships includes material on this subject and concludes that joking relationships do not in fact coincide with patterns of enmity and/or friendship, actual, past or putative (1968: 135–7). Similar considerations would apply to joking relationships between men all circumcised at the same time, and women who all started menstruating at the same time: even if considerations of conjunction and disjunction could apply to the men (group solidarity – conjunction; economic or other competition – disjunction), it would be difficult to apply to the case of the women, because in the instance studied it is clear that such joking relationships between women are based entirely on an analogy with male joking relationships: the women tell the same jokes, and say that they are in a joking relationship because they were all circumcised at the same time – of course, they say, we were not actually circumcised at all, but that is the explanation that we give (Barley, 1987).

Two further criticisms of Radcliffe-Brown's theory are relevant. The first of these refers to the relationships between joking relations and the cosmology of the people involved. Thus Rigby's study of Gogo joking relationships points out that they arise at points in the social structure which Gogo conceive of as full of ambiguity, for example in relationships between clans where the manner in which they received their names (a matter of considerable ritual importance) is in some way conceptually incompatible with some other feature of their relationship – e.g. inter-clan marriage. According to Rigby, there is no objective stress in the social structure at these points, but Gogo cosmology interprets such matters as ambiguous and therefore suitable for joking. This suggests that these joking relationships cannot be interpreted in terms of a latent social function at all, but primarily in terms of intellectual satisfaction: *mutatis mutandis*, this is the brunt of Lévi-Strauss' famous comment that animals are totems not because they are 'good to eat' but because they are 'good to think'.

The second criticism of Radcliffe-Brown's model refers to the type of evidence that is produced for it. As is commonly the case in functionalist arguments, the demonstration of function is held to be sufficient in itself as an explanation, regardless of whether participants are aware of the function in question – indeed, 'latent function' is defined precisely as a function of which participants are unaware. Commonly, participants in joking relations assert that the only purpose of the activities in question is the pleasure involved, and anthropologists themselves observe that this is indeed apparently so:

> Fortes states in a discussion of joking relationships between members of certain Tale lineages that 'Tallensi say that this is just jesting . . . but we see again that this apparently spontaneous jesting acts as a means of reconciling and counteracting the tension of a double-edged relation-ship.' The evidence of the ethnographer's senses ('apparently spon-taneous') and the informants' opinion ('Tallensi say') are both ignored in favour of an abstract argument in which the evidence of inferred potential conflict is largely in the joking behaviour itself. Such observa-tions are commonplace in anthropological literature.
>
> (Kennedy, 1970: 51)

In other words, theories such as Radcliffe-Brown's (based in part upon Fortes' field-work) infer the existence of potential social conflict but do not observe it, and the evidence for this potential social conflict is primarily the existence of the joking relationship which the potential conflict is supposed to explain. Kennedy ignores the other evidence which Radcliffe-Brown cites, namely the common-sense deduction that relationships such as son/parents-in-law are likely by their very nature to give rise to conflict; moreover, it is *ex hypothesi* unlikely that empirical evidence could be found of such conflict, since *insofar as the joking relationships were successful in performing their function*, there would be no such conflict. Nonetheless, despite such caveats, Kennedy's criticism is strong: Radcliffe-Brown's theory is marred by an element of tautology.

Radcliffe-Brown's theory is typical of a certain use of the notion of function: 'functionalism' in the traditional sociological and anthropological sense of the word. Explanation here consists of describing a relationship between whatever is the focus of investigation – here, humour – and the social structure as a whole, where we are shown how the thing examined makes a contribution to the satisfactory integration of the social system as a whole; this in turn is based upon the assumption that any conceivable society must consist of a set of meshing elements whose smooth interaction constitutes the social system as a whole. Alternatively, the object of investigation may turn out to be dysfunctional, to interrupt the smooth workings in question; either way, society is conceived of as the sum of an interrelated set of components, and explanation of any element of society consists of assigning it a place in this process. As is well known, this belief about the nature of societies derives from a biological metaphor, where society is conceived as an 'organic whole', and this is why the description given here fits the function of 'species adaptation' as well as sociological theories.

Such theories have well-known weaknesses when applied to human behaviour and social structures. In the first place, the argument about societies being akin to 'organic wholes' is at best an assumption which can be used as the basis for systematic description; at worst it is an ideological justification for a particular political and social programme. Somewhere between these two possibilities lies the criticism that – at the very least – it omits the crucial dimension of power, since if a society has a power structure it is always possible that the power in question may be being used to create just such a smoothly functioning set of interrelated elements (by for example suppressing anything that gets in their way) and thus creating the illusion that this society is indeed an integrated whole. In the second place, explanations couched in these terms tend to reach completion at the point where a function has been assigned to the object of study: for example, humour is said to relieve anxiety. But this omits two crucial further factors: first, how does humour perform this function (relieve anxiety); second, what do we make of the various other things that also relieve anxiety – e.g. drinking alcohol or playing football. Basically these two points are the same: both indicate that what is missing in the functional explanation is an analysis of what constitutes the object of study in its specificity; providing this element of explanation both shows how humour achieves what it is said to achieve, and distinguishes it from other things that have the same function.

Functionalism lies at one end of a spectrum of possibilities, the strongest form of functional analysis. If it has clear disadvantages, there are weaker forms of ascription of function. To say, for example, that jokes are used to introduce taboo subjects, and form one stage in a negotiation about putting them on a serious agenda is not to make a claim for a total explanation of humour, it is to ascribe a place for humour in a particular process, by bringing it into relationship with another piece of the social structure (here, rules about what can be publicly said); such a description says something meaningful about humour by locating it in a place, showing how it is a part of some wider process and makes a particular contribution to it. This too involves the notion of a function, but in a more limited sense. Here the placing of humour in a relationship with another process shows the function that humour performs within that process, or in conjunction with another process: the relationship is functional in that one contributes to the operation of the other, and such a description constitutes an 'explanation' of humour (at least a partial explanation) insofar as it indicates a use to which humour may be put. Clearly, in the case taken here, no claim is made that this is the only use to which humour may be put, and such a notion of function is restricted in scope when compared with the 'functionalist' approach.

5

GENDER AND HUMOUR

A series of case histories that illustrate this more modest approach concerns the relationship between humour and gender. We might hypothesise that there was a single, unequivocal relationship between humour and gender; if this turned out to be so, we would have traced a systematic relationship between a fundamental demographic variable – or possibly a biological determinant – in human societies and what we are studying. If the hypothesis was correct, then, we would be in the presence of a relationship which was in some sense of the word a functional relationship: its systematic nature would indicate that humour made some contribution to the nature of gender (at least in the society under consideration). We can appproach this subject in two ways: first, by reviewing the evidence of a correlation between gender and patterns of humour appreciation and performance; second, by looking to see whether 'gender', as a discursive construct, has a single place within humour.

Whether men and women have different senses of humour is usually studied in terms of their humour preference as consumers. Such studies reveal ambiguous evidence about differences between men's and women's humour, at least within the Anglo-Saxon culture which is the main source of such information (it should be added that most of this information derives from laboratory experiments in which the overwhelming majority of experimental subjects are students: the extent to which such information is representative must be open to question, both because of the restricted age and class range of the subjects, and because of the untypical circumstances in which they are exposed to humour). Some studies in this area suggest clear and systematic differences: for example that men are more likely to appreciate sexual humour than women (Terry and Estel, 1974) and that men's humour is more aggressive whereas women prefer 'absurd' humour (Chapman and Gadfield, 1976). Other research suggests a more complex pattern. For example, a series of studies by La Fave (1972) indicates that in general people prefer jokes that are aimed at some group of which they are not members, or feel no empathy with. It is important to note that the 'reference group' to which the individual belongs is defined primarily by the individual's sense of identity rather than

68

by objective demographic characteristics such as biological gender. When this principle was applied to gender La Fave found that

> Pro-male males [i.e. males whose definition of themselves coincided with traditional conceptions of masculinity] found pro-male anti-female jokes funnier than pro-female anti-male jokes; pro-female females [i.e. women whose views coincided with feminism] found pro-female anti-male jokes funnier than pro-male anti-female jokes.
>
> (1972: 205)

Roughly consistent with this, Chapman and Gadfield (1976) found that men preferred sexual humour more when the theme of the humour was consistent with traditional definitions of masculinity and the status of men was not under threat, whereas women did not like such humour, especially when they defined themselves as influenced by the women's movement. Otherwise there were no significant differences between men and women where appreciation of sexual humour was concerned, although both men and women who defined themselves as conservative in their value orientation did not like sexual humour in general.

This might appear to be another example of science sadly struggling to follow in the footsteps of common sense; however, other studies suggest a very different pattern: for example, Cantor (1976) found that both men and women prefer the butt of a joke to be female, regardless of the theme of the joke. This finding is consistent with a study by Zillman and Stocking (1976) which found that women prefer self-disparaging humour, regardless of whether the self-mocker is male or female, whereas men prefer humour that mocks somebody else, especially when the other is female; men also dislike self-disparagement by a female, perhaps on the ground that they so much like mockery of female others that self-disparagement by a female takes the fun out of the situation for them. Perhaps the discrepancy between these two results and the La Fave, Chapman and Gadfield results is to be explained by the strong ideological orientation of the latters' subjects, whereas Cantor, Zillman and Stocking's were randomly selected where this variable is concerned. In general, self-disparagement jokes must be taken as contradicting the evidence of studies which indicate preference for jokes that disparage somebody else.

What can this body of evidence tell us about gender and humour? It suggests that men and women do indeed have somewhat dissimilar senses of humour, and that such differences are to be found where jokes are about sex and aggression, if not anywhere else. But the reliability of such studies must be questioned, for the question of context is all-important. For example, the lack of appreciation of sexual humour by those defining themselves as conservative could easily be a product of the circumstances of testing: we could guess, on common-sense grounds, that such people would be very averse to admitting – to themselves as much as to anybody else – that they enjoyed such humour, or indeed averse to actually enjoying it in a public situation, such as an experiment, where members of the opposite sex were present. A follow-up experiment by Gadfield (1977) even suggests that where sexual humour is concerned the presence of a companion of the same sex who is visibly amused by the humour may have a facilitating effect on the enjoyment of such humour, a finding which seems consistent with these common-sense deductions. On the other hand, common sense suggests that the presence of someone who is visibly amused – regardless of gender, regardless of the theme of the humour – would have a facilitating effect anyway. A classic instance of such untheorised extra causative factors is to be found in a study whose initial hypothesis was that men would find sexual jokes funnier when told by an 'attractive' woman (the researchers went to some length to achieve 'reliable' indices of attractiveness). The findings indeed supported the hypothesis. However, the research report indicates that the 'unattractive' woman who was telling jokes was also instructed to wear drab clothing and to tell the jokes in a non-animated manner! Common sense again suggests that it was not the feature of the situation that was being tested that was in fact the causative agent.

All of these studies are based upon showing experimental subjects some isolated piece of humour, often cartoons, sometimes jokes typed out in a booklet. None of them examines the possibility that women's humour may be less oriented towards jokes and isolated pieces of humour and more towards humour which emerges as part of conversations and other everyday situations. Of course such a proposition would be difficult, perhaps impossible, to test in a laboratory situation, but in a personal interview the comedienne Jenny Lecoat gave it as the fruit of her observations of women's humour that such a difference was marked. If this is indeed true, then the results of such laboratory studies are probably not very meaningful.

Studies about who jokes with whom about what and under what circumstances, especially where correlations with gender are concerned, tend to be studies of pre-industrial societies. A rare exception is a study of jokes in a Glasgow printworks (Sykes, 1966), which showed that jokes in the workplace between the sexes were much more ribald than jokes at home, and that in the workplace jokes between potential sexual partners (i.e. unattached men and women in the same age group) were much less ribald than jokes between those who 'could not be' potential sexual partners. A second partial exception is Spradley and Mann's ethnographic study of waitresses which, among other things, considers the role of humour in their relationships to the barmen (quoted Mulkay, 1988). The authors' thesis, based on detailed transcribed *in situ* observations, is that humour between waitresses and bartenders is essentially a form of safety-valve in a tension-laden situation: the demands of the workplace entail that the waitresses should simultaneously co-operate with the barmen and be subordinate to them. But as Mulkay (1988: 146f.) shows, this would only follow if the waitresses initiated the humorous exchanges and were able to develop their own humorous themes; what in fact clearly happens is that when waitresses try to do this they usually fail, and most of the humour observed by Spradley and Mann is in fact male-oriented put-downs of the waitresses by the barmen.

A survey of the literature about 'sexual inequality in humour' concluded that 'women's humor reflects the existing inequality between the sexes not so much in its substance as in the constraints imposed on its occurrence, on the techniques used, on the social settings in which it occurs, and on the kind of audience that appreciates it' although certain social factors such as 'marriage, advanced age and the greater freedom enjoyed by women in groups' to some extent balance out existing inequalities and reduce the differences between men's and women's humour (Apte, 1985: 69). Most of the studies which Apte is summarising are studies of pre-industrial, largely tribal, societies. Although many of the forms of humour which are typical in such contexts do not apply in our society, what such studies indicate very clearly is that there is a link between women's absence from many forms of humour and the forms of social control exercised over them. For example, women do not engage in slapstick and horseplay, in verbal duels and ritual insults; in other words in the most aggressive and competitive forms of humour. These are precisely the forms of humour which are held to be very masculine, even in our society, and the evidence of anthropology suggests, perhaps, that such an atttribution has more to do with forms of social control than with any 'universal' or 'natural' features of either gender. In general, some sociolinguists have suggested, women do not feel that they have the same freedom to speak as men do, and therefore do not develop the verbal, rhetorical skills necessary to be good story-tellers; moreover, the rules of customary politeness may prevent women from telling jokes in mixed company (Apte, 1985: 75). International self-reported survey evidence shows that women are less likely to joke intentionally – as opposed to inadvertently causing laughter – in the presence of males than males are in the presence of females, that women are more likely to joke in female-only company whereas males are likely to joke in both male-only and mixed company, and no woman in the survey could remember passing on, or retelling, a joke, whereas many men could (Castell and Goldstein, 1977: 195–6). On the other hand, the evidence of female anthropologists from many parts of the world suggests that when women are in women-only company a very different situation obtains: vigorous satire directed at men (especially their appearance, their sexual behaviour and any specifically male rituals or activities); obscene songs and dances; all are readily observed here (Apte, 1985: 76–80). Against Apte's conclusion, quoted above, that these circumstances have the effect of reducing the differences between men's and women's humour, it should be pointed out that the fact that women can only pursue these themes in non-mixed company is itself a major difference in no way reduced by these considerations. However, what it does suggest is that there is no universal correlation between gender and sense of humour insofar as the nature of the social occasion is a crucial variable; on the other hand, the 'social rules' of gender are a central part of the nature of the occasion. These findings are consistent with Jenny Lecoat's opinion about the differences between male and female humour.

What can we learn about gender and humour from this evidence? It suggests that the nature of the occasions when humour is possible or permissible vary – among other ways – according to the gender of who is present. Such variation may exclude the possibility of humour, or humour on certain themes, in mixed company: this is usually tantamount to excluding women from being the intentional source of humour in mixed company, and may even prevent women from visibly enjoying humour when men are present (Apte, 1985: 70, 75). This may result in women tending not to develop the skills necessary for humorous performance as well as refraining from using them in mixed company if they have them. Humour is usually thought of as a desirable, even admirable trait, and is conventionally taken as a source of power and prestige; perhaps the traditional division of attributes between masculinity and femininity make the attribute of a sense of humour on the part of a woman a threat to masculinity in its traditional form. Certainly women who have taken the decision to be professional comediennes have said repeatedly that their gender makes it difficult for them (Levine, 1976; Banks and Swift, 1987). Put at its strongest – and no doubt it is now a gross oversimplification – it seems that male attempts to monopolise the right to be funny are a part of male power in the public domain.

Such is the evidence of sociological and psychological studies of humour preference and of the identity of those who joke. What does an analysis of actual jokes tell us?

One obvious way in which gender is represented in humour is in the form of 'dirty' jokes. We have already seen what evidence there is about how appreciation of such jokes is distributed between the sexes. Empirical evidence about who tells them to whom, and under what circumstances, is entirely lacking, to the best of my knowledge, and the evidence of common sense is more or less useless, for what is true under one set of social circumstances may be utterly untrue under another – this is one of the implications of Sykes (1966), quoted above – and common sense is heavily bounded by social experience. Under the circumstances it is probably safest to assume that what is true of jokes in general is a fortiori true of 'dirty jokes', and therefore their main contribution to gender may lie less in the detail of what they say about sexuality and gender than in the fact (if it is indeed so) that in general they are told by men rather than women, at any rate in mixed company.

In the only extended analysis of sexual humour, Legman (1968) concluded that dirty jokes incorporate a vision of women which corresponds to masculinity, for they assert the primacy of coitus, the universal availabilty of women, the subordination of women's discourse to male discourse and in general portray woman as an object. What follows is essentially a test of Legman's proposition (see also Mulkay, 1988: 139–40). Since there can be no question of a survey of the themes of jokes about sex, our discussion must be based upon a few examples; it is not even a question of asserting that they are typical, of anything, and what we can learn from them is only some ways in which gender is represented in jokes.

The first example is a Mediterranean joke – the source is directly relevant, as will become clear. A tourist is driving in the mountains in central Corsica, up a steep winding road. As he slowly nears the crest of a hill, a tall gaunt Corsican peasant with a rifle jumps out from behind a tree, points the rifle at him and yells at him to pull up. Quaking, he does. 'Get out!' yells the Corsican; he gets out. 'Take off your trousers!' – 'What?' asks the tourist in amazement. The Corsican sticks the gun in his ear: 'Trousers! Off! Or I'll blow your head off!' The tourist takes his trousers off. 'And your underpants!' The tourist's jaw drops. 'Do it!' The tourist does. 'Now masturbate yourself' – 'But ... but ....' 'I'll blow your effin head off if you don't!' The tourist starts to masturbate, with some difficulty. The peasant watches him carefully. Eventually he has an orgasm. The peasant waits for a moment and says: 'Do it again!' The tourist looks at him in stupefaction: 'I can't' – 'What do you mean, you can't?' 'I mean I can't, it won't get up' – 'Try', in a menacing tone of voice, rifle again in the tourist's ear. He tries, and slowly achieves tumescence and eventually another orgasm. The peasant looks at him suspiciously: 'Do it again', he says. The tourist just shakes his head, visibly incapable of speech. 'Go on!' Another shake of the head. 'You can't?' A nod of the head. 'You're sure?' Another nod. 'Alright', says the peasant, and puts his gun down. He turns to face the trees at the side of the road and calls out 'Alright, Maria, you can come down now, this gentleman's going to give you a lift into town!'

The humour arises from the utterly unexpected conclusion to the narrative, which arouses our intense curiosity about the peasant's motives. The solution is highly implausible: who would ever go to such lengths to 'protect his wife's virtue'? And yet at the same time it is a little bit plausible, since it is well known that jealousy causes strange behaviour and what he does would indeed produce the desired result![1] Clearly, therefore, this joke is closely related to traditional norms of masculinity, and it is no suprise that it comes from one of the bastions of such norms. In the terms of Legman's analysis, what is striking is that it says very little about women at all, it is entirely about male attitudes towards them. But what is curious is the 'implied listener' of such a joke: it can be enjoyed either by somebody who adheres to these traditional norms and finds this particular version absurdly exaggerated – this is presumably why the joke comes from such a bastion of male traditions – or by someone who finds these traditional norms distasteful and sees the joke as a satire of the entire tradition. 'Alternative' comedians such as Jeremy Hardy whose stock-in-trade consists in large measure of self-deprecation are probably subject to similar strictures. One of Hardy's successful jokes is: 'As far as I'm concerned, a woman who's good in bed is one who goes to sleep quickly and doesn't take up too much room.' The humour in this line derives from its contradiction of traditional male norms, clearly, but it can be enjoyed perhaps in both the ways outlined above: as a satire upon this tradition, or as an 'inadequate' exception to such a norm.

While it is difficult to assert on the basis of two examples that such an ambiguity is typical of reactions to jokes about sexuality, further examples will reveal that it is frequently the case that it is difficult to argue that there is an unequivocal correlation between the content of any joke and an orientation towards any particular set of values associated with the definition of masculinity. This conclusion points in a different direction not only to Legman, but also to this judgment: 'By describing behaviour considered sexually improper (and thus comical), [sexual humour] reveals by implication the correct forms of sexual interaction' (Fine, 1976: 135). The similarity to Powell's (1983) functional definition of humour as a form of social control is striking.

A second example. A blonde woman gives birth to a child with bright red hair. 'Oh', says the doctor, 'father a redhead, is he?' – 'No idea', says the blonde, 'he didn't take his hat off.'

In this very traditional joke, the humour arises from the implausible situation of the punch line, which is nonetheless given partial plausibility by the notion of the 'quickie'. To what extent does the structure of this joke involve reference to notions associated with masculinity? Clearly the notion of the quickie – at any rate of the version of it implied here – is linked to the notion of sex as a form of very brief encounter, perhaps as an anonymous transaction, and the humour derives from the way in which the situation described clearly transgresses, in a very exaggerated form, some norm of sexual encounter. But what is the norm which is transgressed? Is it a norm which asserts that sex ought not to be a brief encounter, but a fully developed relationship? Or a norm which asserts that quickies are indeed normal (and by implication perfectly right), and this instance transgresses it only by its extreme form? It is probably impossible to decide between these two alternatives, since all that can be deduced from the structure of the joke is that the situation in the punch-line is abnormal, and it is abnormal in relation to both of these norms. In fact the most likely situation is that the joke gains its power from contravening both these norms simultaneously: it asserts the justifiability of quickies, in defiance of their traditional moral status, and gains its humorous impact from the exaggeration of the situation. A simple test of this proposition is to ask who would be offended by such a joke instead of finding it funny. In all likelihood anyone with a sincere and deeply-held belief in traditional moral values would be offended, and perhaps feminists. If this is true (it must be stressed that there is no empirical evidence either way), it would be because the joke involves a certain level of cynicism about sexual relationships, implying that although in the abstract it might be better if sex was exclusively a feature of long-term relationships, in practice the search for pleasure is such a normal feature of human behaviour that the quickie is commonplace, even if such a quickie isn't. But then we must ask whether such cynicism towards one version of sexual morality is directly linked with gender roles or not. One answer would be that the generalised hedonism of our society (its 'permissiveness') is not gender-specific; and indeed it seems to be true that the belief that pleasure is a valid pursuit in itself is not a feature of any particular gender role. This is part of a very general value reorientation in our society, in which people increasingly define themselves according to patterns of consumption rather than according to patterns of production. On the other hand, feminists have insisted that in a society where power is distributed unevenly between the sexes, the pursuit of sexual pleasure as an end in itself favours males more than females; whence the commonplace accusation that feminists are puritanical. It is probably true that the distribution of these attitudes between the sexes is extremely uneven at the moment, and that which attitude people take depends more upon their politics than whether they are male or female. Feminists would argue that this is irrelevant, that what matters is how future relationships between the sexes are going to develop, not who believes what now: according to this analysis, the implication of this joke – as of any validation of casual sex – is that woman is seen as no more than the source of male sexual satisfaction, and this is taken to affirm male power.

My last example was told me by a well-known feminist, who had started a collection of dirty jokes which she found acceptable to feminists; the punch-line gains from being spoken.

Three women are talking in a bar, comparing their lovers. The first says: 'My man is like a double Scotch on the rocks. He's smooth and he's cool, and when he gets inside me it gives me a kick that lays me flat.' The second woman says: 'My man is like a bottle of white wine. I like to take him slowly and savour every moment. But when he's all inside me, then I'm out of my mind with ecstasy.' The third one says: 'My man is like Green Chartreuse.' A silence while the first two look at each other and at the speaker. Then one asks: 'What's a Green Chartreuse?' The third replies: 'Some fancy liquor.'

At one level, the pleasure of this joke derives from the ingenuity of the pun, an ingenuity which is partly responsible for the unexpectedness of the punch-line. But this unexpectedness is also due to the reversal of what is asserted as the source of women's sexual pleasure. In the early part of the joke, we assume that it is the man's penis that is being referred to in the innuendo of 'inside', and this assumption coincides with traditional assumptions about sexual 'normality'. The pun of the final word reveals a very different source of women's sexual pleasure, which is at least partially in breach of the earlier traditional assumptions. This revelation is surprising insofar as it is both a linguistically daring and unusual pun and the revelation of a form of sexual pleasure whose presence in the story line was unexpected until that moment. If that unexpectedness derived from the sense that this form of sexual pleasure was abnormal, then it would be difficult to see in what way the joke was compatible with feminism, in the sense that feminism asserts a woman's right to the forms of sexual pleasure she wants regardless of the 'normal' forms of male desire; if on the other hand it derived from the set of expectations created by a very traditional form of innuendo in the earlier part of the joke then this argument would not apply.

Gender may also appear in humour in the form of jokes about features of gender roles that are not necessarily or directly connected with sexuality as such. All the traditional jokes about gay effeminacy, for instance, or about domineering women, would come into this category. As an example we could take some gags from *Some Like It Hot*. This is a particularly good example to take because it was widely held in gay circles to represent a loosening of attitudes towards the gay community, and therefore a partial redefinition of masculinity. An analysis of the humour in the film suggests that this is not so, but it should be added that the mere fact that major Hollywood stars were prepared to wear drag, and that Hollywood felt able to joke about the subject of men dressed as women was in itself an indication of some loosening of attitudes, even if the actual humour was based upon traditional stereotypes. This argument is in line with earlier comments about the existence of jokes demonstrating that the topic in question is not totally repressed.

The first example is Jack Lemmon, in drag (and looking as 'unfeminine' as he does throughout the film), dancing the tango with his elderly millionaire lover, Osgood: he keeps on forgetting that he's the woman and starts leading, to the point of removing the rose that his partner was holding in his teeth and putting it in his own. This comic reversal is based entirely on the presupposition that the man should be the leader not the woman, that is, on an entirely traditional definition of masculinity.

The second example is more complex. In the final scene of the film, Jack Lemmon has to tell Osgood that he cannot marry him. He tries to do so without revealing the true reason, but is eventually forced to admit that he's a man; Osgood's reply is 'Nobody's perfect'. According to Ellis (1975: 115), *Some Like It Hot* expresses the theme of homosexual desire, but in a surreptitious form, by allowing us to laugh at its manifestations:

> Comedy has to effect some kind of reconciliation between the desires it deals with and the society which these desires are disrupting: this is at its weakest in the kind of integration that takes place at the end of *Some Like It Hot....* Here then the scatological theme of homosexuality is integrated on a personal level only. This is the most flimsy acceptance permitted; comedy is progressive in that it reveals the partially repressed areas, the areas of unease, tension, guilt, of potential change, but in the

end it has to effect, in the reading preferred by the film-makers, some kind of re-integration.

(ibid.)

Ellis does not in fact say in what way the film incarnates homosexual desire as a scatological theme, but it is safe to assume it is in the form of the Jack Lemmon/millionaire sub-plot, since here the millionaire desires Lemmon despite his – to the audience – obvious 'unfemininity' and Lemmon at one point becomes 'confused' over whether he can marry the millionaire or not: all of these plot elements could be taken as an incarnation of scatology.

But we should notice two things. First, the presentation of these plot elements is calculated to make the behaviour in question ridiculous: Lemmon's exaggerated response to his engagement and his deliberate misunderstandings of Curtis' objections to the situation produce laughter in the mechanism of their enunciation; therefore the plot element which incarnates the scatological element is doubled (if not totally 'reinterpreted') by the enunciative mechanism of comedy. Second, as a result, the 're-integration' of the ending is not really necessary, since the theme's rendition in the mode of the ridiculous has already done it for us; and anyway, as we have seen, the reintegration is inseparable from the final gag of the film.

Moreover, if we unpack the joke of the final line of dialogue, it is difficult to sustain Ellis' interpretation even where the ending is concerned. The humour of this line derives from the fact that 'Nobody's perfect' implies, in this context, that Jack Lemmon is basically suitable, but marred by some slight failing, in other words that being the wrong gender is only one marginal imperfection from a long list of other possible ones, and is no more important than any of them: wrong colour hair, likes canaries, squeezes the toothpaste from the middle of the tube, etc. This joke is fairly typical of the jokes involving the millionaire, and what they add up to is a comic portrait not of a homosexual but of an obsessive: someone who is so obsessed by 'collecting showgirls', as he calls it, that he doesn't notice, or care, about Jack Lemmon's multifarious 'imperfections': ugliness, disinterest, size, face-slapping, all of which his obsession (with girls) leads him to interpret as playing hard to get. In short, he is ridiculous because an obsessive, and the audience laughs at him; it is difficult to see how this could be taken as a release from inhibitions repressing homosexual desire. In general, this seems consistent with the overall comic theme of the film: a series of misunderstandings and double meanings arising from the false appearance of gender reversal, where the continuous presupposition is precisely that the appearances are indeed misleading. In short, the definition of masculinity implied by the form of the jokes in *Some Like It Hot* is largely traditional; such non-traditional elements as there are derive largely from the fact that homosexuality (or transvestism) is presented as an acceptable subject for humour in public, in other words that the topic is no longer so suppressed that it is unavailable for humour in a public forum such as mainstream Hollywood cinema, as opposed to the more restricted forum of 'dirty' joke telling.

What do these examples imply about a possible functional relationship between humour and gender? The conclusion they lead to must be largely negative. 'Function' is essentially a form of causal explanation, for what is implied in a functional explanation is this: that the thing to which a function is ascribed (here, humour) exists because it has such-and-such a function; even if causality is never mentioned, it is logically necessary in the sense that the being of the functional object, humour, is entirely taken up by its function; there is nothing in humour that is not to be explained by its function. If the object has no properties that are not explained by function, then it must be the case that it is function that is the cause of the object's existence. Even the more modest cases of functional analysis are liable to this criticism, in that while they do not propose any single function, and therefore explanation, for humour, they still propose that such-and-such a form of humour, or such-and-such a circumstance for humour, is entirely circumscribed by its function. The enormous variety of relationships between humour and gender that are to be found in every respect (identity of tellers and listeners, humour preference, joke themes) certainly implies that there cannot be a single functional relationship between gender and humour in our society. Studies of humour preference and performance in relation to gender might be used to reveal some functional attributes, at least as a hypothesis, but the study of the representations of gender in jokes which are explicitly about this topic suggests that even this is a dubious enterprise: the versions of gender that are proposed in such jokes are in the first place remarkably various, and in the second – crucially – often very ambiguous: the same joke may appeal to very different value judgments about gender.

6

FREUD

A major theory of humour which sets out an explanation on the basis of a functional relationship between the joke and the ecology of the mind is to be found in Freud, especially his early work *Jokes and their Relation to the Unconscious*.[1] At the core of Freud's theory is a single, simple assertion: jokes are not distinguished from other verbal phenomena by their linguistic structure – their 'technique', as Freud puts it – but by their relation to the unconscious. Specifically, they relate to it in this way: they give a form of pleasure which is unique to them, which enables them to subserve the interests, so to speak, of 'the major purposes and instincts of mental life' (1960: 133); Freud calls this the 'principle of assistance or intensification' (1960: 135). This is consistent with what is clearly Freud's central tactical concern at this point: to demonstrate that there is something of the unconscious at work in this everyday psychological mechanism, a mechanism which is apparently an entirely conscious matter.

Seen in this context, the long section on joke techniques which opens the book has two clear purposes: to establish that the technical description of jokes tells us nothing about their basis in the mind; and to prepare the ground for the later assertion that different categories of jokes, defined technically, occupy different places in the ecology of the mind. To this end, Freud divides jokes into groups on a basis which is simultaneously technical and ecological. His major distinctions are between verbal/conceptual jokes, and between innocent/tendentious jokes; he also uses the term 'jest' to refer to purely verbal and innocent jokes, and distinguishes between the joke (*der Witz*) and *Schwanke* (funny stories); this distinction is based on the distribution of enunciative roles in the two forms, where *Schwanke* have only two and jokes three. We shall see that it is also possible that there is nonetheless a single fundamental mechanism common to all forms of jokes, jests, etc., indicating a single relationship to the unconscious.

Verbal jokes are ones where the entire impact of the joke relies on its verbal form. When asked about the professions of his four sons, Professor Rokitansky replied 'two heal and two howl' (doctors and singers); the same information is contained in the second formulation as in the first, but the joke has disappeared, for it is the assonance that is its base (Freud, 1960: 129–30). In a joke based upon conceptual play, much of the wording can be changed without any loss of humour:

> A horse-dealer was recommending a horse to a client. 'If you take this horse and get on it at four in the morning, you'll be at Pressburg by half-past six' – 'What should I be doing at Pressburg at half-past six in the morning?'

> (1960: 54)

Here, much of the wording could be changed without losing the humour: any mode of transport, any location, even the wording of the final retort – 'What's so great about Pressburg in the morning?' would do just as well.

Innocent jokes are ones whose pleasure derives entirely from their technique, tendentious jokes are ones that directly subserve the interests of the unconscious. It is through the principle of assistance that joke pleasure helps the interests of the unconscious, for this pleasure enables the joke to overcome repressions and inhibitions. At the moment that the joke is told, Freud hypothesises, there are present in the mind a series of tendencies:

1 to do something that is the object of social disapprobation, e.g. insult somebody;
2 the repression of that tendency;
3 the pleasure specific to joking.

In the absence of (3), (2) will usually overcome (1): the repression or inhibition will operate to control behaviour. But if the joke is introduced into the situation, then the pleasure which it gives will be sufficient to overcome the inhibition and the otherwise repressed tendency will appear. Under these circumstances, Freud argues, a thought which would – for example – be an insult if not expressed in joking form will be expressed (in the form of a joke) and tendency (1) will overcome inhibition (1960: 136).

Clearly under these circumstances two things are central: first, the thought given expression in the joke must be of such a nature as to be relevant to the drive of aggression (in this instance; under other circumstances, a sexual thought would give free rein to the drive of desire); second, the pleasure which is specific to the joke form is responsible for unlocking this process.

The joke pleasure, Freud explains, consists of the capacity to subvert the norms of adult rational thought, which he also often calls 'rational criticism', for it is in these norms that repression occurs. Through this subversion, the adult manages to recreate the sense of pleasure in play that the child loses in the process of maturation. Jests and jokes prolong 'the yield of pleasure from play' by silencing the 'objections raised by criticism which would not allow the pleasurable feeling to emerge'; this is achieved by combining the yield of pleasure with the demands of criticism: 'the meaningless combination of words or the absurd putting together of thoughts must nevertheless have a meaning' (1960: 129). Thus, as Freud insists in the following pages, it is not the techniques of jokes that define them, but their capacity to subvert criticism and give pleasure through the prolongation of the childlike sense of play. The pleasure that is brought about by the subversion of rational adult criticism is a form of the pleasure created in general by the subversion of inhibition, for rational criticism is in itself an inhibition; its subversion corresponds therefore to an economy of psychic expenditure.

We are now in a position to understand the logic of Freud's paradoxical argument that jokes could not be separated from other linguistic forms on the basis of their techniques:

> The technique which is characteristic of jokes and peculiar to them, however, consists in their procedure for safeguarding the use of these methods of providing pleasure against the objections raised by criticism which would put an end to the pleasure.
>
> (1960: 130)

This procedure, which protects the sources of pleasure, is precisely psychic economy, for a procedure which does not consist of the techniques of jokes must be based on the relationship between the joke and the mind of the listener. That is to say, the techniques of jokes are to be found equally in things which are not jokes, and the distinction between jokes and non-jokes is displaced to the manner in which the mind appreciates the technique.

Now it is true that certain other affirmations made by Freud somewhat undermine his insistence that joke techniques do not have a central place in the schema, notably the way in which he returns to the question of the mixture of sense and nonsense in jokes ('the meaningless combination . . . must have a meaning'); for if this combination was specific to jokes it could be considered a way of distinguishing the joke from other linguistic forms on purely technical grounds.[2] Freud's statements are somewhat inconsistent on this point. On the one hand he says 'there is no necessity for us to derive the pleasurable effect of jokes from the conflict between the feelings which arise . . . from the simultaneous sense and nonsense of jokes' (1960: 131), and nowhere does he indicate that in his opinion the combination of sense and nonsense is a technical matter; this is consistent with the position that there is no technical distinction between jokes and non-jokes. On the other hand, he also says (1960: 131): 'the pleasure in a joke is derived from a play with words or from the liberation of nonsense, and the meaning of the joke is merely intended to protect that pleasure from being done away with by criticism'. Two pressures appear to be at play in this sentence: first, Freud appears obliged to admit that the mixture of sense and nonsense is central to the joke process, for it – more specifically, the presence of sense – protects pleasure from criticism; second, it 'merely' does this, and the presence of 'merely' indicates very forcibly the main drift of Freud's thought.

Now it is well known that it is central to Freudian theory that thought can be a disguise for other processes; this is clear in the theory of dreams that Freud had already elaborated before his theory of jokes (Lyotard, 1971: 261–70). Thus, when Freud speaks of the 'sense in nonsense' being a protection for joke pleasure, he has something similar or connected in mind: 'in jokes nonsense often replaces ridicule and criticism in the thoughts lying behind the jokes. . . . (In this respect, incidentally, the joke-work is doing the same thing as the dream-work)' (1960: 107). While it is true that here Freud speaks of 'nonsense' alone, we already know that in jokes nonsense is always partial sense. We shall return to this. But in the meantime we need to follow the implications of Freud's argument as it is put in the argument about technique and ecology.

Freud is in a position characterised by two contradictory pulls: either jokes are technically distinct from other forms, or they are not. If one opts for the first position (which is arguably faithful to the letter of Freud's text, but certainly not to its spirit) then two further problems arise. First, is it true that the mixture of sense and nonsense is specific to jokes? Second, it would no longer be true that the essence of jokes was to allow free rein to the drives of the unconscious, and the ecological dimension of Freud's argument would be weakened. If we opt for the second possibility, then a further problem arises: what mechanism is responsible for the psychic economy which protects the pleasure of the joke from rational criticism? If Freud wishes to maintain the affirmation that joke techniques are not distinct from other linguistic forms, then it is clear that the source of psychic economy cannot be in the techniques, but at the same time there can be no other possible source. The pleasure of play cannot be the source because the joke produces the pleasure of play precisely by subverting criticism – that is to say, it is thanks to jokes' subversive capacities that psychic economy is created. But it is psychic economy that protects jokes and play from rational criticism. The argument is thus strangely circular, precisely insofar as Freud has refused to distinguish between jokes and other linguistic forms.

This paradoxical circularity points us straight at the core of Freud's argument: the relationship between thought, or sense, in a joke and the joke's place in the ecology of mind. Here certain complexities arise.

'Sense' and 'nonsense' in Freud's argument are clearly always forms of thought: nonsense is such in the terms of rational adult thought, and the same is true of sense. Thus when Freud talks about the mixture of sense and nonsense, and their role in the production of joke pleasure, he is always talking about forms of conscious thought, even though the mixture of the two in the form of jokes may allow free rein to impulses of the unconscious. But where jokes are concerned Freud makes assertions that pull in conflicting directions. On the one hand, a long section in the chapter called 'The Purposes of Jokes' consistently promotes the idea that jokes do indeed directly incarnate entirely conscious thoughts, that the best jokes are the ones that have the most substantial thoughts in them, etc. This line of reasoning culminates in a statement that has been the subject of some controversy: 'the best achievements in the way of jokes are used as an envelope for thoughts of the greatest substance' (1960: 92). Here the translation is Strachey's, from the *Standard Edition*. Samuel Weber, in a deconstruction of Freud's ideas, argues that Strachey has mistranslated Freud, and gives a translation that inverts the meaning of this sentence: 'with jokes the best performances may use the most substantial thoughts as their guise' (1982: 89); that is to say, according to Strachey the joke is a disguise for the thought, according to Weber the thought is a disguise for the 'reality' of the joke. Freud's original text reads: '[es mag vorkommen dass] die besten Witzleistungen gerade zur Einkleidung der gehaltvollsten Gedanken benutzt werden' (Freud, 1958: 74). This edition, which is usually taken as the definitive German language edition, reproduces the text of the last collected edition of Freud's works prepared during Freud's lifetime (Freud, 1940), and at this point is identical to the earlier edition of *Jokes* in the first collected edition (Freud, 1925). Weber translates as an active verb – 'uses' – what Strachey translates as a passive verb – 'are used'. It is clear that Freud used the passive voice: 'benutzt werden'; in this instance it is Strachey's translation that is closer to Freud's thought.[3]

And yet Weber's conclusion, albeit based on a mistranslation, is far from inaccurate: 'Meaning, in short, has for Witz no intrinsic value; it is only instrumental, serving to eliminate temporarily the barriers to play' (1982: 93). This principle is to be found at various points in Freud's text. Thus despite the intellectual distinction beween 'good' and 'bad' jokes (it is the presence/absence of a rational thought that is responsible for the difference), in terms of pleasure (and therefore the joke's place in the ecology of the mind) bad jokes may be just as good as good jokes; thus the role of thought in the joke is clearly subordinate to its capacity to produce pleasure in the ways described here (1960: 120n.). By the same token, Freud asserts that when we laugh at a joke 'we do not know what we are laughing at' (1960: 102); the context applies this specifically to dirty jokes, where Freud argues that we laugh because the joke is a disguised form of making visible what is hidden in sex, but there does not seem to be any reason not to extend the principle to jokes in general insofar as in all cases pleasure is allowing the drives of the unconscious to emerge. Moreover, at exactly the point in his text where he is most directly concerned with the question of the intellectual content of jokes, he makes it clear that what he means by thought is by no means 'adult rational' thought. In his discussion of the 'Schadchen' jokes, he shows that it is not really the figure of the poor marriage broker that is the butt of the humour, but rather the institution of arranged marriage itself. Specifically, such jokes have a façade 'in the contemplation of which one person is satiated while another may try to peer behind it' (1960: 106); in other words there is a disguise, which is the apparent meaning of the story, behind which lurks a different reality, another meaning which is a 'forbidden' meaning (1960: 106). And this is true regardlesss of whether the façade in question is a comic façade or a logical façade: either way, it is 'the disguised representation of the truth that gives it the character of a joke, which is thus essentially dependent on its purpose' (1960: 108). Thus in either of these cases, apparent meaning, the meaning which is available to normal rational adult thought, is a disguise behind which lurk the drives of the unconscious.

This principle does not sit entirely comfortably with the argument about pleasure allowing the drives of the unconscious to emerge, in the sense that if the mixture of sense and nonsense gives pleasure by liberating the childish pleasure of play then surely it cannot only be a disguise, it must have some efficacity of its own. Freud moves towards a resolution of this problem by positing two different pleasures which are given in jokes. He distinguishes a pleasure in jokes which is a 'fore-pleasure', which derives from the techniques of jokes and the subversion of adult rationality, from a second 'new pleasure [in] lifting suppressions and inhibitions' operating on the major drives of the unconscious (1960: 137–8). From a psycho-genetic point of view, there is an original state of free childish play with words and thoughts; as maturation bars this pleasure, jests arise to prolong it, then it lends assistance to thoughts that criticism would debar as stupid and finally – in the fully developed form of the tendentious joke – it allows free rein to the drives of the unconscious (1960: 137).

Two focal points are emerging: first, there is the question of the role of 'sense in nonsense', and whether Freud's argument is circular at this point; second, there is the question of the role of conscious, adult, rational thought.

Does the introduction of a distinction between two forms of pleasure have an impact upon the accusation of circularity? If there was only one form of pleasure given by the joke, then the accusation would surely stand. If there are two, they may play different roles. The 'fore-pleasure' that derives from technique and the subversion of rationality alone liberates nonsense from criticism; Freud suggests in a footnote on 'nonsense jokes' (1960: 138n.) that the inhibition against pure childish nonsense may be far weaker than the bars against the other tendencies of the subconscious, and thus the fore-pleasure would arise very easily and open up an arena of free association where the joke would also allow the other subconscious drives direct manifestation in behaviour.

However, this argument does not seem to avert the criticism of tautology, for several reasons:

1 *The subversion of criticism is still central.* The distinction between the two types of pleasure in no way reduces the centrality of the subversion of criticism, since whatever the relation between them, the pleasure that derives from the liberation of childish nonsense is still the trigger of the whole process.

2 *The distinction between verbal/conceptual jokes may not be as clear-cut as Freud makes out.* The distinction between verbal/conceptual jokes tends to

hide ambiguities in Freud's formulations. If we take the example of Professor Rokitansky's four sons, quoted above, it is not only the assonance 'heal/howl' that is involved, but also what Freud calls 'unification', which is explicitly applied to the Rokitansky example (1960: 130): the assonance implies some kind of unity between these two professions; it causes the mind to perceive a link where none would be seen if the assonance were not present.[4] Of course such a unity, or link, is false, or more exactly absurd: it is precisely the mixture of sense and nonsense that Freud discusses; but this should not lead us to dismiss the idea, quite the contrary. By implying a unity based on a pun, the mind is liberated into the kind of 'nonsense' that the childish mind enjoys, and which can be the source of pleasure for the adult mind if there is something that can bypass the repression of adult rationality, i.e. the assonance.[5] Does this unification amount to a 'thought'? Freud says of such 'jests' that in them

> the meaning of the sentence need not be valuable or new or even good; it need merely be *permissible* [emphasis in original] to say the thing in this way, even though it is unusual, unnecessary or useless to say it in this way.
>
> (1960: 129)

Clearly, then, Freud thinks of the unification involved in the Rokitansky joke as having something in common with thought, at least in the minimal sense that it is 'permissible'. On the other hand, Freud immediately says of such jests that they make possible 'what was forbidden by criticism' (1960: 129), indicating that they are not normal adult thought. Since the thought is absurd (sense and nonsense) it cannot be quite the same as a thought in the sense of rational adult critical thought; and yet it seems likely that there is something 'thought-like' involved here, since the statement is not entire nonsense, in the way that Chomsky's famous 'Colourless green ideas dream furiously' is nonsense, or a logically impossible statement such as 'Napoleon is a prime number'. What happens in a statement such as Professor Rokitansky's is that an intermediate realm is opened up, somewhere between the realm of purely rational statements and the realm of nonsensical statements, the realm inhabited by figures of speech in general. When we recognise – as Freud does – that 'heal/howl' has some element of sense in it, we are recognising this intermediate realm. This implies that Freud may be guilty of some over-simplification when he presents the pleasure of such a joke as deriving entirely from the joke technique. This statement is true in his terms, because 'unification' is a technique, but the whole point of defining 'technique' in the way that Freud does is to preserve the distinction between verbal and conceptual humour, and an example such as this suggests that the distinction is by no means as clear-cut as Freud wishes to maintain.

3 *Adult rational criticism is a repression in the fullest sense of the word.* In general the bar of adult criticism in fact appears a major barrier against the

enjoyment of play. Elsewhere in Freud's theory it appears in the form of the distinction between thing-presentations and word-presentations, and this plays a major role in the development of repression and the structure of the subconscious. The barrier of adult criticism is, in fact, an inhibition in the fullest sense of the word, and it seems difficult to maintain that in adults there is a clear distinction between a joke 'fore-pleasure' deriving from overcoming this barrier and a subsequent more complex pleasure deriving from the overcoming of other inhibitions such as desire and aggression. If this argument is correct, then the distinction between two pleasures falls to the ground, and we are still in a position where Freud's argument about a safeguarding procedure is tautologous.

4 *'Meaning' and 'play' may not be as ecologically distinct as Freud suggests in* Jokes. The psycho-genetic argument that Freud pursues in relation to the two pleasures is clearly intended to suggest that they have different sources in ecologically distinct dimensions of the mind. However, as Weber argues: who (or what psychic entity) is the joke pleasurable to/for? The answer must be: the narcissistic ego, which is bent upon imposing its schemata upon everything round it, thereby reducing the sense of otherness (which is in fact the condition of its existence) to a sense of sameness. In this context the opposition between 'play' and 'meaning' loses much of its force, since both play and meaning are ways in which the narcissistic ego seeks to 'appropriate the other upon which it depends and in the image of which it constitutes its identity' (1982: 98).

At this point we may return to the question of the role of thought and sense in the joke. Freud's assertions that the thought in a joke is only a disguise or an envelope suggest that he sees a parallel between this dimension of the joke and the process of secondary revision in dreams. Here the dream is turned into something like a text which is accessible to normal waking thought. The process of secondary revision takes something typical of the dream-work, the condensation and displacement, which is entirely formless, entirely lacking in all the internal distinctions – categories and classifications – which typify normal thought, and subjects it to a process which brings it into some degree of conformity with the order of the latter. As a result the dream becomes partially accessible to normal thought. But at the same time this accessibility, this form-giving, this gloss of legibility is profoundly erroneous, since it is always a travesty of what the dream is 'really' about: the 'truth' of the dream lies in the thoughts which are subjected to the processes of condensation and displacement, and in these processes themselves; the process of secondary revision is profoundly untrue to these elements, and thus the comprehensibility that it produces is always a disguise (Lyotard, 1971: 261–70).

Clearly there are analogies between secondary revision in dreams and the thought contained in jokes: both have a form of comprehensibility, both act as a disguise for another process deriving from the drives of the subconscious.

Certainly the parallel cannot be exact, since dreams and jokes differ in fundamental respects – first, in the role of sleep, which acts to release the mind from certain forms of conscious control, perhaps in this respect paralleled by the role of joke pleasure; second, in the role of the presence of a listener, which is essential to the joke structure (as Freud repeats on many occasions) but which is clearly absent in the dream. We may suspect that Freud is in fact working with two different senses of the word 'thought', since at some points in his argument thought is something on the surface of the (joke) text, and thus conforms to 'adult, rational, critical' thought; and at others 'thought' refers to something buried in the drives of the unconscious, the cynical, obscene or aggressive impulse that is the 'purpose' of the joke and that thus defines it as such. Here it will help to follow Freud's distinction between jokes and 'the species of the comic', as he calls it.

This distinction is fundamentally given in the distribution of roles between joker, listener and butt. In a joke, says Freud, the joker needs the listener, and it is only through releasing the joking pleasure and giving free rein to the listener's unconscious drives that the joker is able to gain pleasure from the joke him- or herself. But in comic situations, the laugher perceives something in the outside world which strikes him or her as funny, and produces laughter, without any need for the drives of the unconscious to come into play at all (cf. Todorov, 1976). For Freud, the comic has the same mechanism of 'sense in nonsense' as the joke – the same semiotic mechanism, in modern terms – but a very different psychological structure. If we apply this to the vexed question of the role of conscious thought in jokes, we can see that there are indeed two types of thought involved: in the first place, the conscious thoughts which produce the characteristic mixture of sense and nonsense, in the second the 'unconscious thoughts', akin to dream-thoughts in *The Interpretation of Dreams* (Freud, 1953) which are hidden behind the façade of conscious meaning. These too, of course, are also meanings, but meanings which operate in an 'other' realm.

But the question of the truth of the two types of disguise is instructive. In a joke, it is surely not the case that the conscious thought is profoundly, completely untrue to the process of the release from inhibitions.

In the first place, the thought must be relevant to the type of drive and the type of inhibition that will be released: an aggressive thought liberates the drive of aggression in joke-pleasure, a sexual thought liberates the drive of sexual desire. Here we see that even if the thought is indeed a disguise in the way Freud says ('we do not know what we laugh at'), nonetheless it can only act as such on the condition that there is a thematic link between the thought and what it is cloaking. The instance of cynical jokes is especially instructive here, since in them what is forbidden and what is conscious is linked in a special manner. In 'Schadchen' jokes, laughter arises because of a breakdown in rational processes – either reason overcomes prudence, when the 'Schadchen' inadvertently lets the truth slip out, or reason is visibly sophistry.

But the unconscious purpose of these jokes, Freud says, is a cynical assessment of arranged marriage; that is to say, an act of aggression based upon the superiority of one form of reasoning to another. And it is no accident that Freud finishes this chapter with the example of a joke about the impossibility of distinguishing truth from lies, to which he gives a different name – 'sceptical' jokes; but the contiguity and continuity are revealing.

In the second place, the way in which a joke makes sense is not only what makes it acceptable to adult criticism, and therefore comprehensible to the joker, it is also what makes it communicable, in other words accessible to the hearer and thereby makes it into a joke (since the listener is integral); beyond this we shall see in Part III that the thought in a joke is also what makes comic narrative possible, where jokes are joined together in sequences and are made to serve the purposes of narrative in general.

CONCLUSION TO PART II

It is difficult to argue with the proposition that humour has a function or functions: it is clear from the kinds of evidence cited here that it enters into functional relationships with many different entities. Even if we dismiss the notion of a direct biological function as unnecessarily speculative, it is hard to avoid the conclusion that humour is in fact used in various ways, in various circumstances, and that in that sense it has functions.

But that is a claim that most functionalists would regard as minimal to the point of insignificance, for a functionalist explanation demands something more than this rather commonsensical observation: it demands that humour's existence as a phenomenon should be understandable entirely and exclusively by showing how it enables an organism to continue to exist in the form proper to it. Now that claim is much more difficult to substantiate, for a number of reasons. The first and most important is a logical one: demonstrating that humour has a function is not the same as showing how it performs that function and any demonstration that only shows what a function is, is by the same token incomplete. Clearly Radcliffe-Brown's studies of joking relationships fall foul of this criticism, but Douglas' does not: her recourse to Freud shows how humour achieves its function. The second reason is that studies of function ascribe such varied functions to it: it is said to relieve anxiety, and yet at the same time being victimised by a joke for censorious purposes is likely to increase it – or provoke some other emotional reaction that is certainly not a reduction in anxiety; it is said to be a safety-valve for dealing with taboo subjects, an indirect recognition of what is repressed, but it can also be a way of negotiating their introduction onto a public agenda. If humour can be shown to have such divergent functions, it is unlikely that we could ever explain it by ascribing it a single function, and if we choose to explain it by giving it several functions, at the very least we must admit that such an explanation demands extension: if humour can perform several functions then it must have some properties that transcend the division between functions.

This is ultimately the import of the analysis of Freud's book on jokes. Freud's tactic is essentially to show the part of the unconscious in an everyday process, to show that jokes cannot be understood as a phenomenon without reference to the unconscious. But on the way he shows that other forms of funniness – the comic, jests and humour – all share something in common with jokes, but do not share their ecological relationship to the unconscious. However satisfactory Freud's analysis of the part of the unconscious in jokes may be – and of jokes' part in the unconscious – we are left with the necessity of looking at the other elements in the various forms of funniness, as we have seen.

These considerations all point in the same direction: it is beyond doubt that humour enters into all sorts of relationship with other mental and social entities, and in that sense it has a function or functions. Indeed, any analysis of humour which omits this dimension is clearly partial. Yet it is also clear that function alone is incapable of explaining humour: at the very least we need to know how humour does what it does. We must analyse the structure of humour.

Part III

THE STRUCTURE OF HUMOUR

7

INCONGRUITY

Debates about the structure of humour are essentially attempts to answer the question: what makes us laugh? What categories of phenomena cause us to experience funniness? Answers do not, of course, consist of lists of features of the world such as fat men on banana skins: such a list would be interminable, and only parts of it would apply to any particular people or groups of people. Nonetheless, within the probably infinite selection of things that have at one time or another evoked mirth there may well be some common features, or some common process of meaning creation; if there is, then this would constitute the structure of humour. In any event, the supposition that this may be so is what underlies all the debates to which the next two chapters refer.

The starting-point for such debates is usually the question: is funniness a feature of what is laughed at, or is it a feature of the mind of the perceiver? The similarity with very traditional arguments about beauty is no coincidence, for in fact this question refers us straight to a central element in the theory of meaning. As is well known, the basis of semiotics is the proposition that a sign is an object that stands in for some other object *for somebody*; in other words, any sign is such only insofar as it has meaning for its user or users. All meaning resides in an interaction between the mind, culture and the empirical world – this is a banality (although attempts to turn it into a precisely articulated description are notoriously difficult and the location of most major disagreements in the theory of meaning). Where humour is concerned, it at least indicates where to look for an answer to our initial question. Specifically, it indicates the sterility of seeking funniness either entirely in the mind of the laugher or entirely in the phenomenon which evokes mirth: it is in the interaction between the two that answers must be sought. This avoids two obvious shortcomings of many traditional conceptions of humour: on the one hand, variations in what is found funny lead to the argument that nothing is inherently funny; on the other, if we say that humour resides entirely in the mind of the laugher, it is difficult to explain collective humour and we would have to hypothesise that indices of mirth would appear random to outside observers, as there would be no framework for explaining why other people laugh. A valid theory of the structure of humour must therefore seek an explanation in the interaction between the laugher and the laughable object, where the object has some describable attributes that make it an appropriate object for mirth, and where the mind-set of the laugher has some feature(s) that produce mirth.

Morreall (1983) has summarised previous theories of humour and laughter into three types: (1) where humour is derived from a sensation of superiority over what is laughed at; (2) where humour derives from a sensation of psychological relief; (3) where humour derives from the perception of incongruity in what is laughed at.

For Plato and Aristotle, laughter derives from the inadequacy of the laughable person, but the pleasure of laughter is in itself not a worthy aim; its justification is that it can serve to educate wrongdoers by deriding them, but even then laughing too much is morally inferior and vulgar; for both, laughter is essentially derision (Morreall, 1983: 4ff.). In the same way, Hobbes conceived of laughter as a 'Sudden glory arising from some conception of some eminency in ourselves, by comparison with the infirmity of others, or with our own formerly' (Morreall, 1983: 6). Hobbes also admits of laughter 'without offence . . . at absurdities and infirmities abstracted from persons', but he agrees with his Greek predecessors that constant laughter at others is a sign of pusillanimity because it is an attempt to seek confirmation of self through favourable comparisons with others (Hobbes, 1651: 101–3). In the twentieth century, zoologist Konrad Lorenz has argued that humour is an evolutionary derivation in humans from animal aggression. In modern treatments of the subject, it is usually recognised that identifying humour with a sense of moral superiority is inadequate, since not all feelings of moral superiority take the form of humour; at the very least then, such a theory needs an additional element.

Theories based on the notion of relief from psychological tension are always in part theories of a function for humour: here humour is defined by its role in the ecology of the mind. The most sophisticated of these theories is Freud's, and we have already seen at its heart the lacuna of a semiotic structure.

There is something approaching a theory of incongruity in Aristotle. In the *Rhetoric* he indicates that an effective device, which may result in laughter, is to set up a particular expectation in the audience, and then to contradict or subvert it: 'He walked, and under his feet were sores', where the audience would expect something like 'stones' as the last word. However, Aristotle is not offering a theory of humour, but an analysis of how metaphor can be an effective tool of persuasion; he notes that witticisms can have the same effect by promoting an unforeseen comparison, and that they can destroy an opponent's attempt to be serious, provided that the joke is worthy of a free man (as opposed to a slave) (Aristotle, 1973: 67–70, 95–6). In general the theory of rhetoric found no place for an explanation of laughter, being content to note its effectiveness.

The recognition of the explanatory role of incongruity starts with Kant and Schopenhauer, who both refer to the contradiction of expectations in the generation of laughter (Morreall, 1983: 16ff.). For Schopenhauer incongruity consists of a mismatch between a concept and some empirical entity in the world: concepts are necessarily universalising, in the sense that a concept groups together all the empirical instances that fall under it in the world, and thought proceeds by organising perception using concepts; when some empirical entity in the world fails to behave according to the expectations set up by the relevant concept, incongruity occurs. For example, Tom the cat is exploded by the stick of dynamite he intended for Jerry the mouse, but survives – albeit in an attenuated form! The concept 'explosion' includes the expectation of death, therefore Tom's survival is incongruous. In the words of a psychologist's definition it is:

> the discrepancy between two mental representations, one of which is an expectation (presumably derived from, for example, the main body of a joke preceding the punch line) and the other is some idea or percept (for example, as contained in the punch line).
>
> (Suls, 1983: 41)

Humour then arises in the discrepant relationship between the two parts of the perception. In a well-known experiment, Nerhardt showed subjects non-representational shapes projected onto two film screens. The shapes moved off one screen onto the one beside it in a way that demonstrated continuity of movement across the gap between the screens. After a series of such movements came one in which there was discontinuity between the two screens: the more incongruous the lack of continuity, the funnier subjects found it (Wilson, 1979: 34). However, many psychologists maintain that what occurs in humour is not the perception of incongruity but its resolution: the punch-line allows the receiver to make some sense or other of what has gone before. Indeed, this notion is included in some other definitions of incongruity:

> With incongruity we see two things which do not belong together, yet which we accept at least in this case as going together in some way. That is, when we notice something as incongruous, we also simultaneously understand it to be in some minor way congruous.
>
> (Schaeffer, 1981: 9)

The incongruity thesis has been tested by giving groups of children a joke in three versions, where one version was the original, and the two others were altered in some way that would change the degree or type of resolution involved (Suls, 1983: 45). This is one example of the joke-variations used:

1 'Doctor, come at once! Our baby swallowed a fountain pen!' 'I'll be right over. What are you doing in the meantime?' 'Using a pencil.'
2 'Doctor, come at once! Our baby swallowed a rubber band.' 'I'll come at once. What are you doing in the meantime?' 'Using a pencil.'

3 'Doctor, come at once! Our baby has swallowed a fountain pen.' 'I'll come at once. What are you doing in the meantime?' 'We don't know what to do.'

According to Suls, in version 1 there is both incongruity and resolution, because of the relationship (a) between the doctor's question and the answer, (b) between fountain pen and pencil; in version 2 there is incongruity (baby swallows a foreign object), but no resolution, because there is no connection between rubber band and pencil; in version three there is no incongruity. The children found version 1 far funnier than the other two.

Clearly there is good reason to find version 1 funnier: the other two are not jokes, as Suls says; but is his description of why they are not jokes correct? In his analysis, in version 2 there is incongruity but no resolution, and therefore the statement is not funny. But version 2 does not present an incongruous situation in anything like the same sense that version 1 does. A baby swallowing a rubber band may well be abnormal, even threatening (if less so than swallowing a fountain pen!), but it is not the act of swallowing the fountain pen that produces the comic incongruity in version 1: it is the parents' response to the doctor that is comically incongruous. Indeed, in version 3, Suls says there is no incongruity, despite the fact that the baby has swallowed the fountain pen. Clearly – for Suls – the incongruity now lies elsewhere, in the relationship between the baby's danger, the parents' action and their reply to the doctor: the 'removal of incongruity' in version 3 is attributed to the parents' response to the doctor, which is entirely plausible, given the incongruous (or at any rate implausible) circumstances.

Suls' difficulty derives from the terms of his analysis: incongruity and resolution are seen as incompatible; any incongruity is either resolved or it is not. The reality is that here (and in this respect his example is typical of joke structure) there is indeed incongruity, and it is indeed maintained in the punch-line, but only partially; incongruity is both maintained and resolved simultaneously. Modified in this way, the incongruity resolution thesis can be assimilated to a semiotic model I advanced in an earlier book (Palmer, 1987: 39–44). Here the structure of the joke is presented as the conjunction of two processes:

1 the sudden creation of a discrepancy, or incongruity, in the joke narrative;
2 a bifurcated logical process, which leads the listener to judge that the state of affairs portrayed is simultaneously highly implausible and just a little bit plausible.

This combination I refer to as 'the logic of the absurd'. Suls' version 1 is clearly 'absurd', in this sense. A threatening situation is evoked (baby and fountain pen), though we should note that the threat will not be taken seriously if the audience knows that a joke is being told – we shall have occasion to return to this theme later. The parents' reply to the doctor is highly implausible: the mistake about the meaning of the doctor's question could only be made by someone of quite exceptional stupidity or callousness. And yet it is a tiny bit plausible, in the sense – as Suls says – that a pencil is a valid substitute for a pen, and the doctor's question could, with some difficulty, refer to this substitution because of its grammatical structure. In Suls' terms, therefore, the incongruity is both maintained (the implausibility of the parents' reply) and yet at the same time partially resolved (the tiny element of plausibility in it). Version 2, my model would predict, is unfunny because the parents' reply is nonsensical; that is to say, their reply is totally implausible, rather than absurd in my sense. Version 3 is entirely plausible in the sense that (assuming the baby did in fact swallow a fountain pen), any parent would be likely to feel threatened and confused; again it is not absurd.[1]

If the weakness of Suls' model lies in his analysis of the internal articulations of the joke, the weakness of my model is that it fails to take into account the incongruity of the preparatory phase – the baby swallowing the fountain pen. As has been shown before (Mulkay, 1988: 8–15), it is commonly the case that what he calls the 'standardised joke' involves all sorts of implausibilities in the way in which the joke situation is set up. For example: one businessman says to another 'What's 2 plus 2?' – 'Are you buying or selling?' asks the other. If the reply is absurd (in my sense), the question is utterly implausible. As Mulkay says, the audience so to speak makes a pact with the joke-teller and makes different demands upon 'humorous discourse' to the demands that it would make of non-humorous discourse; specifically, the demands of common-sense rationality are suspended. The implication is that the logic of the absurd operates within a wider framework of rules that provide the setting within which the absurd is achievable. Of course, this does not mean that all jokes do in fact involve such a suspension in their preparatory phase. The Irish comedian Michael Redmond uses the one-liner 'People often come up to me and say "What are you doing in my garden?"': no implausibility in the preparatory 'people often come up to me and say . . .', which is the kind of thing that celebrities indeed come out with in TV chat shows. However, recognising that 'normal' discursive expectations are suspended in humorous discourse raises the concomitant problem of explaining how people know in advance that what is happening is indeed humorous; we shall return to this question shortly.

At this point we may consider a question which has been latent in the discussion of incongruity and Suls' thesis. Suls' definition of incongruity relates 'expectation' to the flow of the joke statement in time: first there is the creation of some expectation; then there is the device which is discrepant in relation to it, producing the perception of incongruity. Yet in his example, there are in fact two incongruities: first, the statement that the baby has swallowed the pen; second, the parents' reply to the doctor's question; of these two, it is the second that constitutes the major comic incongruity, i.e. the punch-line. What happens at the first incongruity? First, it is clear that a lot turns on whether the audience knows that what is being told is a joke: in this instance, the first incongruity may well be seen as funny since in humorous discourse the normal rules are relaxed, and the audience is emotionally insulated from the 'reality' of a baby swallowing a pen. But if the story was told 'cold', as if it were a true story, it is less likely that the audience would find it funny because the emotional insulation of humorous discourse would be missing, unless they realised immediately that the chances of the story actually being true were pretty low (or they were totally indifferent to the fate of babies!). Second, it is clear that the first incongruity sets up a situation which demands some further development, or resolution; in this respect a joke is typical of narrative in general, where some initial event occurs which demands continuation. Such resolutions are various: the story could end with the baby's death. In the event, a comic resolution has been chosen, and it is comic because the incongruity is both resolved and not resolved, as we have seen. The question which has been latent until now is this: is it always the case that humorous situations consist of two stages, as this analysis and Suls' definition suggest?

It is clear that 'one-liners' can in fact contain these two stages, as the example from Michael Redmond shows. But it is also clear that not all humorous situations need to be set up in this way. Years ago I was walking in the street in Amsterdam with two Dutch actor friends, who suddenly improvised a comic moment (I never found out why!): they started walking along the edge of the pavement very close together, one behind the other, each with one foot in the gutter and one foot on the pavement, perfectly synchronised. Clearly the intention was comic (they were laughing) and I thought this was a wonderful piece of clowning. Whatever the ultimate explanation of why this was funny, it is clear that no composed preparation stage occurred. But it was not necessary to do this because the appropriate background conditions were already in existence and so to speak waiting to be exploited for their purposes: first, the pavement and the gutter, with their usual functions and associations; second, the distinction between 'normal' and 'abnormal' ways of walking. (For what it's worth I think that the explanation of the comedy is this: the incongruity between (1) the ir-rationality of walking on two levels simultaneously, especially when the gutter is designed to separate feet from water and detritus, (2) the elegance of the 'solution' found to the situation of finding yourself walking in this way – they looked like a wonderful but insane machine that was designed to negotiate uneven terrain, but was here employed totally unnecessarily!). Many similar instances could be found in everyday life. For example, in England for many years football fans used to write slogans on the walls claiming that their team was the best, using the form 'Chelsea Rules OK'; many variations on this came into being, all based on the supposition that potential readers were aware of the original format – for example, 'Dyslexia Lures KO', 'Bureaucracy Rules OK, OK, OK', 'Sycophancy Rules – if it's OK with you'. These were ingenious and incongruous variations on a background situation already in existence and readily exploitable for comic purposes.[2]

In reality, this situation is not very different from the situation in two-stage jokes such as the baby and the pen, for in these cases, the preparation consists of lining up a set of expectations drawn from the everyday background culture of the teller and audience in just the way allowed by pavements and gutters, football teams and dyslexia. The way in which these expectations and background associations are mobilised is different in the two cases, and this difference is not without results, as we shall see, but the nature of incongruity and its absurd partial resolution is not essentially different.

It is often argued that incongruity cannot by itself be held to account for humour, since it is clear that not all incongruities are funny. Some incongruities may be so minor that they pass more or less unnoticed, others may be so major as to be positively threatening. It is usually thought that these two thresholds are describable in terms of arousal: to someone in a sufficiently aroused state an incongruity is capable of appearing funny, but if the arousal is excessive some other reaction is more likely (Rothbart, 1977: 87–90). If we think of humour in terms of arousal, we can also ask whether humour arises from the arousal itself or from relief from it. Both answers have been given to this question, but subsequently physiological measures of arousal have demonstrated that experimental subjects remained aroused after the punch-line of a joke, while they laughed (Rothbart, 1977: 88); this suggests that humour derives from arousal rather than from relief. At the same time, if arousal is to be humorous, the situation must be insulated from excessive arousal in some way. In this real-life incident from the Vietnam War we can see the relationship between levels of arousal and incongruity very clearly:

> On the last part of the trip, flying into Dong Ha, the aluminum rod that held the seats broke, spilling us all on the floor and making the exact sound that a .50 caliber round will make when it strikes a chopper, giving us all a bad scare and then a good, good laugh.
>
> (Quoted Mulkay, 1988: 53)

Here, the circumstances give a very high level of arousal potential indeed to the incongruous noise. Subsequent relief lowers the arousal level, while at the same time other incongruities become apparent: the threat was not a real threat, the noise both was and was not the sound of a bullet, etc.

Of course, arousal and incongruity are not the same thing: apart from anything else, incongruity operates cognitively whereas arousal operates affectively. Nonetheless, it appears likely that in many comic instances the arousal will in fact be brought about by the incongruity itself, as for example in the case of Suls' joke about the baby and the fountain pen: here the initial incongruity is sufficiently high to cause some arousal; indeed, if the story was told as a true story the arousal would no doubt be high enough to be threatening (at least until common sense came to the rescue and reminded us that the situation is fairly unlikely).

If we think of arousal and incongruity operating together to cause humour, we confront this situation: an audience either is passive or it is aroused; if aroused, it will no doubt be sensitive to incongruities; if not, an incongruity may well arouse it; provided the combination of incongruity and arousal does not create a sense of threat, humour is likely to result. What mechanisms are available which might set up a mood of arousal and yet avoid a feeling of threat? Obvious candidates are:

1 knowledge that the occasion is 'entertainment' – this has been discussed at length in Part I – which would both act as a humour stimulus and a brake on the sense of threat;
2 the incongruity is itself sufficiently acute to cause arousal but insufficiently acute to provide a threat, regardless of the environment in which it is perceived;
3 locating the comic meaning reveals retrospectively that the incongruity was not threatening.

Any or a mixture of these would act to cause arousal and avert the sensation of threat.

Among other things, it is clear now that the question of whether incongruity by itself is a sufficient explanation of humour is more complicated than first sight suggested. Although common sense indeed tells us that many incongruities are not funny because too minor or threatening, we have seen how often it is argued that the incongruities themselves are responsible for the arousal that is thought to make the incongruity comic. We shall return to this matter shortly.

The most sophisticated psychological version of this theory is that developed by Apter and Smith (1977; Apter, 1982a and 1982b). Drawing on the more general body of 'reversal theory', Apter and Smith postulate that humour is the product of the combination of a series of psychological states. The first of these they call synergy, that situation where any phenomenon is perceived as having two contradictory identities: for example a toy dagger, which both is and is not a threatening object, or Mickey Mouse, both human and non-human. Synergies break one of the fundamental rules of logic, that something cannot both be and not be the same thing simultaneously (cf. Cohen, 1970; Ricoeur, 1979; Palmer, 1987: 62–73). The synergy may be a property of the object in itself, as in the two examples here, or it may be a product of the way in which it is presented, as is commonly the case in jokes. To use Suls' example of the baby yet again, the synergy is the dual meaning attached to the word 'doing', where the doctor's meaning refers to helping the baby and the parents' to writing.

Synergetic identities are not necessarily funny, Apter and Smith postulate, and humour synergies have two further features whose combination is specific to them. In the first place, they are always based in the contrast between appearance and reality: one of the conflicting identities is apparently the true identity of the phenomenon, but the other, opposite one turns out to be the real identity; the parents of the baby with the pen appear to be helping it, but in reality they are not, according to the joke. Second, when the reality becomes plain the process of revelation is always to the detriment of whatever is in question: 'doing' in the baby's parents' sense is inferior to 'doing' in the doctor's sense, thus the baby's parents are revealed to be less than ideal. This second consideration excludes other real/apparent synergies such as the revelation of unexpected guilt at the end of a detective story, because here the reality is shown to be 'more than' appearance suggested, not less. In addition, the real/apparent synergy should be unexpected, and as exaggerated as possible, in order to maximise humour. The example from the Vietnam War would be funny because the reality is less than the illusion. In his discussion of this incident, Mulkay suggests that the joke is the result of the 'inter-pretative work' of the participants; of course this is true, in the sense that it is only a joke because they realise that they have not been hit by gunfire, but the relief in question is comic relief, according to Apter and Smith's theory, because of properties of the object – the relationship between illusion and reality is located in the external world, not in the mind of the observers (Mulkay, 1988: 53). The relationship between real/apparent synergies and the process of disparagement satisfactorily resolves an issue left hanging at an earlier stage, where we saw that a key problem in traditional 'superiority' theories was that not all feelings of moral superiority were funny. It is clear from Apter and Smith's analysis that humorous superiority consists of the use of incongruity – real/apparent synergies, in their terms – for disparaging purposes (cf. Suls, 1983: 51–2; Zillman, 1983: 100).

Thus the first of the psychological states typical of humour is a specific type of contradictory identity; clearly this is closely related to the notion of incongruity, and to my 'logic of the absurd'. The second is a state of playful arousal, which is in reality two distinct states, since playfulness and arousal can exist independently of each other. Apter and Smith's theory of arousal is little different from others, except insofar as they suggest that humorous arousal is usually caused by the incongruous contradictory identity we have seen. In this sense, humour has something in common with a puzzle – for example, in the baby/pen joke the incongruous situation evoked by the first line catches our attention and makes us want to know what is coming next, how the situation will be resolved. The playful state is their way of theorising both the stimulus to humour and the insulation from threat already discussed. They postulate that all human activity is either goal-oriented or non-goal-oriented ('telic' or 'para-telic'); if the mind-set is para-telic, a different set of expectations is applied to any phenomenon observed – the normal laws of rationality, purposefulness, etc., cease to apply and are replaced by playful-ness; this is similar to Mulkay's observation that in humorous discourse different rules apply to those normal in non-humorous discourse. Specifically, the real/apparent synergy causes arousal and either induces a para-telic mind-set, or maintains one already extant. The puzzle constituted by the real/apparent synergy is a 'pleasant challenge' to a mind in the para-telic state, but in a telic state it is perceived as a threat; on the other hand, even if the mind is in a telic state, the revelation of the inferiority of the real identity is likely to dissipate the goal-orientation, since 'what purported to be a genuine puzzle turns out to be only a pretended puzzle', and therefore 'the synergy is only a playful synergy' (Apter, 1982a: 185). The para-telic state may also be induced by a series of cues such as the knowledge that the occasion is 'entertainment', laughter on the part of others or simply the assertion by the speaker that what (s)he is doing is telling a joke.

Thus humour arises when a specific combination of states occurs. Exactly what role each of these states plays is uncertain (Apter, 1982a: 186). On the one hand, the real/apparent synergy (even in combination with the revelation of inferiority) perceived by someone not in a para-telic state causes embarrassment, which implies that this synergy is not capable of inducing humour in the absence of a para-telic state, nor of inducing a para-telic state of mind (Apter, 1982a: 189); but elsewhere Apter suggests that it is the para-telic state which is responsible for the distinction between a pleasant and an unpleasant incongruity (1982b: 67). Yet we have also seen the assertion that the real/apparent synergy is capable of inducing the para-telic state, and that the revelation of the inferiority of the real identity in this synergy is capable of revealing that the challenge was playful, i.e. capable of inducing the para-telic state. Similarly, Apter asserts elsewhere (n.d.: 3) that the topic of the incongruity (e.g. sexuality or personal aggressiveness) is responsible for arousal independently of the fact that there is an incongruity involved. The extent to which these assertions contradict each other is unclear: the independence of the arousal mechanisms from incongruity is not necessarily incompatible with the overall thesis, whereas the uncertain relationship between incongruity and para-telic states would appear to be more difficult to resolve. In any event, it is clear that the basis of the argument is that some combination of the states in question is what is reponsible for humour, and that the exact articulation of the states is flexible.

8

INCONGRUITY AND DISCURSIVE CUES

A number of issues arise from Apter and Smith's theory. The first is the question of disparagement and superiority theory. Here the classic theories made the feeling of moral superiority the distinctive feature of humour: humour is always essentially the act of derision directed at someone – although Hobbes, as we have seen, adds the proviso that the derision may be directed at a quality in the abstract, not attached to an identified individual; at this point Hobbes' theory is little different from Freud's notion of cynical humour, for in both instances the denigration of some value or other is an act of self-aggrandisement on the part of the joker. In this theory too incongruity plays no part, though we have seen subsequent attempts to blend the two ideas. Essentially this traditional theory amounts to saying that acts of symbolic aggression are enjoyed in the form of humour, and that this is the defining characteristic of humour. Apter and Smith too make disparagement a defining feature of humour, but they do so in a way that is significantly different, for the disparagement need not be directed at any identifiable person or quality at all, and does not necessarily involve any sense of superiority for the joker. To take again Suls' example of the baby and the pen: what is put down by the final incongruity? The answer can only be that the inadequacy of these fictitious parents either implies no general disparage-ment, or a metonymic disparagement of parenthood as a social entity; alternatively we may see the joke as a denunciation of stupidity in abstraction from any particular butt. In either instance, (1) no identifiable individuals from the real world are involved, (2) no reason is given to suppose that the joker feels inflated by this 'squelch' of parenthood or stupidity (though (s)he may – and also may feel inflated by the esteem that arises from making others laugh). Thus the superior/inferior reversal that accompanies the real/apparent synergy has no necessary implications for the moral stature of the joker, and this is very different in orientation to the classic superiority theory. In fact we should distinguish between two ways in which disparagement is involved in humour: first, if Apter and Smith are right, humour always involves an act of belittlement; second, humour can be used for egotistical purposes to 'squelch' other people or attributes. Often, of course, the two processes converge, as in

103

the 'ethnic stupidity' jokes discussed in Part II; but occasional convergence does not equal identity. One of these processes is concerned with the identity of the joker and the identity of those against whom the joke is directed. The other process is internal to the structure of the joke itself. The extent to which, and the occasions on which the two processes converge is unclear, and this uncertainty may be central to how humour works. We shall return to this (cf. Palmer, 1987: 87–95, 175–202).

It remains to be asked whether Apter and Smith are in fact correct in their assertion that all humour involves the belittlement they claim. In Apter's words, in a joke the reality should in some way be 'less than the appearance . . . one characteristic must have a positive sign . . . and the other a negative sign, the positive sign attaching to the "appearance" and the negative sign to the "reality"' (1982a: 180). This is what distinguishes humour from other real/apparent synergies such as the end of a detective story, where the revelation of unexpected guilt involves a reversal between appearance and reality but where the reality is 'more than' the appearance and not 'less than' it as in humour. However, we may ask in what sense the revelation of guilt here establishes that reality is 'more than' appearance; certainly in this instance reality turns out to be more complicated than appearance, and different from it. But the essence of such melodramatic story endings is that someone who appeared to be the acme of respectability turns out to be anything but that: he or she is *morally far less* than appearance suggested. What constitutes inferiority and superiority in this instance is not clear.

A second difficult example is the pun, where humour derives simply from the fact that a word turns out – unexpectedly – to have two divergent meanings. Of course, in many cases the divergence in meaning is also a divergence in 'moral level', as is plausibly the case in many sexual puns such as the graffito 'Love Thy Neighbour – Regularly'. Puns may also be used for 'squelch' purposes, such as this addition to the name of a suburban Underground station: 'Morden – Enough'. However, the humour of many puns seems to derive solely from the revelation of unexpected dual meaning, for example the graffito 'Whither Atrophy?' Here the combination of the two words is already incongruous, since the idea that atrophy has a direction is bizarre; the incongruity is maintained and resolved by the revelation of the second meaning through the combination of the two words. Neither of the two 'meanings' of the sentence makes very much sense, and it is difficult to maintain that either is inferior to the other. Certainly it could be argued that in our culture the literal denotative dimension of language is spontaneously considered to be the natural way in which language functions, and therefore any 'deviation' from this literalness – such as the 'revelation' that a word simultaneously has two different meanings – might be considered non-natural; but to go from there to the argument that one type of meaning is superior to the other is an inferential leap that would require some further justification (cf. Palmer, 1987: 218–24; Apter, 1982b: 64–5). Possibly one could claim that first appearances suggest that there is some meaning here, but the reality is shown to be no meaning; it is true, as Apter says, that the 'puzzle' turns out to be a fake puzzle. But at the same time the ingenuity of the convergence of meanings around a single phonic signifier makes the second meaning anything but inferior: it seems equally reasonable to claim that the process is simultaneously implausible and plausible, for in a culture that 'believes in' denotation it is in a sense implausible that two words pronounced the same but spelt differently should happen to have senses that allow them to be brought together in such a combination; yet it is true, and therefore plausible. On the basis of such limited evidence it is difficult to maintain that either model is better or worse than the other: both are reasonably internally consistent, both seem able to ground descriptions of a wide range of examples, and they have much in common.

A more general problem arises in Apter and Smith's analysis of the relationship between incongruity and the playful state of mind which they argue is a central feature of humour. We have already seen that the relationship between these two is uncertain, since sometimes the incongruity is said to induce the playful state, and sometimes the playful state is what distinguishes between pleasant and unpleasant incongruities. If we take as our example the baby/pen joke – or any similar 'standardised' joke – the relationship between incongruity and playful state of mind is scarcely problematic: the incongruity is so heavily marked by the rhetorical structure that it is likely to induce a playful state of mind unless there is some strong factor present in the listener to counteract this influence. In short, on the evidence of the joke structure it will always appear that there is an unequivocal relationship between incongruity and para-telicity. But if we take as our instance a joke and its reception, we can see that the situation may well be different. Some years ago I was on the Greek island of Paxos in mid-summer when against all expectations it started to rain. Looking at the downpour I said to a Greek friend 'What beautiful weather'; my friend totally failed to appreciate the irony (unsubtle though it was) and replied 'Yes! It's saved me 10,000 drachmae!' (to buy water for the cistern). To understand the intended irony, a certain amount of information is necessary, primarily that the English go to Greece to escape English weather. To anyone in possession of this information, my statement about the weather would be marked by a pragmatic incongruity; to anyone who shared my English obsession with getting my fair share of Greek sun an appropriately playful state of mind would not be a difficult achievement at this point. But my Greek friend, despite a good knowledge of the English, had a different agenda, dictated by the chronic summer water shortage on Paxos (it has to be shipped in bulk during the tourist season). Here it is clear that he was not in a playful state of mind, and because of elements of meaning external to the moment the pragmatic incongruity of my words was incapable of inducing it; to the mind-set of an Englishman on holiday, the incongruity would have been obvious.

In an instance such as this the incongruity, the real/apparent synergy, is intrinsically linked to pragmatic elements in the situation: it is only to the holiday-maker that there is any incongruity involved, and for this reason the link between incongruity and playfulness was not activated in my Greek friend. However, it is always the case that incongruity must be perceived as such in order to cause mirth, and although the semantic markers of incongruity may be clear in the case of most standardised jokes, if they are not perceived as such then it is highly unlikely that the joke will succeed; that is to say, the pragmatic dimension is always present.

None of these considerations reduce the pertinence of Apter and Smith's observations about the centrality of a playful state of mind, but the nature of the interaction between it and incongruity is clearly subject to some caution. However, everything said so far has assumed that playfulness and incongruity are the only possible causes of mirth, whereas in pratice there are many other relevant factors; in general, these relate to the context in which the joke occurs, and all are in some sense cues to the nature of the discourse which is under way.

Perhaps the major cue is the knowledge that the occasion in question is one on which humour is normal. In Part I we saw that the social identity of participants in humour and the social identity of the occasions on which humour is achieved cannot by themselves explain how humour occurs. In brief, the reasons are these. Although the social identity of participants and occasions is indeed an integral part of what humour is, there are very few occasions and very few relationships which are exclusively humorous, let alone obligatorily so. That is to say, it is true that humour cannot be achieved on some occasions and within some relationships (usually, in our culture, prohibitions derive from a mixture of these factors) and can be achieved on and within others. But with rare exceptions it is not the relationship and the occasion which are funny, even in combination: they provide a framework within which humour can occur, they even encourage its occurrence, but they do not, in themselves, constitute humour. But although they do not constitute humour, they do induce a state of mind in which the audience is mentally prepared to find humour, the mind-set that Apter and Smith call para-telic. Indeed, it is easy to observe in comedy performances that an audience which is sufficiently in tune with the performer will laugh at practically anything that can possibly be construed as having some incongruity built into it, such as a change of facial expression or tone of voice, sudden movement, etc.

If the social label 'comic performance' has obvious cue properties, it is less clear what other features of discourse can play this role in everday inter-actions where there is no preordained element of performance. What sorts of signs can act as humour cues? Clearly any statement to the effect 'this is a joke' has this property: there are conventional forms such as 'Have you heard the one about . . .?' or 'Three men are shipwrecked, an Englishman . . .' or even the words 'There was this . . .'. There are also many para-linguistic features of ordinary speech which are commonly used, of which probably the commonest in British culture would be: a 'light-hearted' tone of voice (perhaps accompanied by a smile); a tone which was obviously inappropriate to what was being said or the circumstances in question (or both), such as an excessively severe or formal one; facial expression or body posture (exaggeration, mimicry, etc.); a fake accent, such as saying 'I say, old chap, do you mind?' in an exaggerated Oxford accent in order to show that the objection is not to be taken seriously; or saying 'Ve haff vays of makink you talk' to indicate that a request for information ought not to be taken too seriously, gestures of various sorts that may indicate that what is said should not be taken literally.

Of these various signs, the commonest of all no doubt is laughter. It is commonly thought that laughter is essentially a reaction to the perception of humour, but it is well established by analysis of everyday language that people readily insert chuckles or laughter-like noises (usually recorded in transcripts as 'he-he') into conversation in order to indicate that what is in the process of being said should be taken as funny. For example: 'So the next class he-he for an hour and fifteen minutes I sat there and I watched his hands he-he . . .' (Jefferson, 1979: 85; transcription modified). Here it is clear that the speaker is indicating that she finds what she is saying amusing, and is inviting her listener to feel the same. Before the sentence is complete, i.e. before the situation which is to be found amusing has been sufficiently described to make it clear to the listener that it is funny, a chuckle is inserted. Perhaps this is obvious, but it has a less than obvious implication: it can no longer be argued that laughter is only caused by the psychological state of being amused by something that acts as a stimulus, since in this instance laughter is being used deliberately in advance of the stimulus-object making an appearance in order to help make it into an appropriate stimulus. Certainly it could be argued that the laughter is caused by the memory of the event being narrated, but this seems unlikely: given the careful placing of the laughter in the verbal chain it seems more profitable to consider it as a rhetorical device. No doubt the mental state of amusement, or memory of amusement, exists, but the rhetorical care suggests that in this instance the laughter itself is not primarily a response, but a conventional sign used to communicate intent.

By the same token the listener may indicate by laughter whether the joke is found to be funny. No doubt there are many occasions on which laughter is evoked in a way that is more or less beyond conscious control: everyone has experienced those moments when something seems hilarious, under circumstances when laughter is socially inappropriate, and we are forced to disguise our mirth in some way or other (e.g. a fake sneeze). When we are told a joke, it may well seem as though we have no choice but to laugh – the laugh is 'caused' by the joke. But we should remember that being told a joke is a standardised activity, where recognition that what is going on is 'joke-telling' prepares us to be amused and to find incongruity; indeed, it is readily observed that people start to laugh well before the joke is complete, or smile as soon as told a joke is coming. As Mulkay shows, acceptance of the social framework 'joke-telling' involves a change in expectations about the production of meaning (1988: 8–15). We have all also experienced those moments where we have felt obliged to fake polite laughter in order not to offend someone who thought something was terribly funny. Participating in ordinary conversation is an activity which is governed by all sorts of norms, including appropriate behaviour when humour is introduced; to refuse to recognise that a statement is funny when the speaker has clearly indicated a humorous frame of reference is to inflect a social relationship in a particular direction – it may, for example, cause offence, if only momentary.

The turn to humorous discourse introduces a new dimension into our analysis of the structure of humour. Until this point, most of the argument has been pursued in terms of how a single joke arouses mirth; typically, the type of investigation summarised here is concerned with the reactions of experimental subjects (or hypothetical individuals) to a single joke or something similar. However, in real life we rarely if ever encounter a single joke in isolation from any other message; the usual situation is either comic performance or one in which jokes are inserted into the flow of ordinary dialogue. So far this situation has been considered largely in terms of the cue properties which are operated by these circumstances, cue properties defined in terms of the capacity of the circumstances in question to help the single joke arouse mirth. In other words the analysis has been conducted in terms of a foreground (the joke) and a background (the circumstances). Whatever the analytic convenience of this method, it is largely untrue to the experience of everyday life and comic performance, where the division between background and foreground, if it occurs at all, will be based not upon the demands of analysis but upon some feature or other of our personal lives and the circumstances in question. Thus the feature of humour that we need to consider now is the way in which bits of humour are articulated onto each other and onto non-comic features of discourse.

Humour may arise 'spontaneously' in the middle of a conversation in many different ways, as these examples of transcribed natural conversations show.

At a dinner table, as the diners are sitting down, one sets out to tell a standardised joke:

(1) Steve: So should we do that? should we start
    Deborah: sure
    Steve: with the white?
(2) Peter: Didju hear about the – lady, who was asked,
(3) Deborah: I'm going to get in there, right?
(4) Chad: Okay.
(5) Peter: Didju hear?

(6) David: We have to sit boy girl boy.
(7) Chad: Boy girl boy?
(8) Peter: Didju hear about the lady who was asked,
(9) Chad: There's only two girls.
(10) Deborah: What?
(11) Peter: Did you hear about the lady who was asked. . . Do you
     Chad: Boy girl boy
     Peter: smoke after sex?
(12) David: I don't know I never looked. (nasal tone)
(13) Deborah: And she said? What?
(14) Peter: I don't know I never looked
(15) Deborah: Oh (chuckles).

(Tannen, 1984, quoted Mulkay, 1988: 57)

Here considerable effort and time are put into persuading the assembled group to accept that a joke is being told and that they are meant to listen, as another agenda is in competition with the would-be joker's. His attempts to move into a joking frame of reference meet with repeated rebuffs and he is unable to introduce the joke until he gets co-operation from another participant (Deborah's 'What?' in utterance 10 seems to indicate she is now listening). Once he has actually launched the joke with the necessary acceptance, at least one other person joins in, adding the punch-line in a tone of voice presumably intended to indicate that someting non-serious is being said; perhaps it is intended as a sarcastic comment on the feebleness or predictability of the joke, perhaps just as a contribution to the collective elaboration of a joking frame; without knowing more about the people in question it is difficult to know exactly what was intended here. Deborah then provides an opportunity for Peter to say the punch-line. Perhaps she felt sorry for him because his punch-line had been stolen, perhaps she did not hear David say it; either way, she then indicates by a chuckle that she accepts that what has just occurred was indeed a joke. As Mulkay says, the joke becomes the 'joint accomplishment of the group's members' (1988: 58). Clearly the boundary between the joking frame and the non-joking frame is very permeable, in many directions: the joke-teller has to negotiate his way into it; other participants choose the moment at which they accept the movement into the joking frame; moving into it can involve different sorts of participation – David either contributes or tries to wreck it, depending upon the interpretation of his utterance, Deborah constitutes herself as the facilitator and willing audience (cf. Handelman and Kapferer, 1972).

In this instance, there is no thematic connection between the joke and the preceding conversation, and therefore the negotiation of the entry into the joking frame is not motivated by thematic continuity, but commonly jokes can be based on some previously announced theme, as in the dinner-table conversation recorded by Tannen where somebody refers to a part of the turkey they are eating as the 'Pope's nose', and this provokes a joke about the (Polish) pope's supposed miracle – 'He made a blind man lame' – which in turn turns into a serious discussion of Polish jokes.

Later in the evening, participants comment on the fact that the tape recorder has been running throughout the meal, which they knew but had forgotten; they had been told that the conversation had been recorded because Deborah was studying conversational misunderstandings:

(1) Steve: Be uh have we been . . . taping? This whole time?
(2) Deborah: I'm glad I didn't notice until just now.
(3) Chad: She keeps that thing running.
(4) Steve: I keep I . . . I say, get that thing off the table. She says. . . yeah
         okay I'll take it off the table and I look . . . . two minutes later
         it's back. (laughter) . . . What's to analyze. There hasn't been
         one misunderstanding, we've all understood each other per-
         fectly.
(5) Peter: What do you mean by that. (Loud laughter).

(Quoted Mulkay, 1988: 62)

In this instance, the transition to joking occurs in a very different way. There are no cues before Peter's remark to indicate that this is intended as a joke – although it is true that the mood of the preceding conversation is clearly such as to encourage jokes, and this may act as a cue. Nonetheless, the whole audience immediately assumes that it is a joke, intended or otherwise; in all probability it was intended, since the literal meaning is unlikely. Clearly what has happened here is that the listeners have all noticed the incongruity involved in Peter's pretence of not understanding. Even if a light-hearted conversational frame is absent, incongruity may still work to arouse mirth, as in this instance of a serious conversation – at least, apparently so – turned into a joke. Two friends are studying together, and in the course of a serious discussion of academic matters one says 'I'm going to teach you something. It's going to take a few minutes . . . some other time' (Solis, 1992). Here the incongruity derives from the contradiction of the obligation assumed by the first part of the statement: no cues are offered, nothing in the surrounding circumstances prepares the participants for the incongruity, which works entirely according to pragmatic, or enunciative, rules. We may note that incongruity would still be funny even if unintentional: the *Guardian* (20.8.91) quoted a British doctor who said on radio that 'In terms of medical priorities, vasectomies are close to the bottom', where the unintended pun is nonetheless humorous, and perhaps more so, for being unintended. In such cases, where the humour is intended, we are likely to laugh with the humorist, where it is unintended, we laugh at him or her. No doubt, as Mulkay says, the attempt to maintain that such-and-such a topic is humorous will not last very long unless someone in the audience indicates that they find it funny.

9

HUMOUR AND NARRATIVE STRUCTURE

The common feature of the situations analysed here has been that all are directly dialogic: the way in which participants move in and out of utterance is predicated essentially upon the fact that in dialogue any participant can be both listener and speaker. In formal comic performances of any kind this is not so. Of course, communication is essentially dialogue, in the sense that virtually all discursive acts are aimed at someone (even a prayer!), but the nature of the dialogue is different when the participants are unable to swap roles at will. The act of reading a novel, going to the theatre or watching TV or a movie does not allow this exchange, and mass communication is usually distinguished from other forms of communication on these grounds: here asymmetry of access to the means of communication distinguishes audience from performer. Thus when comic narrative is formalised as a performance it is subject to different rules to those that regulate humour in everyday dialogue. Indeed, we have already seen one fundamental difference: in comic performance, the institutional fact of performance is a permanent cue to humour.

Our starting-point is a discussion of the silent screen clowns' terminology for their own activities (Agee, 1963).[1] The clowns distinguished both between different degrees of laughter and the type of gag appropriate to evoke them, and between the different stages of a gag. Laughter was divided into four categories of ascending hilarity: the titter, the yowl, the belly laugh and the boffo. The meaning of titter is obvious, the yowl is a single short yelp, the belly laugh is profound and protracted and the boffo leaves the audience rolling helplessly on the floor, assassinated with mirth. They also distinguished between the gag, milking the gag and topping the gag. For example, a small car pulls up and a very large man gets out of it, followed by another very large man: a gag, albeit minimal. A long line of very large men follow them out – this is 'milking the gag'. Then a midget gets out – 'topping the gag'. Finally the car collapses – this is 'topping the topper'. The principle is clear: each stage in the development of the gag builds on the previous one and each is calculated to produce an increment in laughter, creating a crescendo effect. Moreover, gags could be arranged in sequence, perhaps with different gag series intertwined, in such a way as to give increments in laughter over a more extended period. In Laurel and Hardy's *Wrong Again* the basic narrative drive comes from a simple error they make: overhearing that there is a reward for the return of the stolen 'Blue Boy' they mistakenly assume it is the horse under their noses; in reality it is a painting. By the time they find out their mistake they have obeyed the owner's unfortunate instruction to 'take Blue Boy inside and put him on the piano' – with predictable results! The first indignity they inflict on the decor involves Ollie tripping over a statue and breaking it in three pieces – a very conventional pratfall gag. Ollie sets about repairing the statue – a little gag in its own right, since the idea of repairing a statue involves an obvious contradiction in terms. He sets the statue's feet upright and lifts up the trunk; as he does so he realises that his hands are firmly clasped over the buttocks, and a look of outraged modesty crosses his face; averting his gaze, he takes his jacket off and decently swathes the offending organs. As he then lifts the trunk there is a cutaway shot of Stan nodding approval. Ollie reassembles the legs, trunk and upper torso and delicately removes his jacket; as he steps back the statue is revealed: the buttocks point in the same direction as the knees and the face.[2] In this instance, each joke is distinct from the others, the theme of each is clearly different, and yet, at the same time, they are organised together into a tightly linked sequence in such a way that each one lays the ground for the next. It is because the statue has broken at the points that it has that Ollie ends up with his hands on the buttocks. It is outraged modesty that leads him to avert his gaze while wrapping them up and the aversion of his gaze plus the wrapping that ensures he puts it back together (literally) 'arse about face'.

So it is that jokes can be organised in articulated sequences, in such a way that they form miniature narratives. But jokes are also articulated onto non-joking narrative, a topic with wide implications.

It is obvious that the kind of narrative referred to here is comic narrative, despite the hesitation marked by the phrase 'jokes articulated onto non-joking narrative'. This hesitation derives from a long debate within literary criticism about what the term 'comedy' means.[3] In brief outline the debate centres on whether there is any unequivocal relationship between comedy as a literary form, and funniness; in general, the conclusion has been that there is no necessary relationship between the two, even though in practice many if not most comedies are also – at least in part – funny; perhaps the briefest summary would be that these debates conclude that there is an elective affinity between the two. At the centre of this debate are two points: first, that many texts labelled comedies – and that includes funny moments – are not primarily laughter-evoking machines, but have some other purpose which is arguably more fundamental to their structure; second, that even if some texts are primarily designed to evoke laughter, not all of each of the narratives in question has this purpose. Each of these points indicates a problematic relationship between the creation of mirth and the narrative structure of comedy, which is to be found in the majority of comic texts, at least in the European tradition. If there is a long history of farce, in which the overwhelming bulk of each narrative is either directly intended to provoke mirth or to prepare for the moment which does have this aim, nonetheless there is much writing in the canonical literary tradition, labelled comedy, funny in part, where intuitively we know that much of the narrative has a very different purpose: Molière, Dickens, Gogol, Beckett . . .

What lurks behind this obvious point is the recognition that much comedy, no matter how funny, commonly uses a narrative form which is not essentially dissimilar from realist narrative in general: even a Laurel and Hardy film has an outline, a narrative skeleton, which follows the norms of realism in the minimal sense that the characters progress from point a to point b for a reason; that the spatial relationships between the two points are portrayed in a way roughly consistent with the laws of the known universe (the same is true for time, by and large): in short, that the norms of realist film-making are preserved. Even though this stable framework may be subject to interminable disruptions of every variety – and especially levels of co-incidence that are not very compatible with scientific stochastics – the stable framework is indeed there.

A convenient starting-point for the analysis of this subject is the remarks made earlier about Freud's theory of jokes. There we saw that the 'thought' contained in a joke has an equivocal relationship with the pleasure given by the joke-form: for Freud the pleasure of the joke – which is what makes it into a joke – does not derive from the thought but from an ecological relationship with the subconscious. Moreover, we saw, the term 'thought' in Freud's *Jokes* seems to refer to two very different types of entity. Under the circumstances, we may wonder what type of effectivity conscious rational thought is capable of having, despite Freud's assertion that the best thoughts make the best jokes. It is not that conscious thought is devoid of effectivity, but that it is there to be the bearer of another meaning which is established elsewhere, in the unconscious, a meaning which is not reducible to the categories of conscious thought nor even to the processes by which such categories are constructed; in this respect it is similar to the process of secondary revision in dreams.[4] The ambiguity of Freud's argument is at its greatest in his assertion that there is a difference between good and bad jokes, given by the 'substance' of the thought contained in the joke; we have seen how this idea is worked out in detail with reference to 'Schadchen' jokes.

Accepting such a view of mirth has many potential implications for the study of comic narrative. Insofar as narrative is usually held to be a form of cognition of the world, it suggests that narrative and joking are based in largely different structures, and this fundamental divide can ground various critical strategies. The fundamental difference of joke and narrative could be

113

taken to indicate that traditional canonical theories of comedy are right to assert the separation of comedy and funniness. In such theories, the difference is based largely in the perception that funniness is no more than a passing pleasure, whereas comedy is a narrative form that in itself tells us something about the world around us. In short, narrative can have a truth value, whereas jokes are devoid of it.

The cartoon reproduced here (Plate 1) is marked by a truth of the kind Freud identifies in 'Schadchen' jokes. Steve Bell's cartoon summarises one dimension of the public debate over a book allegedly revealing that Princess Diana was very unhappy in her marriage and had even attempted suicide (*Sunday Times*, 7.6.92). Much was said in print and on television about the Royal Family's right to privacy and the unwarranted intrusion represented by the stories in question. Steve Bell's cartoon, with its exaggerated insistence on the public dimension of the privacy in question, refers to a well-established assessment of the Royal Family's own policy of actively seeking publicity and using such publicity as a means of promoting its role as the symbolic place of the unity of the nation. No doubt the cynicism of Bells' assessment goes beyond this thesis: the aggressive implication that the Princess' alleged suicide attempts were part of the process of Royal public relations is – to say the least – implausible. No doubt also the pleasure the cartoon gives derives from this cynicism and aggression. Yet there is still a massive nugget of truth in the cartoon: anyone who has watched the development of the relationship between the media and the Royal Family with any care is likely to come to the conclusion that it was at least in part a matter of policy, or – to put it in moral terms – of collusion. Of course, this is scarcely a truth that has been 'scientifically established'. Other considerations apart, the nature of the events in question is such that location of responsibility for their appearance is very hard to establish: in general, public relations is all the more effective for hiding the process by which it is produced.

What do these considerations about the ambiguous role of thought in Freud's analysis tell us about the nature of comic narrative? We can most easily see what is involved by an example.

In Molière's *Tartuffe* a good-natured, naive man welcomes a religious charlatan into his house; among other depredations the hypocrite eventually tries to seduce his wife. To fight him off, and to reveal the truth of the whole situation, she hides her husband under the table while Tartuffe is persuading her that because he doesn't deserve her love he absolutely needs proof of it, that sin is fine provided nobody knows, that he accepts all the moral responsibility and that her husband is such a fool that he'll never suspect anything. She counters his demands for instant satisfaction with moral scruples, but eventually allows herself to be 'persuaded' by his casuistry, giving this as her final argument:

Plate 1 (© Steve Bell 1992)

Since you insist on bringing me to this point, since you won't believe
what I say, and you want a convincing proof . . . then resolution is
what's needed, I must satisfy you. If this consent involves offence, too
bad for the person who forces me to it; the fault certainly isn't mine.

(Act IV, Scene 6)

These words are very carefully chosen to have two meanings. For Tartuffe,
they imply acceptance of his seduction; for him, the 'you' who is so
demanding is himself. Similarly, the 'proofs' are the proofs of her love that he
has demanded, the satisfaction is sexual; the 'fault' of the last sentence is her
sexual willingness. For her husband, under the table, and for the audience,
there is a second meaning as well as this, where 'you' refers to himself: the
French 'on', which I have translated as 'you', allows this ambiguity more
easily than any English version, for it is more obvious that the impersonal
'on' can equally refer to the husband; possibly the impersonal 'on' makes her
statements as interpreted by Tartuffe himself more plausible to him, since the
impersonality of 'on' makes her sound more modest than the directness of
'you', and Tartuffe could readily interpet this modesty as fake and therefore
seductive. To her husband, the 'proofs' are Tartuffe's behaviour and the
'satisfaction' is demonstrating the truth; the 'fault' of the last sentence is the
appearance of accepting Tartuffe as a lover. Under the circumstances of a
comic performance the ironical double meaning is funny – although certainly
under different circumstances the same mechanism may give rise to tragic
ambiguities, as we shall see. This humour conforms to the model of the joke
found in Freud and elsewhere: what we see is simultaneously sense and
nonsense (or: is incongruous, a mixture of plausibility and implausibility)
because words 'ought' not to have two diametrically opposed meanings in
this fashion, and yet they do. As Freud says, the element of sense – the reality
of both meanings – is what allows the 'nonsense' to pass: that such clear
statements can be so duplicitous. In that sense, the 'thought' implied in the
joke (that discourse can be ambiguous, that words can hide thoughts as well
as reveal them), is an envelope for the pleasure that humour gives, it is a
disguise, it is false in relation to the 'truth' of the matter, which is the childish
sense of play which derives from the mixture of sense and nonsense. At the
same time, the husband's indignity and Tartuffe's approaching humiliation
are also presented in a comic light, thus allowing the unconscious drive of
aggression to pass the barrier of repression. All of this is true about these
lines. And yet, at the same time, another level of these lines is a set of
thoughts about the events portrayed in the play which is perfectly coherent,
which constitutes a truth about these events as they are portrayed, which
connects with other segments of the play and with the moral thought of
seventeenth-century France (and bourgeois civilisation in general). Here are
revealed the strengths of femininity and domestic common sense, of quiet
intelligent courage and commitment to what one knows to be true. Here her

husband is forced to reassess his gullibility and his estimation of his wife. Can we reasonably say that these 'thoughts' are no more than an envelope, or a disguise, for some passing comic pleasure? Certainly there is a way in which thought performs this function here, as elsewhere in jokes, but the thoughts just presented are not found only in this joke but elsewhere in the text of Molière's play too (as well as outside it, in the moral commonplaces of a civilisation). Indeed these thoughts constitute one of the ways in which the play achieves meaning; they are an integral part of the structure of the text, of its textuality. Thought here is not reducible to an epiphenomenon of the pleasure of humour, for it has a real effectivity of its own operating on a quite different modality. First, its coherence is given outside of the joke itself, in the links between the scene quoted and other elements of the play. Second, the meaning of the thought refers to elements of experience which are independent of the joke framework as it is used here. Third, the impact of the joke on the audience produces not only the pleasure of humour, but also the pleasure of justice: the husband is being punished for his stupidity by the indignity of his situation; the hypocrite is clearly about to get his come-uppance. In each of these ways the joke seems to produce psychic entities that are distinct from the pleasure of the joke itself. Of course, it is also true in Freudian terms that all attempts to make sense of the world around us, i.e. all conscious coherent thought (among other things) is a product of the ego's attempts to impose order on 'its' world, an attempt which is (again among other things) a dimension of the relationship between the ego and the unconscious. Clearly also, referring the thoughts contained in this scene from Tartuffe to the emergent domestic ideology of a bourgeois order in no way reduces their relationship to the unconscious, for the same reason: belief in a moral order is one of the prime ways in which the ego attempts to make sense of its world. Certainly the desire for justice may also hide an aggressive impulse. Perhaps we might think of such conscious thought within a comic framework as a form of sublimation. Nonetheless, it seems certain that the ways in which a joke works within a larger scale comic narrative make it unamenable to *reduction* to the status that one reading of Freud accords it, even though it is clear that this status is indeed an integral part of how it works in such a context.

So it is that comic narrative is semiotically ambiguous. On the one hand, we can see that one dimension of it is constituted by the semiotic structure of the joke: incongruity, or simultaneous plausibility and implausibility. On the other hand, other semiotic structures are also intrinsic. First, the narrative framework which in the instances quoted is essentially the narrative form of realism. Second, the characters, sites of emotional investment for the audience, clustering around a name, and revealed in a sequence of actions.[5] Third, the sequence of actions with their own schemata of intelligibility. In any extended comic narrative, the jokes interact with these other semiotic mechanisms in a vast array of possible ways. At the most general level, we can say that the point of each joke is fixed in and by this interaction. For example, in the instance of irony, it has often been pointed out that a consistent formalised distinction between the mechanisms of comic and tragic irony is not possible.[6] However, it is in fact perfectly possible to make such a distinction in practice, since audiences clearly do so; what makes it possible is the way in which the other semiotic mechanisms referred to act as cues, or markers, within the ironic moment, indicating whether it is comic or not. In the 'Friends, Romans, countrymen' speech in *Julius Caesar* for example it is clear that any audience will see this speech in the context of the narrative up to that point as a whole: they are perfectly aware what is at stake in Mark Anthony's manipulation of the audience in the forum, and this sense of direction provided by the narrative makes the irony in question tragic (or at any rate serious) rather than comic. In the instance of the passage from *Tartuffe*, the many jokes earlier in the play indicate that there is a humorous dimension to this scene – the husband's ridiculous gullibility introduces a humorous dimension, as does the way in which the wife's deliberate ambiguity clearly deceives Tartuffe himself. In these examples, what is happening is that one of the semiotic mechanisms that compose narrative is interacting with an incongruity to make that incongruity either humorously or seriously ironical.

This principle is extendable still further. In *The Logic of the Absurd* I argued that comic identity was a discursive construct in the sense that the themes of jokes were derived from entities external to the semiotic structure of the joke itself (Palmer, 1987: 153–74). In other words, the difference between one comedian and another, or between one style of comedy and another, can be described by looking at how they construct jokes. That principle is extendable to cover such major distinctions – often used as the basis of genre distinctions in popular fiction, film and television – as 'black comedy' or 'romantic comedy'. Black comedy would be a style where the borderline between humour and suffering is consistently blurred, or where a mechanism such as irony persists in presenting under both its tragic and humorous guises (see Part IV).

Similarly, 'romantic comedy' would be a style where it is erotic complications that are made funny, in other words where the humour derives from our sense of the characters' investment in a particular valuation of each other in combination with a particular set of frustrations, deriving from the complexities of the relationship (as opposed to purely external frustrations such as are common in farce). A good recent example is *When Harry Met Sally*, where the central characters pursue a long if ambiguous friendship deliberately uncontaminated by sexuality. The basis of their restraint is that Harry maintains that friendship and sexuality are incompatible, despite a disastrous series of relationships based upon sexual attraction alone; Sally, although less convinced of the theoretical truth of his assertion, nonetheless seems to act upon it in practice, with similarly disastrous results. At the same time, there is an obvious attraction between them, and at a certain point Sally decides that the theory is wrong and seduces Harry. As they start to make love the film cuts to the moment of afterglow: Sally is visibly content, Harry equally visibly astonished and baffled. The expressions on their faces form a caricatural contrast, heightened by the fact that neither is looking at the other's face. It is a rich comic moment, whose comedy derives from the incongruity constituted by this sudden reversal of the apparent norm of their relationship, and especially Harry's inability to grasp quite what has happened despite the fact that in a sense it is obvious. More precisely, this moment acts as a summation of the central theme of the film. In the yuppie culture of the 1970s and the 1980s, a central element of lifestyle was the possibility of a sexuality separated from fundamental emotional commitment; at root, it is this value which structures Harry and Sally's ambiguous relationship. The narrative asserts that such a separation is not ultimately sustainable – or only at the cost of emotional stultification. This is clearly seen in the failure of their attempts to provide for each other through friendship: their attempt to provide each other with a partner on a double date backfires classically when the partners they each intended for the other decide that they prefer their own company, and go off in a taxi – obviously in the direction of bed – leaving Harry and Sally to a disconsolate late evening; the couple in fact soon marry very happily. It is only when Harry and Sally come to the conclusion that the film presents, 'realising the obvious', that happiness is possible for them.

Thus the comic moment illustrated here is only comprehensible in the light of the general structure of the narrative in which it is a central moment. Most of the incongruities that produce the laughter grow directly out of the contradictory position that Harry and Sally have put themselves in: it is because of their wilful adoption of a self-identity that is flawed in this way that the incongruous situation arises. Alternatively, to consider the topic from the point of view of ideology, the fact that absurd incongruities arise is a 'proof' of the obviousness of the film's central proposition about identity and emotional responsibility.

10

COMEDY, FARCE AND NEO-CLASSICISM

Tartuffe and *When Harry Met Sally* were introduced to exemplify an argument about the relationship between funniness and narrative. In each case we see a text which is funny, but which is also something else too, a serious statement about our world. Both texts are clearly comedies, both in the sense that they are funny, but also in the sense that they are not only funny, i.e. they are not farce. In other words, they are both clearly comedies not just, or even primarily, in the sense that they are funny, but in the sense that in them funniness is subordinated to some other meaning, or at least interwoven with it in a way that makes the non-funny meaning at least as important as the process of mirth creation. In general this is the way we commonly distinguish between comedy and farce: comedy is not just mirth creation, it also has serious, important themes; farce is a form where everything is subordinated to laughter production.[1]

So far this distinction has been discussed in terms of its internal semiotic mechanisms, especially the way in which meaning is organised by the interaction between narrative and the structure of the joke. However, it is well known that the distinction between farce and comedy also has a social value: farce is part of 'popular' or 'mass' culture (depending upon the period under discussion); comedy readily forms part of 'culture' in the sense of 'national', 'high' or canonical culture. For this reason, comedy readily forms part of the literary canon, and appears on academic syllabi and national theatre production lists – Molière, Shakespeare, Beaumarchais, Wycherley, etc. The reasons (or at any rate the justification) for this distinction are readily found in the semiotic analysis: it is comedy's greater claim to aesthetic value based upon truth and narrative complexity that allows it to take its place in canonical culture. Correspondingly, it is the subordination of everything in the text to the pleasure of laughter which is responsible for the relegation of farce to mass culture. In general comedy shares with other canonical forms a particular guarantee of 'superiority': a taste for them in some way improves their user. This comment by Michael Ignatieff in the course of a recent debate in Britain about the value of popular culture is typical of a century of such judgments, from Matthew Arnold onwards:

Art that demands the maximum of both its creator and its audience is better than art that entertains or amuses. Demanding art – art that required labour, ingenuity, humour, wit, skill and a fearlessness about human emotion in its making – is better than art that just makes me feel better. I'd take Chuck Berry to the desert island to keep me dancing on the sand, but I'd also take Beethoven piano sonatas to remind me of the fuller range of what human beings can think and feel.

(Ignatieff, 1991; cf. Williams, 1958: 125–36)

Clearly we must ask whether such a distinction is justified (see below, Conclusion), but it is nonetheless certain that this situation is historically local, at least where comedy is concerned, since in the Middle Ages the institutions of comedy were not divided in this way: all comedy was basically farce, albeit that farce had profoundly serious meanings, deriving from the medieval sense of 'folly' (see above, Chapter 3). The opposition to comic forms on the part of the Church was not derived from the sense that 'serious comedy' was more 'improving' than farce – other considerations apart, the notion of 'improvement' was close to blasphemy. At the same time it is clear that the new situation fundamentally affects the nature of comedy and mirth creation, since the split into two levels of funny/comic texts is responsible for the internal structuration of each. How did this new situation come about?

The rest of Part III is devoted to answering this question; in crude outline the answer is that in the Renaissance and the neo-classical period of the history of European culture there occurred a general separation of cultural 'levels', in which what has come to be called 'culture', or 'canonical culture' constituted itself by creating a series of norms which were based on the explicit rejection of what became, as a result, 'popular' culture. While a complete account is beyond the scope of an essay on comedy and humour, we can at least see the elements most directly involved in changes in the nature of the comic. They are: (1) the separation between comedy and farce; (2) the marginalisation and eventual suppression of popular cultural humorous institutions; (3) the reorganisation of vocabulary and literary style.

At the end of Part I we saw that the demise of the medieval French *sotties*, or fool plays, was connected with the rise of comic forms based on the imitation of classical antiquity, which – in Barbara Swain's words (1932: 112) – presented satire of human follies and foibles in a more 'acceptable' way. The word 'acceptable' indicates the location of all the themes to be dealt with here: why was one artistic form more acceptable than another? And acceptable to whom?

We may start with the way in which comedy was classified in the formalised genre system of seventeenth-century conceptions of literature and the theatre. Some attention was still paid to genre distinctions based upon Platonic arguments: genres were distinguished according to whether the artist spoke in his (the possibility of 'her' was largely disregarded) own voice or someone else's, or whether both occurred; lyric forms were distinguished by metre, stanza length and rhyme scheme – ode, sonnet, etc. But increasingly – and especially in what rapidly became the dominant form, the theatre – the basis of genre distinction was the social 'level' of the actions portrayed, an idea inherited from Aristotle (Palmer, 1991: 117–20; Schaeffer, 1989: 25–34). Tragedy and the epic – distinguished by their media – were concerned with the actions of illustrious men and women, in other words the political elite of the ruling class; the other genres were concerned with the actions of lesser mortals, or the lesser actions – for example, love affairs – of the illustrious. For Hobbes, there are three fundamental genres: the heroic (tragedy and the epic); the scommatic, which represents the actions of the bourgeois in the forms of satire and comedy; and the pastoral, which deals with love in an imaginary setting; this tripartite division corresponds to a tripartite division of the world into court, city and country (Hobbes, 1860a). In France it was commonly held that tragedy was concerned with the actions of the uppermost layers of the nobility, that as a result it ought not to include any actions unworthy of them, but that comedy was concerned with the lives of the common people and could therefore involve undignified actions (Palmer, 1971: 162–7).

The fate of Rabelais in the seventeenth century is emblematic in this respect. As is well known, *Gargantua and Pantagruel* (Rabelais, 1955) is a mixture of every form of writing, from learned disquisitions to obscene knockabout farce, with the two extremes often mixed together in the same passage. His work was well known in the seventeenth century; indeed, passages were adapted into court revels in Henry IV's and Louis XIII's reigns, just as the contemporary English court used popular culture devices such as mock battles and the Lords of Misrule in their masques (Bakhtin, 1970: 109; Burke, 1978: 60–1). Now the purpose of the genre system of the seventeenth century was essentially to create and preserve a decorum based on the social hierarchy, a decorum which dictated that a single action could not be simultaneously noble and funny: the realm of the serious and the realm of the comic were to be radically distinguished. Rabelais thus became a very difficult author for the later, more thoroughly neo-classical generations to understand; this judgment by La Bruyère is typical:

Rabelais [is] inexcusable for the muck he spread in his writing. . . . [He] is incomprehensible: his book is an enigma, whatever one says, inexplicable; it's a chimera, it's the face of a beautiful woman with the feet and tail of a snake or some other even more misshapen beast. It's a monstrous assembly of fine and ingenious observation and foul cor-ruption. Where it is bad, it goes well beyond the worst, it's the kind of

thing that charms the rabble; where it is good, it is even exquisite and
excellent, it can be a dish fit for the most delicate.

(Quoted Bakhtin, 1970: 114)

As Bakhtin says, what was unacceptable was the scatology and all the 'below-
stairs verbal comedy', but it is especially the mixture of levels that La Bruyère
cannot stomach, whence his image of the 'chimera'.

Dryden held that comedy was an inferior sort of art because it dealt
with inferior classes of people, like paintings of clowns or a 'Dutch
kermis': comedy is a 'Lazar in comparison to a Venus' (i.e. a diseased
beggar). Running all through these arguments is the assumption that
comedy is inferior to the noble and heroic genres because dealing with
inferior actions, of the sort more typical of the inferior social classes.
Indeed, corresponding to the hierarchical division of genres was a hierarchical division of styles: the sublime, the low and the middle; this
distinction was a commonplace in theories of rhetoric from Quintilian
onwards, and was commonly applied to fictional genres in the neo-classical
period (see for example Chapelain's preface to Marino's *Adonis*, in
Chapelain, 1936; cf. Schaeffer, 1989: 31–2). This version of decorum,
making style suitable for a socially defined subject matter, is echoed in
Pope's lines in *Essay on Criticism* (Pope, n.d.: 40):

> Expression is the dress of thought, and still
> Appears more decent, as more suitable;
> A vile conceit in pompous words expressed,
> Is like a clown in regal purple dressed:
> For different styles with diff'rent subjects sort,
> As sev'ral garbs with country, town and court.

But even below comedy – says Dryden – is farce, the grotesque, 'a very
monster in a Bartholomew Fair, for the mob to gaze at for their two-pence';
laughter may indeed be the mark of humanity, but only just enough to
distinguish our species from the animals – ''Tis a kind of bastard pleasure too,
taken in at the eyes of the vulgar gazers and at the ears of the beastly
audience' (quoted Stallybrass and White, 1986: 71f.). What we see here is the
result of the process of separation and distinction which relegates farce to the
nethermost reaches of the aesthetic and social hierarchy. As the theatre re-
emerged in Europe as a distinct form, farce was normal on the stage, as we
have already seen. But in the early seventeenth century – at least in England
and France – it was progressively excluded from the theatre properly
speaking and relegated to the fairground, the carnival booth and other
locations away from the sites of literature proper. In the early theatre of the
seventeenth century in France it was still common practice to complete the
performance of even the severest of tragedies with a farce, and the main
Parisian theatre troupe, the Comediens du Roi, was most noted for its three

great clowns: Gaultier-Garguille, Gros Guillaume and Turlupin. However, during the 1630s, as the new neo-classical repertoire gained in prominence, and as the theatre audience became more censorious, farce was progressively eliminated from the repertoire. In the later 1630s public esteem moved away from farce actors and towards actors who specialised in serious plays. Mondory, who was in the Marais troupe that Corneille wrote for in his early days, was the first actor who did not play farces, according to the diarist Tallémant des Réaux. Although farces were also performed at ceremonial entries into towns, and at court masques, few farce texts have survived. The writers of the neo-classical generation of 1630 considered the theatre of the previous generation to be below them – the actors were all seen as scandalous ('thieves and whores') and the plays were dismissed as banal farces. Part of the reason for the rejection of the farce was the participation of women in the theatre both as actresses and as spectators: generally women left the audience when the farce started, since it was commonly full of broad sexual innuendo, and it seems unlikely that actresses played in farces (Carrington Lancaster, 1929: 665–6, 737, 748; Faivre, 1988: 119, 121–4).

Farcical elements still abound in Shakespeare, of course – for example *The Comedy of Errors* and *Midsummer Night's Dream* – but farce is more and more marked by a high degree of marginalisation. In *Midsummer Night's Dream*, for instance, the farcical misidentifications of Bottom and Titania are the obverse of the noble 'self-misidentifications' of the young lovers, and the farcical inadequacies of the final playlet are firmly placed in the framework of condescending aristocratic comments. Farce is not there for the sake of its own pleasures alone, but for narrative purposes; Jonson's *Bartholomew Fair* is another text in which farcical elements are frequent. However, Jonson was very aware of the socially dubious nature of the theatre as an enterprise, when conceived in the terms respected by the learned and the noble, for the theatre was – in his eyes – contaminated by its 'vulgar' public:

> Again and again Jonson defines the true position of the playwright as that of the poet, and the poet as that of the classical, isolated judge standing in opposition to the vulgar throng. In this of course he was not alone. Few 'serious' poets prided themselves on their plays.
>
> (Stallybrass and White, 1986: 67)

Bartholomew Fair's 'Induction on the Stage' opposes a stage-keeper, who speaks for the popular public, the 'groundlings' who stood under the stage, and who accuse Jonson of not understanding what they want, and a 'scrivener' who reads out a mock contract between author and audience, prescribing the proper duties of each. Mock though it is, it presents Jonson's own arguments. For the stage-keeper, things were done better 'in Master Tarlton's time'. Tarlton was Elizabeth I's court fool, and his performances consisted of improvised clowning – exactly the sort of performance most appreciated by the popular audience and exactly what Jonson and the new generation of 'serious authors' loathed most profoundly because of its vulgar connotations. To use Dryden's words again:

> I think or hope, at least, the Coast is clear,
> That none but men of Wit and sence are here:
> That our Bear-garden friends are all away,
> Who bounce with Hands and Feet, and cry Play, Play.
> Who to save Coach-hire, trudge along the Street,
> Then print our Matted Seats with dirty Feet;
> Who, while we speak make love to Orange-Wenches,
> And between Acts stand strutting on the Benches:
> Where got a Cock-horse, making vile grimaces,
> They to the Boxes show their Booby Faces.
> A Merry-Andrew such a Mob will serve,
> And treat 'em with such Wit as they deserve.
>
> (Prologue to *Cleomenes*, ll. 1–12, quoted
> Stallybrass and White, 1986: 84).

For Dryden it is those who cannot afford coaches and who treat the theatre as a common entertainment who are not fit to be in 'his' audience; traditional farce ('a Merry-Andrew') is all they deserve, just as Jonson's 'groundlings' only deserve Master Tarlton. For Jonson's scrivener, on the other hand, the audience is divided between patrician and plebeian on an imaginary scale of wit as well as on a scale of purchasing power, and it is clearly to the patrician part of the audience that Jonson would wish to be able to address himself exclusively. Yet, on the other hand, in *Bartholomew Fair* he wrote one of the most genuinely Saturnalian plays of the time, a 'pig-wallow' as he described it, which did not figure in his published works during his lifetime (Stallybrass and White, 1986: 78).

In the early seventeenth-century theatre the improvising clown is increasingly subordinated to the text created by an author, and in most cases the text progressively marginalises farce elements, to the point of eventual near-exclusion. Molière's *Tartuffe* is a case in point. In the scene already examined, Orgon is underneath the table while Elmire brings Tartuffe to say enough to condemn himself; at various points in the conversation the text indicates that she coughs and knocks on the table, and it is common – at least in modern productions – for Orgon to keep on trying to scramble out and confront Tartuffe, while Elmire pushes him back underneath. These are farce elements, albeit restrained by decorum, but it is clear that Orgon's undignified position is part of his punishment for his absurd credulity: the farce is strictly subordinated to the demands of a neo-classical structure dominated by moral and ethological concerns.

At the same time as neo-classical decorum institutes itself in this marginalisation of popular humour, the farce survives, but in a different location: it is excluded from the theatre but survives in the fairground, the carnival and similar places. In Paris, the fair in Saint Germain des Prés was open for between three and eight weeks of the year during the seventeenth century, and always featured charlatans and farce performers, as well as rope dancers, puppet masters and so on. Later in the century permanent theatres were built in its vicinity. The Saint Laurent fair, then outside the city limits (where the Gare de l'Est now is) also had charlatans, tumblers and farce performers; it lasted from 9 August until 9 September. Until roughly the mid-seventeenth century the Paris theatre audience was very mixed socially; thereafter, it became more 'cultivated' and upper class, and the popular part of the audience went back to the little theatres in the fairs. Later in the century the fair theatres began to put on entire plays, which aroused opposition from the regular theatres because the fair theatres started to take their public, instead of just getting an audience of the poor (Wiley, 1960: 124–32; Lagrave, 1988: 175–7, 238–43). A famous example is the 'medicine show' of Tabarin, which flourished on the Pont Neuf in Paris until his death in 1626. His farces were written down by a spectator, and were published in twenty-four editions before 1664 (a significant testimony to his sustained popularity). Tabarin and other 'charlatans' were attacked in a series of books and pamphlets from the medical profession which indicate how successful they were both as entertainers and salesmen; it is clear from these attacks, as well as from contemporary diaries and correspondence, that such entertainers were commonplace in the streets of Paris and at fairs (Wiley, 1960: 72–8).

Clear evidence of the survival of the popular comic forms in the sphere of non-polite culture is to be found also in the *Bibliothèque Bleue*, the cheap publication house in Troyes which printed books, pamphlets, almanacs, etc., for distribution by pedlars from the early seventeenth century until the mid-nineteenth (Mandrou, 1964; Dotoli, 1987). A substantial part of its catalogue was made up of the texts of theatrical farces and 'récits burlesques': for example, *Till Eulenspiegel*, stories of randy and ingenious apprentices, anti-clerical parodies and plain scatological stories. These were written in a popular style: a lot of slang, largely Parisian in origin, a Rabelaisian delight in word play and verbal luxuriation, Spoonerisms and scatology. In short, it contained everything that was evicted from polite culture during the seventeenth century, which is a clear mark of the divergence between the two cultures (Mandrou, 1964: 99–110).

The process that we have seen within comedy is reproduced on a larger scale within culture as a whole: just as comedy becomes distinct from farce, and validates itself as a feature of polite society by excluding its uncouth brother, so in general the various places and activities of popular culture become marked by a similar separation and marginalisation. The history of this process is protracted and extensive, and only its outlines are necessary for our purposes. By the end of the eighteenth century the division was so clear that for most people the separation between the two levels was very conscious; for example, an editor of popular tales feels obliged to justify publishing a collection of stories that are read by 'the dregs of the population', so that not even 'the lowest of the bourgeoisie' would be willing to admit to having read them. He records that a ladies' maid blushed furiously when her mistress asked her to produce a copy of one of these stories (Mandrou, 1964: 12f.).

In the first instance, folly lost all the positive connotations it had had in medieval culture. In medieval culture, the sacred and the profane had been allowed to mix in many ways, and folly was one of the most marked. At the same time, medieval religion accorded a relatively low place to reason, but increasingly over the neo-classical period, reason came to occupy a central place in religious belief: for example, the educated – while perfectly orthodox in their beliefs – also think that they

> have the right to ask for a justification of a belief, which the populace accepts because it is everybody's belief. . . . [They] question God and his servants, demanding explanations. . . . [For them] faith will no longer be simply faith; it will no longer be one with existence itself; they will no longer find it 'natural' to believe. Also, eventually, [they] will consider belief to be an acceptance of propositions which one puts to the test of examination, placing themselves, so to speak, outside faith.
>
> (Groethuysen, 1927: 10)

The new validation of reason went hand-in-hand with the marginalisation of unreason: no longer the universal condition of mankind, it becomes something that is locked away, to be inspected at a distance, as Foucault shows in his history of the treatment of mental illness (Foucault, 1961).

Since folly no longer had any justification, since it was simply the negative Other of a Reason which was the very basis of humanity, none of the institutions that were the preserve of folly could have any justification for their existence. For many years they had been under attack, perhaps even more strongly in Protestant countries than Catholic, for they were tainted with a Catholic heritage: for example, many of the games involved were played on Saint's Days, which were anathema to Protestants since (among other things) they implied that some days were more holy than others. But more fundamentally, all such occasions came to seem the very incarnation of disorder. As Burke shows, the English Puritans were fundamentally opposed to Lords of Misrule, May Games, Xmas feasting, Church ales, wakes, bearbaiting and dancing; the same antagonism is to be found in Holland. The festivals were denounced as immoral, as contrary to the new values of 'decency, diligence, gravity, modesty, orderliness' (Burke, 1978: 212–19). Fairs, which had both an economic and an 'entertainment' function, became increasingly subject to social controls aimed at reducing their 'rowdiness'. In their economic function fairs were an integral part of the social and economic order, and could scarcely be suppressed. Yet they were also the location of community experienced as good fellowship, filled with food and drink and 'entertainment', to use an anachronistic term. Their regulation was aimed at the unbridled elements in them: games, drinking, etc., and during the eighteenth and early nineteenth centuries the authorities were largely successful in their attempts at suppression (Malcolmson, 1973; Stallybrass and White, 1986: 27–43). The entertainment elements of the fair were condemned as uncouth:

> a Dutch poet, describing a country fair, chooses a mock-heroic style to express his attitude of amused detachment from the proceedings, while a French writer, later in the eighteenth century, found the Paris Carnival an embarrassment even to watch, for 'all these diversions show a folly and a coarseness which makes the taste for them resemble that of pigs'.
>
> (Burke, 1978: 273)

Certainly, the respectable person might go to the fair or carnival, but in a very detached frame of mind. Stallybrass and White quote a seventeenth-century father's letter to his son, recommending the boy to go to Bartholomew Fair in Smithfield, in order to learn discernment. In order to profit from the experience, the boy must sit at a high window, overlooking the fair; in this way he will constitute himself as 'pure gaze', as pure externality to the events of the fair. In general, the spectator must always constitute himself as such by non-participation, by this critical distance, and must be allowed the space to do so. The respectable classes in part constitute themselves by this pure gaze of exclusion (1986: 41–2, 118–19).

In general, the seventeenth and early eighteenth centuries see the withdrawal of respectable people from all forms of popular culture. Here the history of the English alehouse is instructive (Wrightson, 1981). In the sixteenth century the alehouses served clear economic functions for the poor, who had most of their food there; they also were the location of good fellowship and good neighbourliness; drinking was a popular pastime for the poor, mostly but not exclusively men. But the alehouses were castigated by moralists for impiety, and wrecking family life. During the seventeenth-century the 'better sort' in rural parishes withdraw from alehouse company. The sixteenth and early seventeenth centuries see renewed attacks upon the alehouse; there is a growing concern with public order generally. Customary behaviour had recently been made subject to legislation and the courts were used to suppress things such as drinking and disorderliness; the introduction of poor relief created a focus for the desire to impose behaviour appropriate to the 'deserving poor'. In the eighteenth century, there was some relaxation, but within a framework of firm control by a new middle class which had a clear sense of 'normal decency', and enforced it. But also in the eighteenth century the new respectable middle classes created a new forum for public intercourse which was to be free of the 'carnivalesque' excesses of the alehouses and taverns: the coffee-houses. Coffee-houses were decent, because free of the grotesque, unruly behaviour associated with taverns, primarily drunkenness and sexual licence; they were democratic – anyone could come in and sit and converse for the price of a cup of coffee. Because the norms of behaviour in them conform to respectable ideals they become prime sites for the emergence of the new respectable public realm, the arena of civil order (Ellis, 1956).

What does this material about comedy and humour in the Renaissance and neo-classical periods tell us?

From this point onwards in the history of our civilisation, the line which separates mirth creation from other elements of our culture is drawn in a different place, and this relocation of the separation is one way in which our culture institutes itself in its distinctively modern form. Underneath the mass of empirical details about the separation of popular and polite cultures, we perceive a unitary process, part of the general 'civilising process' charted by Norbert Elias (1978). Among other things, civil, polite manners dictate a certain decorum which excludes those forms of humour or mirth creation which come to be regarded as vulgar because excessive, grotesque: belly laughs, obscene puns and Spoonerisms, knockabout physical farce, insults, etc. This new prohibition coincides with the condemnation of laughter – by then traditional – by the Church: the gross opening of the mouth and raucous laughter had a theological significance, as we have seen, established by the Church Fathers in the Dark Ages; in the neo-classical period this is doubled by the new regulation of bodily habits which forbids the 'excessive' revelation of bodily apertures (Bertrand, 1991: 75–6). Of course, none of these things are abolished, but they are relegated to the margins of a culture which becomes the dominant culture, the one practised by those sections of the population with the wealth and the power to make their definitions of the world into the public definitions. In this marginalisation, the old culture becomes 'popular' culture. As Burke notes, before the Renaissance, in a sense there was no such thing as a popular culture: there was the universal culture of customary practice, adhered to by the entire population (an adherence somewhat differentiated by rank, occupation and gender); for a minority, there was also learned culture, with its own language (Latin) and a set of practices restricted to a small section of the population for some of their activities. The idea that the population might be fundamentally divided into two cultures, a popular one and an elite one, only arose in the Renaissance period and the new elite, respectable, polite culture was created in the process of self-differentiation from the older universal one, which became 'popular' culture insofar as it was marginalised (Burke, 1978: 24ff.).

This separation and marginalisation can give rise to a great variety of social, political, aesthetic and moral judgments. For example, one might nostalgically regret the vigorous, frank, open, boisterous culture of the repressed margin – to some extent, the set of activities now known as 'the sixties' was an attempt to recreate at least some aspects of the 'world we have lost', and the fact that this attempt dwindled into consumerism should not blind us to its meaning. Or we may denounce certain elements of incoherence or hypocrisy in the exclusions and marginalisation in question. As Stallybrass and White argue, the repression of the boisterous margin goes hand in hand with an unconscious desire for exactly the activities which are being repressed, and the more they are subjected to this marginalisation and repression, the more tainted they are with the 'dirt' of their origins, the more attractive they become (1986: 5f., 149–70). One may regard this as hypocrisy, or one may lament it as a double bind: it is hypocrisy insofar as those who adhere to the respectable morality condemn those whom they desire – perhaps most visibly in the traditional sexual double standard and the associated stereotype of the 'bad' girl – and it is a double bind insofar as those who adhere to the respectable morality are obliged to condemn what they most want, and to most want what they most condemn.

Perhaps what is most relevant for our purposes is to recognise the way in which these processes have affected the nature of laughter in the modern world. As Bakhtin argues, in the Middle Ages and still in the Renaissance, laughter is not just the act of derision, it is a valid expression of an attitude towards the world as a whole; by the following century it is only derision, since anything which is noble cannot also be funny (1970: 75–6). Similarly, in Rabelais everything scatological is part of the evocation of the grotesque, of the 'low corporeality' that is integral to popular cosmology; for example, faeces and urine are ambivalent, they are positive as well as negative, for they are part of the cycle of death and rebirth; thus jokes about them, smearing people with them, etc., are both an insult and at the same time the opposite. Only in the next century do they become nothing but cynical grossness (1970: 149–55). In the same way, insults and beatings – a commonplace element in Rabelais (e.g. 1955: 475–83) – derive from ritualised elements of carnival; here a 'king' is elected by the people, to be dethroned and beaten at the end of his reign, and dressed as a clown. It is the beating that dethrones him, thus making him a clown. For Bakhtin, this is to be understood within a generalised anthropology of such activities, seen as symbols:

> Insults represent death, youth which has become old age, the body become a corpse. Insults are the 'mirror of comedy' face to face with life as it drifts away, with that which is condemned to historical death. But in this system death is followed by resurrection, by the new year, by new youth, by the new spring. So praise echoes rude insults. This is why insults and praise are two aspects of the same two-bodied world.
>
> (1970: 198–9)

This comment has a double significance. In the first place, it indicates a link between the popular culture of the Middle Ages and a generalised anthropology of calendrical events – although whether such a link is valid is a topic for specialist debate. Second, and more importantly, it indicates that stock comic devices have a deeper level of meaning than mirth creation, by locating them within a cosmology. Such devices remained a commonplace in popular culture – for instance, the ritualised aggression so common in silent screen farce – but it is very unclear whether they can have the same meaning in the new context of industrial popular culture.

In short, for Bakhtin, mirth creation is never just mirth creation in the Middle Ages and the Renaissance, it is always at the same time the incarnation of something more fundamental; the individual's place within the community and the community's place within the continuity of the world:

> Laughter in the Middle Ages is not the subjective, individual, bio-logical sensation of the continuity of life, it is a universal, social sensation. Man feels the continuity of life in the public square, mixed in with the carnival crowd, where his body is in contact with those of people of all ages and conditions; he feels himself a member of a people in the constant state of growth and renovation. This is why the laughter of the popular festival contains an element of victory [over death and temporal power].
>
> (1970: 99)

Before the seventeenth century, in short, laughter is inseparable from a cosmology in which the events that provoke laughter simultaneously have a second layer of meaning which is anything but 'mere mirth'. The grossest laughter is perfectly compatible with the deepest seriousness. For us today, even if we have largely abandoned the rules of neo-classical decorum in the arts (and some in everyday life), there is still a tendency to make a clear distinction between what is funny and what is serious. As a result, laughter tends to be reserved for the recognition of some isolated artefact or incident – say, a joke – that we find funny. Of course, this is not absolutely true: laughter is also a marker of embarrassment, and laughter may also be no more than the incarnation of a sense of happy exuberance, a mood in which more or less anything may seem funny. Nonetheless, it seems to me that we practice a fairly rigorous separation between the funny and the unfunny, and that laughter is reserved for the former. Especially, comedy is something that is distinct from other aesthetic artefacts precisely on the grounds that its function is to make us laugh (more exactly, this is one of the two meanings of the word – the other one being the literary meaning already discussed, where the link with laughter is secondary).

11

MANNERS, WIT AND THE REFORM OF LANGUAGE

Along with their withdrawal from the social occasions of the old popular culture, the respectable classes acquire – during the neo-classical period – the new norms of social intercourse that are nowadays called 'manners', but which in the neo-classical period were more usually called 'civility' or 'politeness'. The core of these manners is twofold: first, a certain policing of the body; second, the acquisition of a certain gracefulness.

By 'policing of the body' I mean the norms of personal bodily behaviour studied by Norbert Elias (1978). As Elias shows, from the late sixteenth century onwards, the basic bodily functions, such as eating and excretion, become subject to increasingly stringent regulation, much of which is published in treatises on civility, many aimed at educating parents in how to bring up their children. For instance, people are taught to eat with implements instead of their fingers, and not to use the same implements for transmitting food out of the serving dishes as they are using for putting it in their mouths. Blowing the nose should be discreet, and the handkerchief should be preferred to the fingers. The excretion of urine and faeces is privatised. All of this new self-regulation involves a break with previous norms of behaviour (Elias, 1978: 53–160; Magendie, 1925: 149–70).

By 'gracefulness' I mean all those skills which indicate that one is subjecting one's communication with the outside world to a set of aesthetic norms; in dress, in comportment, in speech, in the mastery of dance, etc., the 'man of the world' should demonstrate an easy, totally natural-appearing capacity to do anything demanded by the social occasions on which he will meet his equals and superiors (Magendie, 1925: 312–15; Castiglione, 1967: 60–5). Above all, this involves knowledge of the rest of the world, but a knowledge which is primarily practical and which should never be paraded in an ostentatious manner – pedantry of any sort is incompatible with politeness (Mornet, 1929: 21–4). Central to this process is the art of conversation, and therefore the acquisition of linguistic skills is a *sine qua non* (Castiglione, 1967: 71–83; France, 1992: 55–9; Mornet, 1929: 81–6). Book 1 of Castiglione's *Courtier* – which is the starting-point for a two-century long tradition of books on civility, manners and how to exert personal influence in society – includes a long debate about the nature of the kind of language skills necessary for the perfect courtier.

Clearly these two sets of norms do not operate in the same way. The new regulation of bodily functions rapidly comes to be seen as the minimal attribute of a civilised person, whereas the skills of gracefulness operate as a distinction between 'ordinary' and 'superior' people. As Peter France shows, in France the terms *civilité* and *politesse* refer to these two distinctive sets of attributes. *Politesse* is held to derive largely from the experience of court life; it is the opposite of provincialism, it is that extra polish, that extra *savoir-faire* that comes from mixing with the great and powerful of the land. It derives from frequenting a particular, narrowly defined world – the Royal court and the salons with their noble female company; it involves a high degree of learning provided it is not pedantic. *Civilité* refers to the more basic set of attributes of self-regulation – the minimum refinement of ordinary manners as taught to children. This distinction is therefore also the distinction between two social groups, where 'politeness' is the manner typical of the urban upper class, and 'civility' a state to which all but the most loutish can easily aspire. In the eighteenth century, the Enlightenment *philosophes* attempted to produce a sense of politeness that would be less hierarchical, an easy but refined mode of intercourse between equals (France, 1992: 53–8, 65–72). In Germany, the same distinction is caught by the usage of the terms *Zivilisation* and *Kultur*, where the former refers to the development of refined manners in noble and court circles, and the latter refers to the forms of intellectual self-development typical of the emerging bourgeois intelligentsia of the eighteenth century (Elias, 1978: 8–9).

Language skills derived largely from the new educational programme based around rhetoric. This was originally developed in the English and German 'grammar schools', but slowly permeated the rest of Europe; a turning point was its adoption by the Jesuits (Mornet, 1929: 141–2). The skills which were valued were by and large those taught in this tradition: the capacity to find something apropos to say on any subject; the ability to present one's thought with clarity; correct grammar, syntax and vocabulary, in other words following the rules of language as developed in polite society, avoiding provincial, archaic, pedantic and lower-class modes of speaking; the capacity to organise one's speech elegantly and to adapt its organisation to the audience in question (Mornet, 1929; France, 1992: 53–73).

Thus command of a certain language was central to the new manners. Now this language was also subject to rapid change in its own organisation, largely in order to function as the language of this new 'polite' social group, and the way in which it was changed is directly relevant to how humour – at any rate verbal humour – operates.

In the first place, the new 'politeness' excluded the use of linguistic forms that derived from outside the social group in question: specifically, it excluded the language of the universities – too pedantic – the provinces and the lower classes. Slowly, this new 'national' language spread outside the capital cities where it most often started, and even in remote areas the upper and middle classes started to use the metropolitan version (Moriarty, 1988: 49–53, 93–8; Burke, 1978: 272). Still today, the use or non-use of the 'standard' version of a national language is a profound mark of social distinction – as one brief instance, we may recall the incident in the Taviani brothers' film *Padre Padrone* where the Sardinian peasant boy, on joining the Italian army, is reprimanded by his officer for speaking in dialect. This historical dimension reinforces Noam Chomsky's famous remark to the effect that a language is a dialect that has an army.

In the second place – and more importantly for our purposes – this new polite language was organised on discursive principles that were significantly different from those typical of what it displaced. I refer to the development, during the seventeenth century, of a literary and polite spoken 'plain style'. Indeed, it is a cliché of the history of the seventeenth century in England and France that both the written language and the spoken language of polite society became increasingly plain as the century progressed. The typical public language of the early century came to be seen as bombastic, precious, exaggerated, inflated . . . in short, rhetorical, in the modern pejorative sense of the word. No single process can account for this change, which is manifest in various activities: science, religion, literary taste. That the spoken and written language overlapped substantially is basic to the changing nature of the spoken language and the way in which it related to culture (Williams, 1965: 237–54).

In science, the methodological innovators of the early century – for example, Bacon and Descartes – held that the operation of rhetoric impeded the growth of reliable knowledge. For their predecessors, public persuasion was the same thing as scientific proof, and therefore effectively the same thing as truth, insofar as it was accessible to humanity. Both Bacon and Descartes rejected this tradition as a dead weight impeding scientific investigation (France, 1972: 44; Howell, 1961: 68ff.). For both of them, rhetoric was 'mere ornamentation', which would get in the way of observation and demonstration (France, 1972: ch. 2; Jones, 1953: 76ff.). The culmination of scientific distrust of the traditional use of language is is to be found in the Royal Society after 1660. The Society's attitude is summarised in often-quoted passages from Thomas Sprat's *History of the Royal Society* (1667), which recommends the abolition of eloquence as it puts people off the truth, is contrary to reason and abets passion, therefore promoting change instead of the stability of reason, and is full of the 'mists and uncertainties' induced by figures of speech. Royal Society style is plain and natural, marking a return to 'the primitive purity and shortness when men delivered so many things, almost in as many words' (quoted Jones, 1953: 85f.). Here the empiricism which underlay English objections to traditional style is clear: words are to be transparent, to present things to the mind in the sense of 'render them present to the mind'. This is in accordance with the seventeenth-century conception of language in which it is nouns that are the basis of all language, since in nouns language was felt to be marked by the maximum proximity to things (Hobbes, 1651: 102ff.). Here too is to be found the grounds of the mistrust of metaphor: the transferred sense of a noun used metaphorically is a betrayal of its natural transparency to the world of things. In this new tradition, metaphor comes to be defined as a 'transferred sense' of a word, and thus as an abuse of meaning. In Foclin's *Rhetoric* metaphor is 'a style by means of which the proper and natural meaning of a word is changed to another'; for Locke they are 'perfect cheats', to be avoided in all 'discourses that pretend to inform or instruct' (Cohen, 1979: 2); for Hobbes it is one of the four abuses of language, which can never be the 'true grounds of any ratiocination', for metaphors openly 'profess their inconstancy' (1651: 102, 109f.).

In religion too plain language became increasingly central, in both France and England. The growing role of reason in religion is part of the motive force, for traditional rhetoric was held to fuel enthusiasm – still understood in its etymological sense of 'possessed by God' – rather than calm conviction (Willey, 1962: 124; Pooley, 1981: 192–8). No doubt in England this was in part due to fear of the sectarianism that had fed the Civil War, but in France the same tendency is visible without the overtly political reason for this 'politics of the signifier'. In the first half of the century, in both England and France, the majority of pulpit oratory was still flamboyant in style, regardless of sectarian adherence. In England, during the Civil War and the Common-wealth, stylistic level was a political matter, but there was no single, simple divide between one politics and high style, on the one hand, and another politics and plain style on the other (Pooley, 1981). After the Restoration English high style became polemically associated with the Puritan divines of the Commonwealth, and conforming clergy – as opposed to non-conformist – claimed simultaneously rational religion and plain style as their own. The proponents of plain style urged that it was a mark of sincerity, and thus more appropriate for God's message than ornamental style, which was simul-taneously obscure – that is, not in accordance with the language of reason – and sterile, mere verbiage instead of genuine spiritual comfort and instruction (Jones, 1953: 78, 115–18; cf. France, 1972: ch. 4).

The proponents of plain style were not seeking to abolish all 'play of the signifier'; what they sought was subordination of the signifier to the order of denotation. Moreover, it is obvious that scientists and preachers were far from the only players in the game of linguistic norms. What we are observing is in fact a change in taste on the part of the educated urban elite. When Pope condemns 'vile conceits' as clownish and boorish, he is giving precise expression both to the rejection of a linguistic norm and to the social base of the rejection.

Both in England and in France we see this process at work. In Bouhours (1687) we find a discussion of epigrams which aims to regulate the play of the signifier in wit. He discusses an epigram by Tristan (already old by this time) on the fire that destroyed the Palais de Justice (Law Courts) in Paris:

> Certes l'on vit un triste jeu,
> Quand à Paris Dame Justice
> Se mit le Palais tout en feu,
> Pour avoir mangé trop d'épice.
> [For sure it was a sad sight
> When in Paris Lady Justice
> Set her palace/palate on fire
> By eating too much spice.]

The pun on *palais* (palace/palate) is combined with a second pun: *épice* (spice) in seventeenth-century France also meant 'bribes', and the epigram is about the notorious venality of the legal system. For Bouhours the punning is beyond the pale of good taste:

> what is called 'spice' in the courts has nothing to do with the fire; and the palate, by eating too much pepper, does not lead to a fire in a building where justice is performed or – if you will – sold.

He objects to the 'pure equivocation' involved here, and offers as a counter-example this epigram by Martial in praise of the Emperor: 'The peoples of your empire speak with many tongues; but they speak with one voice when they say that you are the true father of the country.' (In Latin 'tongue' and 'voice' are the same word, *vox*, which Bouhours translates in both cases as *langage*.) Here there are two meanings to the same word, and even antithetical meanings, but each meaning is the true meaning of the word, and therefore the words are 'in agreement with each other, and the conjunction of these opposed senses creates something ingenious'. Even if the terms of Bouhours' argument are not always clear, the gist is: Martial's epigram involves less equivocation, less 'conceptual distance' between the terms in which it is formulated, and this is more acceptable to the new taste that Bouhours represents (1687: 17–22, 380–6).

In England, the changing sense of the word 'wit' indicates the same process. To the Elizabethans, 'wit' meant simply 'intellect', as opposed to 'will'; subsequently it came to mean ingenuity. Hobbes defines it as 'Fancy', the opposite of 'judgment'. In the later seventeenth and eighteenth centuries it means something pithy, penetrating, profound, aptly and forcefully expressed (and by extension, someone who is apt to speak in this way). In Pope's words:

> Some to conceit alone their taste confine,
> And glittering thoughts struck out at ev'ry line;
> Pleased with a work where nothing's just or fit;
> One glaring chaos and wild heap of wit.

Poets like painters, thus unskilled to trace
The naked nature and the living grace,
With gold and jewels cover ev'ry part,
And hide with ornaments their want of art.
True wit is nature to advantage dressed,
What oft was thought but ne'er so well expressed;
Something whose truth convinced at sight we find,
That gives us back the image of our mind.

(Essay on Criticism, n.d.: pt II)

Pope distinguishes 'wit' from 'true wit', thus indicating some tension in contemporary culture; he speaks no doubt for the most 'refined' taste of his period. But the terms of the debate are shared: forcefulness and truth to experience. Hobbes' definitions already imply a pejorative sense for 'wit', and the post-Restoration writers undertake to change the practice of wit so as to escape Hobbes' strictures, by making judgment the basis of wit (Spingarn, 1908: xxix). In France there is no single word whose vicissitudes reveal changing conceptions with the clarity of 'wit' in English, but the changing applications of the word *vraisemblable* (plausible) reveal an essentially similar process. That there was a similar change in language is shown clearly by Molière's *Précieuses ridicules*, where the women of 1660 who are ridiculed for affected language are using the normal literary language of the 1630s.

Dr Johnson's comments on the Metaphysicals clearly represent the same tendency: they were neither wits nor poets, since they were excessively 'singular in their thoughts' and 'careless in their diction'. Wit on the other hand is something 'at once natural and new, that which, though not obvious is, upon its first production, acknowledged to be just; . . . that, which he that never found it, wonders how he missed'. The Metaphysicals' 'wit' is certainly novel, but neither natural nor obvious nor just, so that far from the reader wondering how he missed it he wonders 'by what perversity of industry [such thoughts] were ever found' (Johnson, 1905: 19–20).

What the insistence on plainness reveals is an attempt to create a language which would be transparent, a language in which the materiality of the signifier would have disappeared. This is most clearly revealed in Sprat's definition of pure language as language which 'delivered so many things almost in as many words', or in Hobbes' conception of language as a mere notational convenience for helping the mind in its operations with things, but it also underlies the attempts to rationalise metaphor. The signifier should be no more than a window onto the material outside world. Nowhere is the materiality of the signifier more starkly revealed than in metaphor, for here the manner in which meaning is transferred along the signifying chain depends absolutely upon the nature of the signifier, which is the link between different regimes of meaning. Hence the centrality of metaphorical meaning in the attempt to create a transparent language. Such a programme is impossible, of course, and the neo-classical moment did not seek literally to abolish metaphor, persuasion, ornamentation or any of the other features of language it sought to regulate – except in moments of aberration, such as the English clergyman who sought to abolish ornamentation of speech by Act of Parliament (Jones, 1953: 81). What was sought was the sense that transparency was the norm, and that everything else was deviant, secondary, marginal, in relation to it.

To fully understand the scope of what happened in the language of the seventeenth century, we need to make a comparison with what preceded it: the medieval and Renaissance discursive formation, in which the sense of a language transparent to the order of things was rigorously impossible. We will follow the first part of Foucault's *The Order of Things* (1966).

For the early Renaissance, Foucault shows, the universe consisted of an immense network of resemblances, and knowledge of the world consisted of their exploration. Everything in the world is related to everything else through the play of resemblances; everything is caught in this play somehow, and knowledge consists of deciphering the resemblances, finding out what types of relations of similarity and dissimilarity the object under investigation has with such-and-such another object. But these resemblances, which are inscribed in the very heart of everything in the universe, might easily escape our attention but for the presence of marks, of indications, which bring them to our notice. There is sympathy between aconite and the eyes, which enables it to cure eye infections, but this sympathy would not be noticed but for a visible indication: aconite seeds are little dark balls in a white skin, just like eyelids and eyes. The analogy is thus a sign, a signature, of the profound resemblance between the two; indeed, any of the forms of resemblance is capable of serving as the visible signature of the hidden, profound resemblance which guarantees the reality of the sign.

Everything in the universe is a sign of something else as well as being itself, and knowledge starts with reading these signs, which point to the fact of Resemblance itself as the fundamental structure of the natural order. These signs are in principle no different from the signs that emanate from God (the words of the Bible) and signs that emanate from the ancients (their writings, which were also considered divinely inspired). Thus observation of the external world has no clear privilege in this epistemology: it is in no way superior to, or even fundamentally different from, erudition; hence the sixteenth-century encyclopaedias, in which what the modern mind would recognise as science is inextricably mixed up with legend, folklore, mythology, etymology, travellers' tales, etc.: all are equally relevant to the development of knowledge, since all are indicative of the play of resemblance.

Within this system, language shares the characteristics of all other things. Originally, language was genuinely transparent, they thought: it was the incarnation of God's knowledge. But sin destroyed this state and Babel was the result; a situation in which language shared in the properties of a fallen world. Just as things hide their true nature in the infinite play of resemblance, so words too are mysterious things that need to be deciphered; they too are subject to resemblance, analogy, etc.

This first similarity between language and the realm of things is paired with a second. If there was an original discourse about the world – God's word – which was both entirely adequate to its subject and completely transparent, then the language of the post-lapsarian state must incessantly strive to reconstitute that original meaning, in the form of commentary, a process that is infinite because each comment is another element in the play of resemblances: no comment can uncover the truth of the original text. Thus the knowledge of things and the knowledge of words is essentially the same: knowledge of things consisted of deciphering the play of resemblances on the basis of signs, but these signs were in their turn no more than a series of resemblances. Commentary is the perpetual, infinite exploration of resemblances in language, since it can only approach the true text of the original discourse by saying things similar to it. But because similarity is simultaneously identity and non-identity, difference, the gap can never be closed.

This epistemology, and particularly the place of language within it, is in direct and dramatic contrast with the epistemology implied in the development of plain style in the seventeenth century. Within the earlier epistemology, there can be no single normal established meaning for a word, in relationship to which another usage would be deviant. The fact that a word can be made to mean something new or different is an indication that another element in the infinite network of resemblance has surfaced. Under these circumstances, what the modern mind calls 'metaphor' is an element in the perpetual approximation to truth that was called knowledge: in a metaphor a similarity is revealed, and similarity is an objective feature of the nature of the world.

Here all meaning, any relation between signifier and signified, is inherently unstable, inherently liable to the revelation of layers of meaning, based on resemblances that were previously unsuspected, and this process was an intrinsic property of language, of sign systems in general. We can see an example of this process in this passage from Rabelais' *Gargantua*, where he is proving that the colour white signifies joy:

> That is the reason why the Galli (that is French who are so called because naturally they are as white as milk, which the Greeks call 'gala') like to wear white feathers in their caps. For by nature they are joyful, frank, gracious and kindly, and have for their sign and symbol the flower that is whiter than any other: the lily, that is.
>
> (1955: 61)

Clearly this argument is absolutely dependent upon the play of resemblances, the word-play surrounding 'Galli' and 'gala': the argument only makes sense because of the overlap at the level of the signifier between the Latin and Greek words. This overlap, this pun, is then referred to the occult qualities of whiteness as its underpinning: the material echo of the two signifiers only has any significance because it can be traced further into the network of resemblances, but it is the polyphony of the signifiers that is the starting-point of the argument. To the modern mind, this is no more than a bad pun, at best; to the sixteenth-century mind it is a serious argument, and its seriousness derives from what they considered to be the nature of sign systems. The erudite puns that were a constant feature of sixteenth-century writing, and that so infuriated the neo-classical writers of the seventeenth, were no ornament: they were an intrinsic part of the process of knowledge, of that revelation of Resemblance in the play of the signs of resemblance that was the purpose of knowledge.

In this respect Renaissance epistemology stands at the end of a tradition stretching continuously back into antiquity. In the ancient world reasoning of the type Rabelais employs was frequent and appears to have been regarded as normal: Cicero, Ovid, Virgil, Plato . . . the list of major authors in whom it is to be found is long. Not only the pun but also the anagram and the etymology were taken to be valid bases for logical deduction (Ahl, 1988). For example:

> Augustine argued . . . that Christians must sacrifice to no God *nisi Domino soli*, 'except solely to the Lord', as Exodus 22.20 states. Unfortunately the Latin text does not help his argument because it contains a (possibly unintentional) pun. *Soli* does not just mean 'alone' or 'solely' but 'sun'. And some Christians chose to interpret the passage as meaning: 'Except to our Lord Sol'. This pun was not risible hearsay to Augustine. It was heresy. . . . Augustine urged his readers, if they would not accept his assurance, to look at the Greek.
>
> (Ahl, 1988: 33)

Augustine had to take the 'argument' seriously because he lived in a culture where it was taken seriously. The book which argued the case most consistently, the *Etymologiae* of Bishop Isidore of Seville, was written in the seventh century and was one of the most used textbooks throughout the Middle Ages.

In such a conception the distinction between normal and deviant usage is elided, and the relationship of pure equivalence between signifier and signified becomes difficult to maintain: all signifier/signified relationships become inherently unstable and shifting, apt to turn into the sort of punning pseudo-argument – as the modern mind would see it – that Rabelais advances.

What do we see in this historical process?

Essentially the process which occurs is the marginalisation of all linguistic forms in which the play of the signifier is foregrounded – puns, jokes, metaphors, etc. Of course, none of these forms are suppressed or altogether excluded from normal language, but they are relegated to the margins of two norms of discursive organisation which become increasingly dominant within civilised culture: the representation of truth and politeness. They are marginalised in the search for and representation of truth because truth is held to reside in the relationship between signs and referents (reality), not in the nature of signifying systems themselves. Any 'play' which results from the nature of the signifying system is now seen as 'play' in the mechanical sense – a dysfunction of the system. And play of the signifier is marginalised in polite conversation because it comes to seem uncivilised, associated with the speech of the unsophisticated, uneducated 'ordinary people': the 'wit of crassitude' (Ahl, 1988: 21). An example of such a marginalisation is to be found in Dr Johnson's condemnation of Shakespeare's taste for the 'quibble' (i.e. pun). Shakespeare's use of puns is well documented, even at points of high drama in his plays: Mercutio, dying, says 'Ask for me tomorrow and you shall find me a grave man'. For Johnson, such abuse of language, as he sees it, is unworthy: 'A quibble was to him the fatal Cleopatra for which he lost the world and was content to lose it' (Culler, 1988: 7–8).

Of course, this new linguistic propriety, associated very directly with the programme of neo-classicism, came to be seen as stultifying by the Romantics, who in reinstating the claims of the imagination also insisted on the modification of linguistic propriety, at least in poetry. However, this programme did not affect the position of humorous forms, especially the more popular ones. Subsequently, linguistic nonsense came to occupy a certain place in English literary culture – Lewis Carroll's Alice books, Edmund Lear's 'nonsense poetry', clerihews, etc. Freud's *Jokes and their Relation to the Unconscious* is among other things a testimony to the popularity of – and Freud's own taste for – riddles; crossword puzzles are based on similar principles. Anecdotal evidence suggests that such verbal 'nonsense' came later to French culture than to other European countries. Baudin (1991) recalls hearing a typical English music-hall joke on the radio shortly after World War II, which he found wonderfully funny, but which his parents thought was merely stupid. In general, French usage distinguished between the *mot d'esprit* (typically French, linguistically very refined) and *l'humour* (absurd and English) (Baudin, 1990: 2). At the same time the *Almanach Vermot* – a monthly collection of jokes, cartoons and riddles published since 1886 – makes it clear that popular French humour contained many jokes based on similar verbal play mechanisms to popular English humour (Chanfrault, 1990). With the Surrealist movement, verbal nonsense of every kind became valued in its own right.

Yet none of these considerations contests the basic point made here: that such forms are marginal in relation to the major forms of post-Renaissance culture and are clearly located on one side only of the 'Great Divide', to use Andreas Huyssens' phrase (1988), between 'culture' and 'mass culture'.

CONCLUSION TO PART III

We have seen that structure is necessarily one dimension of humour: this is logically necessary because neither occasion for humour nor negotiation about humour can explain the existence of humour. Occasion fails because it is permissive rather than prescriptive, negotiation because it must occur on specifiable grounds in order to avoid being random. We cannot avoid postulating structure as an immanent feature of humour. But it is also clear that it is not a feature of an artefact in itself: it must be seen as existing in the relationship between the artefact and its perceiver(s). Any mechanism such as the one commonly labelled incongruity exists on this borderline: its properties are part of the symbolic order of a culture; they derive from discursive organisation. This order or organisation both exists as one dimension of a society and is also a structuring principle of mind. At the same time we have seen that there is a strictly subjective dimension involved too, in the sense that the individual receiver must be minimally receptive. We have also seen the difficulties involved in understanding how this receptiveness is structured: in part it is a question of occasion, which acts as a cue; in part it is a question of a playful state of mind, which may be cued by the occasion, by some property of the artefact or by arousal. But nobody has ever succeeded in an exhaustive description of all the possible ways in which receptiveness may be organised.

Such difficulties do not reduce the necessity and centrality of structure. That said, the notion of structure turns out to be more complex than is usually recognised. Most semiotic and psychological analyses are based on the single joke or gag, or a selection of them, where their articulation into a sequence is not taken into account – Mulkays' (1988) *On Humour* is an exception here, because his grounding concept of 'humorous discourse' as a self-contained discursive entity necessarily includes principles of internal organisation. But observation of comic performance – including under this heading, for the moment, joke-telling in everyday life – reveals very clearly that what may be broadly called narrative context is intrinsic to the organisation of humour. Professional comedians select jokes on the grounds of their suitability for their public persona, rejecting others or passing them on to colleagues. Jokes in silent screen farce, sitcoms and other similar narrative forms which emphasise the regular production of laughter depend upon a fit between narrative flow and joke theme, despite their overwhelming emphasis upon the flow of gags.

Ultimately, in the culture of the modern Western world, this principle produces the distinction between 'comedy' in the canonical sense, and more popular forms – 'farce' is a convenient label for them, even though historically farce is a particular sub-genre of theatrical comedy. This distinction in its turn is part of a far wider set of distinctions which, cumulatively, have produced the fundamental distinction between 'polite' or 'respectable' culture, and 'popular' or 'mass' culture: the 'Great Divide' within our societies. At one level, this division is one of the fundamental marks of the nature of occasions in our culture: we do not have the same expectations when we go to 'art' as when we go to 'entertainment' – although no doubt there are many borderline phenomena, and recent practices in the arts have tended to erode the difference. At another level, the distinction is a fundamental organising principle of texts themselves: in popular entertainment the production of laughter is a valid aim in itself and requires no particular placing within some larger artistic scheme of things; in the canonical tradition laughter is never an aim in itself, it is always part of the larger scheme of which form is the incarnation.

Such conclusions are obvious in this context. However, one further implication of the analysis in Part III is less so; it refers to the question of function.

It is commonly the case that analyses of function are based upon the forms of humour to be found in modern society (clearly the anthropological literature about joking relationships is an exception here). In the preceding pages we have seen good reasons to suppose that the form of humour which is most often held to be the universal form – incongruity – may in fact be distinctly local. There are two grounds for supposing this. First, the nature of carnival, as Bakhtin presents it: here – if Bakhtin is right – mirth occupies a different place in medieval cosmology to the place it occupies in post-Renaissance society; indeed, quite conventional analyses of the place of the fool in medieval society suggest the same. Second, the reform of language in the neo-classical period also suggests that verbal humour at least shifts its place, not just because neo-classical decorum marginalises the grosser jests and the more baroque forms of wit, but because congruity and incongruity acquire a new epistemological status. It may well be the case that the semiotic mechanisms of incongruity existed in medieval society – indeed we saw a sixteenth-century nobleman refer to the 'happy-unhappy' answers of a fool, which suggests a close parallel with modern wit. But medieval epistemology and cosmology give a different place to such incongruity, or perhaps several different places. The strict decorum of the later neo-classical period – after the quarrel of the ancients and the moderns – is arguably of lesser importance than what was common to the whole period, the rejection of medieval reasoning and representational norms. In analyses such as Freud's and Jonathan Miller's we can see that the semiotic form of wit, incongruity, is central to the functional or ecological account which is the authors' main purpose: the 'cognitive rehearsal' of new possibilities, the free rein momentarily given to the subconscious. If, however, the semiotic form of wit occupies a different place in culture – as in medieval Europe – it is arguable that it cannot play the same functional role. But it must be stressed that such a conclusion is to say the least speculative.

Part IV

THE LIMITS
OF HUMOUR

12

COMPREHENSION AND HUMOUR

Most professional comedians have had the experience of failure to raise a laugh. Most of us have probably, at one time or another, told a joke that has utterly failed. In that sense, we can say that humour is a fragile thing. Of course, within our own culture, we can point to circumstances which reduce the chances of failure: the comedian who has already had a warm-up man at work on the audience; telling a joke to friends where there has already been a lot of laughter (and maybe some drinking), for example. In tribal cultures we could point to the role of customary relationships in fixing a framework where joking will succeed; in medieval Europe the fact of customary roles and calendrical occasions such as the Feast of Fools would no doubt act as a similar form of insurance. These caveats about limited circumstances notwithstanding, the central point holds: jokes and other humorous attempts operate within a framework where they may not be received as such. And if they are not received as such, it is very unclear whether they are in fact humour: as Douglas says, a joke must be permitted as well as intended in order to accede to the status of joke.

The point is perhaps obvious, but it has an implication which is less so: it is that any theory of humour, jokes and comedy which does not have the principle of potential failure built into it, as one of its fundamental axioms, is a defective theory. In the apocryphal words of the English comedian Ken Dodd: 'The difference between Freud and me is that he never had to play the Glasgow Palais on a wet Monday night'. Of course, at one level this merely insists on the superiority of practice over theory, but it is interesting that the element of practical experience that is chosen as decisive is the high risk of failure.

Now in practice the great bulk of the major theories of humour, jokes, laughter and comedy are based on the presupposition that the jokes in fact succeed. For example, in Aristotle laughter is treated in various ways: it can be the mark of a perceived superiority to what is found derisory; it can be effective in destroying an opponent's argument by confounding his (*sic*) attempts to be serious. In the case of laughter as a mark of superiority, this derives from the theory of genre in Aristotle's *Poetics*: the coherence of a genre is given in two dimensions; first by the enunciative relationship between the text and the audience; second by the type of pleasure that is proper to the genre in question. In comedy, the enunciative relationship is the recognition of the audience's moral superiority to the events portrayed on stage, and the type of pleasure proper to the genre is laughter (Genette, 1986: 97–100). In this theory, the success of joking is doubly inscribed at the centre, in the recognition of superiority and in the pleasure; indeed it is successfully evoked laughter that acts as the hinge between the two panels of the theory, binding them together. Comedy is only such in this theory if the allocutionary and the illocutionary force of the utterance are the same, or – in another terminology – if the encoding and the decoding are homologous, if the real reader accepts the subject position offered as the position of the implied reader (Palmer, 1991: 24–32).

Freud's theory too is marked by a stress on success. While it must be said that Freud explicitly recognises the possibility of the failure of jokes (thus anticipating Ken Dodd's practical considerations, if not in detail!), the main body of his theory pulls in the opposite direction. Jokes are not 'technically' distinct (i.e. semiotically distinct) from other forms of statement, but the form of pleasure that they give is distinctive. This pleasure derives from their relationship to the drives of the unconscious, and especially from the procedure which safeguards them from suppression by 'adult critical rationality'. Now we know that for Freud jokes must have a listener, and implicitly at least this listener must find the joke funny: Freud insists that jokes give pleasure to the teller so to speak by ricochet, or via the pleasure the listener takes in them. To that extent the success of the joke is an integral part of Freud's theory. However, this pleasure and the procedure which protects jokes, or – as Freud also calls it, this 'forepleasure' – is also to be found in other species of the comic and in humour, and here there is no need of the listener, for the comic and humour are distinguished from jokes precisely by the different distribution of enunciative roles in them, as we have seen. Jokes, humour and the comic appear to have a single semiotic mechanism in common – the mixture of sense and nonsense, as Freud puts it – but only in jokes is the successful reception of this mechanism a relevant consideration.

Aristotle and Freud are typical of the major theories of jokes and the comic in that the place of successful reception of the joke is either simply assumed, or left ambiguous. The exception to this rule is modern social scientific thinking on the subject, where, as we have seen, it is an integral part of the theorising. For Douglas, permission must ratify intention before an act can be held to accede to the status of joke or humour, and although we shall see that there are important restrictions on this principle, notably surrounding the identity of the person or persons who must grant permission, nonetheless it is clear that Douglas' central perception – that the joke must pass a reception threshold – is correct. For ethno-methodological analyses such as Mulkay

(1988) and Jefferson (1979), the prime focus of study is the social process whereby the entry into what Mulkay calls 'humorous discourse' is negotiated; here it is appropriate to emphasise that such a process is indeed negotiated, that is to say unless both (or all) parties to the negotiation are satisfied that what has occurred is indeed the movement into humour, then the transition has not in fact occurred.

On the basis of this principle, it then becomes possible to study the set of conditions that obtain when success or failure occurs. For example, we have seen that gender is a variable in sense of humour, and we might expect that a would-be humorous activity likely to be successful with one gender might be less successful with the other. However, another line of enquiry will be pursued here: we will see what occurs at the limits of humour, at those moments when the negotiation of permission to be funny is in question, and we will be less concerned with empirical questions (since there are few studies) and more with what can be deduced from various examples about some general principles.

The first of those principles is the borderline between comprehension and incomprehension.

Clearly a joke must be understood in order to be found funny, in order to fully accede to the status of joke. At the Massachusetts Institute of Technology some years ago this joke was very successful: 'What's a goy?' – 'If examined at or before time t it's a girl; if examined after, it's a boy' (quoted in Cohen, 1979: 9). Here it is apparently lack of some piece of information or other that makes the joke incomprehensible, and we can imagine that if we had been in possession of it we could have enjoyed the joke as much as the people who did. Apparently some knowledge of information technology and Yiddish is necessary for understanding. Importantly, such knowledge must be available in advance of the joke being told, since its explanation afterwards will never make up the deficit, and simply destroys the joke; this implies that the information in question must be part of the culture of the individual who responds to the joke.

A couple of years ago I heard on the English TV news that a group of English soccer fans, *en route* to the European Cup in Sardinia, were appalled by the luxuriousness of the shops in Bologna: in an act of humorous derision they walked through the streets with their underpants on their heads. Here there must have been some element in the original situation which made the choice of the form of derision comprehensible, at least to the participants, and again it is not difficult to imagine that if we had been participants (which would probably have ensured that the 'we' was young and male), we could have appreciated the circumstances in the same way: walking around with your underpants on your head is easily assimilable to forms of clowning or horseplay that are relatively traditional.

This example is to be found in a study of Navajo humour:

A Navajo man out hunting is surprised by a rainstorm and takes shelter in a cave. After a while a coyote does the same, and doesn't notice the man. The man goes up to the coyote, approaching him from behind, and speaks to him. The coyote falls down dead.

Apparently the Navajo think of the coyote as the ultimate incarnation of cunning, the one who is always prepared, always ahead of the game, and Navajo humour in general refers to elements of disharmony in the universe (Cunningham and Lorenzo, 1991). Once we are told this, we can probably see why the Navajo would find the story funny, but even with this information it seems difficult to imagine someone brought up outside this culture actually being amused by the story. What is missing is not simply a piece of information, or being present at an event – as in the first two instances – but an entire culture: we do not merely need to know something about the Navajo, we need to share their belief system in order to make sense of this story in a Navajo way. Belief, in this sense, is not just a matter of information, but of emotional investment in a particular symbolic order: the notion of the coyote as supreme cunning must be written into the fibre of our being before we can see the event in the joke as humorously incongruous.

Clearly this point is part of a much larger debate about the relationship between culture and identity. What is suggested by these brief – and speculative – comments about the reception of humour is that the preconditions of its success include a very tight fit between the culture out of which a joke is produced and the culture of the receiver; this tight fit produces something like a common 'frame of mind', in which the stock of information held by participants has at least sufficient in common and, crucially, the participants are agreed on the emotional significance of the events that are portrayed. Although this description is not the same as saying that personal identity derives from culture, it does suggest that the layer of identity that can be derived from culture is more than just cognitive, it is also affective and motivational, since here shared pleasure seems to depend upon some common agenda.

Incomprehension may be written into the structure of humour in other ways too. In the cartoon 'Club Ability' (Plate 2) the multiple play of irony depends in large measure upon the incomprehension of the participants. The basis of the joke is that even the most absurdly exaggerated versions of male chauvinism are perfectly acceptable as literal statements of commonplace attitudes; however, this needs to be demonstrated through ironical displacement of meaning in order to be funny, and here this is done through the incomprehension of the two male interlocutors, one of whom fairly soon comes to realise that his daughter is being ironical, and whose warnings serve to underline the naivety of the other (and perhaps to make the irony clear to the reader). If this explanation seems pedantically unnecessary, it is because the mechanism of irony is well known: a dual meaning where one is

150

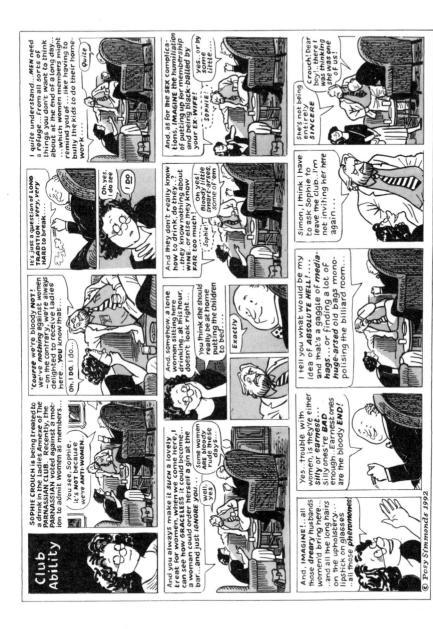

Plate 2 (© Posy Simmonds 1992)

pragmatically marked as a disguise for the other; in this cartoon the obvious irony is doubled by another, where the interlocutor's total incomprehension reveals just how utterly prejudiced he is, so prejudiced that he can mistake ironical exaggeration for truth. His incomprehension is the real basis of the joke.

Such a use of irony is well known in canonical literature, as we can see in this passage from Chapter 15 of Jane Austen's *Persuasion*. Here Anne Elliot is reunited with her family in Bath, and among other new information finds that her estranged cousin has renewed acquaintance with her father and sister, and has been forgiven his earlier distance from them on the grounds that it was the result of misunderstandings and extenuating circumstances. Anne's reservations about such a renewal have already been well established, and it is clear that her delicacy and tact may well be excessive and caused by a disappointed earlier love affair.

The scene which presents this is narrated in the past tenses:

> But this was not all which they had to make them happy. They had Mr Elliot, too. Anne had a great deal to hear of Mr Elliot. He was not only pardoned, they were delighted with him. He had been in Bath about a fortnight. . . . They had not a fault to find in him. . . . The circumstances of his marriage too were found to admit of such extenuation. This was an article not to be entered on by himself, but a very intimate friend of his, a Colonel Wallis, a highly respectable man . . . had mentioned two or three things relative to the marriage which made a material difference.
>
> (Austen, 1965: 152–3)

The use of the past tenses serves to underline the interplay of conflicting, or possibly conflicting, perspectives. They indicate to us that everything is being filtered through Anne's point of view: these are matters that her father and sister have narrated to her, not just events that the narrator is narrating to us, the readers – 'he *was* not only pardoned, they *were* delighted . . .'. In this multi-layered writing, how and where is the reader positioned? Without wishing to try and interpret the passage, in any traditional 'authoritative' sense, we can see that the positioning derives from the process of enunciation. The tense structure indicates the interplay between the 'normal' simple past of realist narration and the representation of Anne's point of view. In the play between these two arises the irony: we can see that Anne is not at all impressed by the arguments presented by her family, even though this is not directly said; we can also see that Anne's attitude is not unequivocally to be approved – she is perhaps over-reacting. Now whatever the 'meaning' in the traditional sense of this scene – which would need a far wider-scale interpretation of its place within the novel as a whole to establish – it is clear that it depends upon the play of irony outlined here, and it is Anne's family's ignorance of her evaluation of the situation, presented in the indirect narrative of their comments, which produces the effect in question. The family's ignorance is the mechanism which allows meaning to ricochet between what they say (indirectly narrated), what Anne makes of what they say and what the reader – aware of the long-term context – makes of her attitude towards what they say.

These examples show that incomprehension is not in itself inimical to mirth. Freud stresses that the joke always has three enunciative roles: the speaker, the listener and the butt. Incomprehension kills a joke if it is the listener who fails to understand, but incomprehension on the part of the victim not only does not kill the joke, it may well be the condition of the joke's existence, as in the Posy cartoon, or the irony, as in the Jane Austen passage. Alternatively, it may serve to increase the pleasure of the joker and the listener, as in the rather condescending witticisms of the courtiers watching the artisans' performance at the end of Shakespeare's *Midsummer Night's Dream*.

As Cohen says, jokes and metaphors – among other purposes – serve to create intimacy through mutual comprehension (Cohen, 1979: 6–10). This they do through the role of presuppositions inherent in them, the 'background knowledge' they always mobilise in their structure, without which they are incomprehensible. This background knowledge is part of the culture which joker and appreciative listener share. To share something like a joke or a metaphor, something whose presence in a culture is by no means predetermined, and which is not shared by others, no doubt creates an even greater degree of intimacy, especially if those who do not share it are the butt of it as well as not understanding what is going on. This is the process which is the basis of the end of *Midsummer Night's Dream*, where we see the division of society into courtly elite and the gross others reproduced exactly along the fault line of comprehension and incomprehension of the jokes of which the artisans are the butt. Even more importantly, we can see how these examples, and the principle to be deduced from them, demand a modification of Douglas' omniparent rule that a joke must be permitted: clearly it does not have to be permitted by everybody, since the victim's incomprehension may be what produces it in the first place.

Thus what we see occur at the border established by the divide between comprehension and its opposite is a process of inclusion and exclusion with respect to some section or dimension of the social order. And this despite the fact that the incomprehension involved is of two forms: in the instance of a joke such as the 'goy' joke, the standardised format would no doubt make it clear to anyone in American or British society that what was being said was indeed intended as a joke, but the absence of relevant information would make the joke incomprehensible. In the case of the victim of the irony in the Posy cartoon, the incomprehension is more fundamental, being unaware that a joke is being made, and that he is its butt through his very incomprehension. In both cases, a process of inclusion and exclusion occurs.[1] In our next case, the ambiguity which occurs at the borderline of comprehension is of a different nature, for here it is a question of an ambiguity which is built into the core of the humour: it is the case of the grotesque and of black humour.

During World War II this joke circulated in Nazi-occupied Central Europe:

A rumour goes round that the Nazis are going to kill all the Jews and all the barbers. One evening, in a bar, a group of citizens are pondering this rumour. Eventually one says 'Of all the nonsense. Why the barbers?'

(Quoted Skvorecky, 1986: 252)

This joke is very typical of a style of humour widely practised in Central and Eastern Europe, characterised by a degree of irony which is so extreme that it is more than usually ambiguous. For instance, in this joke, we may hesitate about finding it funny because we are unsure whether it is a piece of brutal anti-Semitism, or somthing very different. It is easy to interpret it as anti-Semitic: the speaker (in the joke, not the person who tells the joke) has simply assumed that the first part of the rumour is utterly unimportant (or so obviously true that it is not worth mentioning), and it would be easy to laugh at the implied insult to the Jews derived from the incongruous reasoning process he has followed. But it is equally possible to see it as a joke aimed at anti-Semitism: seen in this light we would laugh at the exaggerated nastiness and stupidity of the speaker's reasoning process, and in wry recognition of its frequency in less exaggerated form. In either case the source of the humour is the incongruous reasoning process, and it will probably be some feature of the circumstances under which the joke is told that is responsible for its reception: for example, its meaning could diverge fundamentally depending on the identity of the joker, for instance whether (s)he was Jewish or not. Most importantly, the joke must have had a very different meaning in Nazi-occupied Central Europe to the meaning it has in the post-war period, where the reality of the threat in question has receded. People who have lived through this threat may feel that they alone have the right to tell and enjoy such jokes: the sense of intimacy that Cohen argues is the basis of jokes and metaphors may be a very exclusive mechanism.

The English comedienne Jo Brand is a person of considerable girth, and makes no attempt to hide it. For many months she opened her nightclub act by walking onto the stage dressed in tight sports trousers and a sweat shirt, taking the microphone off its stand and saying 'I'd better stand to one side of this thing, or you won't be able to see me'. After the laugh that this always got, she would move the mike stand in front of her and away again, saying 'Now you see me, now you don't'. She continued with this: 'People say to me "Jo, you're not exactly anorexic, are you?" Well, I don't know. Anorexics stand in front of the mirror and say "God, I'm fat!" I stand in front of the mirror and I say "God, I'm fat!"'.' Given the pressure placed upon women to conform to a standard of slim beauty, which is held to be synonymous with personal attractiveness, it is likely that there is a certain amount of personal pain involved in this humour, and it is certainly easy for audience members to be aware of this possibility (not because of indications in her performance, but just from ordinary empathy); thus the laughter has an edge to it which derives from the ambiguity.

In the film *No Surrrender*, one of the central characters is a Protestant Irish community leader, who is blackmailed into harbouring a Protestant terrorist on the run from the British police; the terrorist is also a friend from his youth. This occurs on New Year's Eve, when he is taking a party of Protestant old age pensioners to a party in a local dance hall, which a joker has also booked for a party of Catholic old age pensioners, one of whom is a blind ex-boxer who used to fight the Protestant leader in the ring when they were young. As the result of a complicated and farcical series of events, a situation arises in which the Protestant kills the terrorist in a toilet cubicle in the dance hall, and shortly after finds himself obliged to join in a boxing match in the same toilets with the blind Catholic ex-boxer, watched by a large percentage of the two groups of old age pensioners, who have all crowded into the toilets. At the height of the fight, the Protestant knocks the Catholic out and as the latter staggers away from the blow he falls through the cubicle door and straight on top of the dead terrorist. The coincidence, especially in the context of the brutal knock-out blow to a blind man, is farcical. Yet at the same time it is horrible, and in this moment are summarised many of the main narrative strands of the film. The Protestant killed the terrorist because of the threatening situation, but in doing so he has cancelled a lifetime's commitment to the Protestant militancy that was the focus of his working life. The boxing match is effectively the last act that he undertakes which is consonant with his commitment, but he does it only because he's forced into it by the blind man. Thus the outcome of the fight is both hilarious and tragic simultaneously.

Moments of ambiguous humour such as these three are typical of a style of humour which is widespread in our culture, and typical of a set of narrative devices which are widely found in twentieth-century fiction. The examples quoted above are clearly intended to be funny, and their reception is usually appropriate. In other examples the role of humour is more equivocal. In Philip Roth's *The Breast*, a professor of Comparative Literature becomes – by some inexplicable process – a six-foot 'high' bosom. This transformation is presented as both horrifying and funny. In the narrative of the weeks preceding his transformation, the first-person narrator refers to himself as a 'devout hypochondriac' who had recently quit a 'Grand Guignol marriage' (Roth, 1973: 4, 9). The actual transformation itself is referred to in a way that mixes the emotions of mirth and fear:

> The bulk of my weight is fatty tissue. At one end I am rounded off like a water-melon; at the other I terminate in a nipple, cylindrical in shape, projecting five inches from my 'body', and perforated at the tip with seventeen openings. . . . As I am able to understand it without the aid of

diagrams – I am sightless – . . . My nipple is rosy pink in color. This last is thought to be unusual in that in my former life I was an emphatic brunette. As I told the endocrinologist who made this observation, I myself find it less 'unusual' than certain other aspects of the transformation, but then I'm not the endocrinologist around here.

(Roth, 1973: 13)

What happens in all these examples is that we are in the presence of two semiotic mechanisms simultaneously: the structure of the joke, and whatever other narrative structure is in place in the particular instance involved; we have already seen the principle involved in the instance of romantic comedy (see Part III), except that there the mixture juxtaposes humour with a narrative in which the ego comes to be founded securely, whereas in black humour the juxtaposition is with anxiety.

This mixture of emotions is often referred to with the term 'grotesque', which has a long pedigree in Western European cultural history.

The term 'grotesque' derives from the word 'grotto'. At the end of the fifteenth century, excavations in ancient Roman buildings revealed a series of underground chambers (*grotte*, in Italian) ornamented with murals in a style previously unknown: fantastic landscapes and creatures, part human, part animal, part vegetable, all intertwined and growing out of each other. This was a revelation in more than the physical sense, for in the Renaissance the assumption was that all antique art was characterised by strict decorum and a sense of mathematical proportion; the luxuriating abundance, 'unnecessary' ornamentation and pure fantasy – in the sense that what was represented was not subject to any laws of resemblance to anything recognisable – clearly derived from an aesthetic that was radically different from the 'classicism' that the Renaissance had chosen as its legacy from antiquity. But quickly the 'fantasy' elements derived from the grottoes were used as ornamentation in sixteenth-century painting and architecture (Barasch, 1971: 17–31; Kayser, 1963: 19–24).

Throughout the neo-classical period (sixteenth to eighteenth centuries), arguments about taste and style in the arts were dominated by discussion of the appropriate degree of decorum, and the grotesque (with its various approximate synonyms, such as 'arabesque' in France, and 'antick' in England) was seen as the maximum degree of indecorousness. For example, caricature: in relation to a highly normative order, deviation was readily seen as inferior and ridiculous, and comedy and caricature were justified uses of ridicule to correct it. But in the fantastic elements of caricature we see the inscription of a mixture 'of surprise and horror, an agonizing fear in the presence of a world which breaks apart and remains inaccessible', an inscription organised through 'a clashing contrast between form and content, the unstable mixture of heterogeneous elements, the explosive force of the paradoxical, which is both ridiculous and terrifying' (Kayser, 1963: 31, 53).

156

With the abandonment of then traditional notions of decorum, especially in the arts, the value of the grotesque as a breach of decorum becomes lost. No longer can fantastic apparitions and grossness appear as the irruption of another conception of the world order inside the rationality and decorum of the neo-classical order: once the value of decorum is abandoned, such irruptions are only either funny or terrifying. In nineteenth-century writers, such as Poe and Hoffman, the fanatasy elements and the fear they represent become divorced from comedy; the grotesque in this version is little different from Todorov's 'fantastic literature' (Todorov, 1970). Subsequently, the term 'grotesque' becomes largely associated with forms of comedy that are either gross or mildly frightening, as the elements of fearful fantasy turn largely into the Gothic heritage of horror stories. This is a turning point in the history of the term 'grotesque', since from now on it becomes more and more associated with broad humour and the burlesque: 'the measurable psychic effect of laughter [becomes] the legal basis of . . . [its] definitions' (Kayser, 1963: 103–4).

Regardless of historical variations in its meaning, the term 'grotesque' refers to the possibility of mixing the fearful with the comic:

> The grotesque object must always display a combination of fearsome and ludicrous qualities – or to be more precise it simultaneously arouses reactions of fear and amusement in the observer. . . . In view of the disturbing nature of the fear current and the well-known capacity of the playful, comic tendency for providing relief . . . it seems reasonable to suppose that . . . there is a disarming mechanism at work. The formation of fear images is intercepted, at its very onset, by the comic tendency, and the resulting object reflects this interaction of opposing forces.
>
> (Quoted Steig, 1970: 255)

For Steig, it is essential to distinguish between what Freud calls 'the uncanny', and the grotesque. In the uncanny, there is no defence against the arousal of anxiety; in the grotesque, comic elements provide such a defence, but it may well be that it is only a partial success:

> the defence is only partially successful, in that it allows some anxiety to remain, and characteristically will even contribute to the arousing of some anxiety. This is the basic paradox of the grotesque: it at once allays and intensifies the effect of the uncanny; in pure comedy, at the other end of the spectrum from the uncanny, the defence is complete and detachment is achieved.
>
> (Steig, 1970: 258)

Typical examples of grotesque characters are to be found in Dickens. Our first example is Miggs, in *Barnaby Rudge*, who moves from being nothing but a ridiculous hypocrite to a very threatening figure, albeit ridiculous at the same time. We first meet her in Chapter 7, as Gabriel Varden comes home late from a concerned visit to Barnaby and his mother, which gives rise to the blast of domestic propaganda about his selfishness that we soon come to recognise as the normal accompaniment of such circumstances:

> 'Master's come home, mim,' cried Miggs, running before him into the parlour. 'You was wrong, mim, and I was right. I thought he wouldn't keep us up so late, two nights running, mim. Master's always considerate so far. I'm so glad, mim, on your account. I'm a little' – here Miggs simpered – 'a little sleepy myself; I'll own it now, mim, though I said I wasn't when you asked me. It ain't of no consequence, mim, of course.'
>
> (Dickens, 1973: 103)

To underline the obvious, her reaction is clearly to be seen as hypocritical, in the sense that its purpose is to sow discord between husband and wife: Varden 'very well knew for whose ears it was designed', and it soon becomes clear that Miggs uses Mrs Varden's own sense of matrimonial martyrdom to create a space in which she can cause mischief and pursue her own ends.

In Chapter 70 Dennis the hangman realises that now that the riots are over, and many men made prisoner, his own chances of survival depend in part upon hiding the role he played in the abduction of Emma and Dolly. His plan is to have them abducted again – preferably to eternity, we understand – under the guise of a rescue, but as Miggs is locked up with them, he needs to persuade her to go along with this plan, and not to make a fuss when she is apparently not rescued. He persuades her by pointing out that if it were not for Dolly's coquettish wiles, Sim Tappertit would no doubt be more enamoured of herself. Miggs' vanity makes her an easy target, and she easily agrees that Simmun would be better off preserved from the attentions of 'designing and artful minxes (she would name no names, for that was not her dispositions) – *any* designing and artful minxes' (Dickens, 1973: 634). She can see that Mr and Mrs Varden might regret the loss of their child, but as human beings are such sinful creatures we rarely know what is really in our best interest. All of this is presented with a degree of irony that amounts to a savage indictment of Miggs' hypocrisy.

The presentation of Miggs is instructive, for here we see the construction of a character through irony changing meaning as the story progresses. What starts off as comedy threatens to become something far more serious, for Emma and Dolly's fate hangs by a fine thread at this point. That this is possible is due to the structure of irony, which is such that it is equally capable of giving rise to humour or to a sense of disaster: comic and tragic irony are equally possible, in the abstract, and the way in which this structure is read depends entirely upon the discursive context within which it is placed. In the context of Miggs' first appearance, the irony is comic, though perhaps less so than subsequently as the constant repetition builds up comic effect; it is comic for reasons to do with the discursive circumstances in question, among them certainly the lack of threat that is implied by her behaviour; certainly it is a nuisance, since it encourages Mrs Varden's sense of matrimonial martyrdom, but at this stage it is no more than this, and Varden seems well able to cope with it. That is to say, this incongruous behaviour – incongruous because of the incompatible meanings attached to it by the participants – is judged largely in terms of its causes, i.e. hypocrisy. Subsequently, it has to be judged as much in terms of its likely effects. Under these new circumstances, the distance between the two contrasting sets of meanings attached to the words in question, while perhaps no greater, is certainly different in impact. To use terms developed in the discussion of the structure of humour, the balance between plausibility and implausibility has shifted in this discursive replacing. What we observe in the early presentation of Miggs is how implausible or incongruous her behaviour is, and therefore how ridiculous, or absurd; we judge it largely in terms of the extra-textual discourses which make it comprehensible. In the later presentation we are all too aware of the motives which make her hypocrisy under much more dangerous circumstances so plausible, and we are aware of the likely effects that it will have: thus our estimation of her behaviour is caught in a chain of reasoning in which its implausibility is counterbalanced by calculations about the plausibility of the chain of events in which it is one link.

Mrs Gamp, in *Martin Chuzzlewit*, is another often-quoted Dickens' grotesque. She is made ridiculous in two ways. First, through her laziness and greed for liquor, which are presented ironically: her appetite for liquor is presented as its opposite, in her own words – she doesn't drink but would like to have a little dram available when she feels like it. Second, she is made ridiculous through her language. Dickens readily – though not always – makes fun of working-class speech rhythms, and in the case of Mrs Gamp this is a primary source of humour: the use of imprecisely formulated relative clauses to link together totally unsuitable pieces of information is a common technique (cf. Wegg and Jenny Wren's drunken father in *Our Mutual Friend*). In Mrs Gamp's case this is doubled by a level of pretentiousness of vocabulary that makes the inexact and ambitious syntax seem even more ludicrous. Finally, she has an intensely personal abuse of the English language which consists of frequently substituting a 'dj' for a hard 's' inside words – 'suppoged' for 'supposed', 'dispoged' for 'disposed', etc.

When we see her with her first patient – the man we later learn is Newsome, the pharmacist who supplied Jonas Chuzzlewit with poison – her laziness and drunkenness are still primarily ridiculous rather than threatening: only in her selfish appropriation of the sick man's pillow do we see a foretaste of what she is capable of. Subsequently we realise that her greed, hypocrisy and venality are indeed threatening: we see her cruelty to old Chuffey, and we eventually realise that she has known all along that Jonas has probably murdered his father, and is prepared to live with that knowledge on condition that she (along with others, notably Tigg/Montague) can profit from it.

Steig analyses Sairy Gamp in somewhat different, Freudian terms. In his analysis the anxiety-arousing qualities in her character derive from the reader's identification with her based on her utter selfishness (which corresponds to the pleasure principle), but she is also ridiculous; because she is ridiculous we do not consciously identify with her, but unconsciously do so in the very enjoyment of the comedy; we are 'delighted by the childishly playful free associations of her speech, her indulgence in oral pleasures, and her strong assertion of self against the world'. Thus the grotesque is not just a defence against anxiety through comedy, but:

> To the extent that these techniques disguise the repressed material, they are defensive, but they *also allow* for the expression of this material, in part by virtue of their being in themselves a reflection of childhood impulses, but primarily through their function of allaying anxiety, and hence weakening inhibitions.

(Steig, 1970: 259)

That Dickens constructed grotesque characters is far from a novel claim. What has been demonstrated here is the way in which the grotesqueness is directly related to the structure of humour as conventionally analysed, and the way in which this grotesqueness is a product of a particular type of ambiguity: the mixture of comedy with something fundamentally opposed to it. It is clear that this profile of characters has a well-defined place in the moral universe that Dickens constructs, and nothing said here has attempted to deconstruct that universe. Nonetheless, we may ask why it should be that Dickens uses this particular tactic. On the one hand, it seems likely that Dickens owes much to a popular tradition: the tradition of gross caricature. Of course, this is scarcely a Bakhtinian celebration of corporeality, and Dickens' celebrations of bonhomie are tempered by a concern for respectability and decorum; the grossness of the caricature would seem to refer rather to a firm moral vision within which ridicule is indeed visibly such. On the other hand, rendering this moral vision by a mixture of aesthetic levels of the type we have seen is not without its effects: to grasp something as simultaneously threatening and ridiculous, or pathetic and ridiculous, is tantamount to asserting that it has no single meaning. Perhaps this is an overstatement of Dickens' modernism, since unequivocal meaning is often in fact achieved: Miggs' hypocrisy ceases to be funny and is more likely to arouse anger than laughter, no doubt. But fundamental ambiguity is a dimension of the popular tradition that the gross caricature derived from, and perhaps something of this survives in Dickens despite the enormous weight of Victorian moral decorum that underpins the unequivocal judgments he offers. It would take a sensitive study of Dickens' relation to the culture of his readers to unearth all the different resonances of his use of grotesque comedy in contexts such as these.

13

PERFORMANCE AND OFFENCE

A second reason for the failure of humour is performative inadequacy. I have heard it said by a professional comedian that even the tritest joke in the repertoire can get a laugh if delivered right; the example he gave was 'Who was that lady I saw you with last night? – That was no lady (pause – two – three) that was my wife!' The example may be dubious, but the principle is beyond doubt: all jokes, and much humour, are dependent upon performance skills. Naturally there are exceptions, such as incidents in everyday life where someone provides unintended amusement to others. But the intention to arouse laughter commonly calls for performance skills, albeit of a minimal kind. My daughter aged around 11 once tried to tell me a joke that I remembered myself from school-days: 'Did you hear about the two worms who went to the graveyard to make love in dead earnest/Ernest?' Unfortunately she forgot the name, and said '. . . in dead Arthur'. Actually – since I remembered the original while she was talking – the result was funnier than the intended joke, but not for reasons that appealed to the teller. Of course, in most performative situations, such a degree of incompetence is rare – though we may recall the psychological experimenter, already quoted in Part II, who was instructed to read out a series of jokes in an unvarying monotone. Amateur performances may fail for a variety of reasons: insufficient rhetorical skills or bad timing in the sense of not picking a good moment for delivery, for example. Professional performances are more likely to fail because of some mismatch between repertoire and audience: different audiences have different stylistic and thematic preferences in comedy. This is the basis of Trevor Griffiths' play *Comedians*, which the author uses to explore the political role of rhetoric: pandering to the audience's lowest prejudices through a series of vicious racist and sexist stereotypes is clearly condemned (Palmer, 1987: 15–18). In this respect, Griffiths' play resembles Scorsese's *King of Comedy*, which pursues Scorsese's favourite theme of opportunism through a would-be comic who resorts to kidnapping to get on TV, and then delivers a performance of exactly calculated mediocrity which is successful with the audience.

If professional comic performance demands adjustment to local conditions, it is unsurprising that – when recorded – it may not survive historical change. It is noticeable that much Hollywood silent farce is not well received nowadays (at least in the UK): if the great stars (Laurel and Hardy, Buster Keaton, Chaplin) are still respected and occasionally viewed, most of the other products of the period would rarely raise a laugh today, or perhaps would go down well with a pre-teen audience (or an audience which had loved this style in their youth). There are many possible reasons for such a failure to survive. One is that jokes may not survive repetition, and the sorts of pratfall-based gags that were the stock-in-trade of the silent screen have become so well known that any such gag is nowadays virtually an nth time repetition. Another possibility is that most pratfall gags rely on the impression of painful indignity, and animated cartoons such as *Tom and Jerry*, *Road Runner*, etc., have long since developed degrees of painful indignity that are only attainable with live actors through the use of intricate (and expensive) special effects; in comparison with Tom the cat being blown through a keyhole by a dynamite blast and surviving keyhole-shaped, a banana-skin pratfall or a pie in the face is a minimal stimulus. A third possibility is that the cinematic technique of much silent farce is primitive, and may be unacceptable to an audience used to the colour stock, deep focus lenses, far more fluid camera movements and editing techniques of modern film. This statement does not apply with great force to films made at the end of the silent period, such as most of the Laurel and Hardy shorts, since camera and editing techniques were well advanced; although even here technical features such as the monochrome stock and lenses with a restricted depth of field give a distinctly period feel. But with earlier film it is difficult not to be aware of the relatively or literally static camera frame. The English music-hall comedian Little Titch was filmed around the turn of the century doing his stage act in front of a totally static camera, whose frame simply reproduces the proscenium arch. Titch's act, which involves acrobatic clowning with a pair of shoes whose length is nearly half his height is still very fresh, perhaps because that skilled clowning is so rare today, but the static frame somehow reduces the impact, as does his evident haste to get as much of his act as he could into the few minutes he presumably had available.

Amateur performance, in the course of everyday life, without the benefit of the stage or screen space and audience attentiveness premised upon particular expectations, is dependent upon other considerations, as a moment from Tannen's analysis of a dinner conversation shows (quoted on pp. 108–9 above). Here the difficulty that Peter has in gaining acceptance for his attempted joke-telling, and the limited success that it has even when granted the status of a joke, is probably due primarily to the obvious alternative agenda: a group of people are sitting down to dinner and trying to organise various features of the table. Their dispersed attention and the 'serious' frame of reference of this agenda makes joke-telling difficult. Equally, other frameworks may readily promote attempts at humour: as Douglas remarks, if the bishop is stuck in the lift, suddenly many things become funny, for the basic framework of everyday expectations has been subverted and it is easy to see other incidents in the same light (Douglas, 1968: 368). In Coser's study of humour on hospital wards, it is clear that the threatening situation patients find themselves in gives added meaning to the smallest incongruities, that readily become seen as jokes (Coser, 1959).

It is at this point that the study of humour and aesthetic theory converge, a point to which we will return. Any study of humour is forced to confront the elementary truths of communications theory, that the receiver of a message is as integral to the communication process as the sender, the message or the channel and context in which the transmission occurs. But beyond that the question of performative adequacy reminds us of a further truth, that any act of reception is also an act of evaluation, at any rate where fictional messages are concerned, or more generally any messages whose purposes include entertainment. Communication models evolved for the study of news flows and suchlike tend to omit this dimension of analysis, but it is integral to European reception theory, developed on the basis of response to literature (Striedter, 1989: ch. 4).

The final way in which humour may fail is by being found offensive rather than funny.

In 1934 in the former British colony of Tanganyika (now Tanzania) a joke turned into a court case (Pedler, 1940). A woman from the Sukuma tribe lodged a complaint in the British-run court about a man from the Zaramu tribe, who had pushed her to the ground and manhandled her. The man admitted the act, but claimed in his defence that she was his joking partner, that he had already behaved in the same way with her several times before, and that the act was therefore a joke and not an assault. It was established in court, on the basis of witnesses' accounts, that the Sukuma and Zaramu tribes were indeed in a joking relationship with each other, and that the man and the woman were certainly acquainted. The court found that the act was indeed an assault, but that the nature of the joking relationship was a mitigating factor.

We saw in Part I that it was of the essence of joking relationships in tribal societies that they were reciprocal and non-optional; if it were indeed the case that these two people were in a joking relationship, how could it be that the woman came to regard the event as offensive, instead of a joke? How could she opt out of the joking relationship? Pedler's interpretation of the court proceedings suggests that something in the circumstances was responsible, such as the fact that the event occurred in a town, rather than in an African village, and in front of various witnesses who might not have known about, or rejected, the relevance of the joking relationship. The woman's own evidence appears to support the contention that she was afraid of appearing non-respectable. Perhaps various features of the colonial situation had converged to make the joking relationship untenable in this particular instance. We may guess that either the presence of witnesses who the woman thought would not accept the validity of the joking relationship, or the nature of the act that was intended as a joke, or the conjunction of the two, brought about a counter-vailing definition of this would-be traditional behaviour. Certainty of inter-pretation seems unlikely, but the principles involved here are clear: a joke may become offensive if something in the circumstances is held to make the behaviour in question inappropriate, even if it is clear that what was intended was a joke and the circumstances are in principle favourable to humour. Here the 'misunderstanding' arises – probably – because the event occurs at a point where two social systems are intersecting, and perhaps because one of those systems has more power to impose itself than the other.

So it is that humour may fail because it offends the listener instead of amusing him or her. Indeed, this is the grounds for failure that Freud mentions in passing: a joke at someone's expense is unlikely to succeed if the audience consists of that person's friends, just as a cynical joke is unlikely to appeal to those who believe in the value or institution in question (Freud, 1976: 197). In what ways, or on what grounds, is an attempt at humour likely to be offensive rather than funny? There are three main variables involved in this process, which may then figure in any combination in individual circumstances:

1 the structure of the joke itself, considered as a representation of the world external to the joke;
2 the relationship between the joke-teller and the others involved in the enunciation – the butt and the audience;
3 the nature of the occasion on which the attempt at humour is made.

We have seen in Part I that the occasion is central to the nature of humour, and that definitions of occasions for humour are specific to different social orders (and perhaps to sub-sections of social orders). As a result it is impossible to generalise about which occasions might be deemed suitable for humour and which ones not. For example, in our own culture, it is clear that religious occasions are on the whole not suitable, whereas in many tribal societies clowning is a part of the institutional structure of religious practice. In the European Middle Ages, the Feast of Fools was a form of religious clowning that lasted for centuries, but which many prelates regarded as only partly compatible with the dignity of the Church. Here we have a humorous practice which is the subject of a fundamental disagreement within the institution inside which it is located; presumably those who felt that the Feast was contrary to Church dignity were not amused by the antics involved. But this does not alter the principle that there is indeed a fundamental distinction here between suitable and unsuitable occasions. Just as suitable occasions facilitate humour by acting as cues and preparation for it, so unsuitable occasions have the reverse effect. We should note the possibility of a further inversion, where the 'unsuitableness' of the occasion, its dignity, makes any subversion all the more readily comic for those who do not appreciate this would-be dignity.

Where 'joking relationships' exist (in African and some other societies) the occasions that are suitable for humour appear to be premised primarily on the relationships between participants. However, in modern Western culture it is clear that the sociological definition of an occasion is analytically independent of the identity of the participants: for example, the behaviour usually considered appropriate for a funeral, or a job interview, does not depend upon the identity of the participants, but upon the roles they occupy within the occasion; conversely, the role a priest plays during a service is largely different from the role that he (or occasionally she) may play on a different social occasion – say, a party. We saw in a study of American longshoremen that the sort of humour they regard as normal among themselves at work they would not accept in their homes. All of these examples demonstrate the same point, the autonomy of the occasion. Nonetheless, it is clear that the identity of participants in an occasion is also relevant, partly because different participants have different roles within the occasion, partly because their identities are aligned with structural positions within the society at large which bring different roles in general and different degrees of power. For example, in a study of jokes among medical personnel in professional meetings in a hospital, Coser (1960) showed that senior doctors are more likely to make jokes than junior ones, and that ancillary staff – primarily nurses – never do. Clearly, the hospital hierarchy, which operates as much outside the meeting as inside, is largely responsible for this difference, but if the nurses were predominantly women (unclear in Coser's study) then different social expectations in general are relevant, particularly the differential definitions of modesty that help to distinguish masculinity from femininity.

The Central European joke about the Jews and the barbers has already been quoted, in the context of a debate about its meaning, whether it is anti-Semitic or anti-fascist. One of the variables in establishing its meaning would be the identity of the speaker: if told by a Jew, the joke is clearly an ironical statement about anti-Semitism; if told by an anti-Semite, it would have the opposite meaning. Of course, the question remains whether either of these groups would in fact tell such jokes. About Jews telling them there is no question: it is well established that a recurrent feature of Jewish humour is its wry irony about many features of Jewish life, a mordant wit that attacks the teller him- or herself. One can thus easily imagine that the same joke would give pleasure to anti-Semites. We may equally imagine that a wry joke told against some Jewish characteristic would arouse laughter in a Jewish audience if told by a Jew, but indignation – or at least an ambiguous response – if told by a non-Jew whose motives were suspect or unknown. Jewish humour is a response to a particular situation, and the identity that came to be formed therein: from the eighteenth century the cultural movement Haskala promoted an exit from the ghetto in Central Europe, and secular-minded Jews tried to assimilate to the modernising nations surrounding them; the difficulties they experienced became the subject of much of the humour that has become known as 'typically Jewish', and the theme of the difficulty of assimilation in a hostile or at best indifferent environment both creates the humorous style in question and gives a particular meaning to the jokes for an audience which has this life-experience (Stora-Sandor, 1992). By the same token, no doubt, the same joke told by someone without that experience may appear ambivalent.

Thus the nature of the occasion and various features of the relationships between the parties to the enunciation may act to make a joke offensive rather than funny, regardless of the nature of the humorous activity which is undertaken. But clearly also the nature of the joke or other humorous activity is relevant too. This story appeared in the *Guardian* newspaper on 23 January 1991:

> Scantily clad, glamorous women sell everything from chocolate and cars to holidays. No surprise then that the Swedish-based chainstore Hennes should use a photo of a woman reclining in underwear in their advertising campaigns both last year and this. They do, after all, sell lingerie.

> What has provoked an outcry, however, are the copylines placed with the photos. Last winter's ad read 'This is what the au pair will be wearing this winter'. The Advertising Standards Authority received 34 letters of complaint. Rather than retreat from the flak, Hennes went on the attack. This winter the copyline was, 'Last time we ran an ad for Swedish lingerie 78 women complained. No men.'

According to a spokeswoman from Hennes the second ad was intended to be humorous, although she admitted they had received complaints (including some from men). No doubt also many people were amused by it and did not complain. Leaving aside the possibility of an absolute judgment of right or wrong in the case, it is clear that the joke caused offence, partly no doubt because of the 'cynicism', as one complainant called it, of this response to earlier complaints which had been upheld by the Advertising Standards Authority. Perhaps the offensiveness is partly a matter of the public nature of the joke, but it is likely that the nature of the joke itself is at least as much the cause.

Although there are no systematic studies of this principle, it is not difficult to imagine similar scenarios: contexts where jokes or humorous activity in general would be perfectly acceptable, but where particular themes in jokes would not. For example, in a business meeting an elegant witticism about something to do with the matters under discussion might easily be successful where an irrelevant obscene joke, or a piece of physical horseplay would probably be unacceptable. The successful British TV comedy show *Spitting Image*, which specialises in grotesque puppets of famous people performing less than dignifed acts, was shown briefly in the USA but was taken off the air

– according to reports in the British press in 1987 – after a flood of complaints about repeated treatment of President Reagan as a doddering old buffoon. A group of feminists would be likely to find many (but certainly not all) obscene jokes offensive on the grounds that they are demeaning to women and an assertion of male privilege (see Part II). Professional comedians pride themselves on being able to select from their repertoire according to the nature of the audience.

So far this discussion has referred to scenarios with a single common feature: in each case there is a situation, in which one person makes, or tries to make a joke, and some feature of the situation dictates either success or failure. In other words, on one side of the equation we have the joker and on the other a group consensus about what the situation is and its suitability or otherwise for humour. But it is clear that in reality situations do not always conform to this model. Three examples illustrate this assertion.

When I was at boarding school, attendance at Church services on Sundays was compulsory; several of us found these occasions excruciatingly boring, and used to enliven them by passing notes along the pews, with various irrelevant or derogatory messages; these caused laughter, largely by virtue of being subversive of the occasion. Had we been caught, no one would have been amused and the defence of comic intention would only have aggravated the offence. Here permission to make a joke is incompatible with the occasion, but is 'granted' by a small sub-section of the participants for subversive purposes.

The second example is an anecdote told me by a colleague. Several women go into a pub during a local festival, where a lot of drinking and merriment has been going on; as a joke, one of the men in the pub 'gooses' one of the women – they have never met before – presumably thinking this is acceptable behaviour under these circumstances. The woman objects and complains to the landlord, who takes the man's side and asks her to leave. In this incident we can see very clearly the conflicts investing sexuality, and particularly the conflicts easily aroused in sexual humour; crucially, it is clear that the conflicts are located at the division between the genders. This can be represented in a value-neutral way thus: one person's humour is another person's offensiveness, and the dividing line between the two definitions is the way gender is lived by the participants. We should of course add to this the dimension of power: the woman's attitude towards the incident is less powerful than the man's, because only accepted by a minority of the population; the majority either accept that such behaviour – at least during a festival – can indeed be a joke or, if they disagree, are not prepared to make a stand about the issue, for one reason or another. The implications of this analysis will become clearer if we look at the incident from the point of view of the man.

From his point of view there is a clear distinction between what he has just done, and sexual harassment: such a joke is not sexual harassment, according to this version of the world, and this judgment is reasonable, to this extent; if it is an act of sexual harassment, it is one that is different in kind, not just in degree, from the forms of sexual harassment which can be the subject of criminal proceedings (i.e. sexual assault). That is because in this incident the occasion is crucial – it is a festival and a pub, an occasion on which transgressive behaviour is commonly felt to be acceptable. Clearly there are intervening varieties of behaviour, where the distinction is more difficult to maintain than in this example (e.g. bottom-pinching in the office). Thus, making this incident humorous (in intention) enables the perpetrator to say (implicitly) 'I do not mean this to be sexual harassment, because it is a joke', despite the fact that the basis of the joke clearly is sexual, and enables him to say (probably explicitly) 'What's the matter with you? Can't you take a joke?' Such a definition of the incident, it must be stressed, is – as a matter of fact – perfectly possible within the social structure of contemporary Britain, and although of course the hidden, ulterior purpose of the joke is to assert the continuity of patriarchal relations, what is of prime importance is that on this occasion the tactic which has been chosen for this assertion is a joke, not a sexual advance or an overt insult. Now we already know that permission is an integral dimension of a joke. If permission is integral, then the incident in question may not be a joke, despite the intention. In this instance, it is clear that the implicit insistence upon the humorous dimension of the incident *is indeed valid*, in the sense that such a definition is genuinely possible within the set of social circumstances in question – this is the burden of the sociological analysis above – and therefore *permission has been given*, even though not by all the participants, and no amount of insisting that it is not funny, but offensive, will alter the fact that it is objectively funny to the extent that its funniness *for some participants* is guaranteed by features of the social structure.

A third example. Many years ago Winston Churchill so incensed a Labour member of Parliament called Paling that the latter called him a 'dirty dog' in the House; to which Churchill replied 'If he is not careful, I will show him what a dirty dog does to a paling' (quoted Knight, 1990: 41). This witty put-down no doubt delighted Churchill's supporters in the House of Commons and did not please his opponents, let alone the unfortunate Mr Paling. The point is that in humour directed at a butt we do not expect the butt or their friends to enjoy the joke, but that will not prevent others from doing so, even in the presence of the butt. In such a situation, there is no question of the joker being an isolated figure in relationship to the consensus about the suitability of the occasion and the theme of the joke; the public in question is no doubt thoroughly divided about the merit or otherwise of the joke, about whether its offensiveness makes it unacceptable as a joke, and so on. Those who accept the pleasure offered by the joke-structure (including the identity of the butt) in effect assert the suitability of theme and occasion; those who are not amused are refusing their assent. Both assertions are present in the situation, and one cannot say that no joke has occurred because the victim refuses the definition 'joke'.

In the second and third of these examples we see cases where in general there is not much doubt that the occasions and the relationships between participants make joking an acceptable form of behaviour, and conflict arises because of the nature of the jokes. All three examples indicate that the question of the permission to make a joke is more complicated than first sight suggested. Specifically, they demand a modification of Douglas' principle that a joke must be permitted; the principle is indeed true, in the sense that someone must permit the joke, for if everyone refuses to allow that a joke has occurred then in truth no joke has occurred, but it is not the case that everyone is obliged to allow that what has happened is a joke. Of course, in each instance, refusal to allow that a joke had occurred would be a way of taking sides on the issue involved, and this would be a legitimate political tactic, but it would bring in its train the possibility of being accused of lacking a sense of humour, and a concomitant loss of sympathy.

We have seen that humour is capable of performing serious tasks, in the sense that it is used for purposes that have a serious dimension: squashing a political opponent is one such, and although in everyday life we may like to focus on the intense emotional satisfaction to the speaker given by getting home a barbed shaft like this, we should not be blind to the properly rhetorical work being done too. Paling's insult might have provoked the kind of row in the House of Commons that results in a speech failing to make any impact; Churchill's wit effectively restored his place in public attention (if it had ever been threatened). Why should humour be so effective in this role? What is it about its rhetorical structure that gives it this capacity? In the first place, at least in our culture there is an unwritten rule that the only effective answer to a witty put-down is an equally witty rejoinder (cf. Palmer, 1987: 10–11): any other answer is likely to be held inferior, unless it can be shown that the joke was unworthy of the circumstances – this must be roughly what Aristotle had in mind when he said that a joke was a good way of ruining an opponent's speech by stopping people taking him seriously, *provided the joke was worthy of a free man.* In the second place, mockery and humiliation devalue the butt and thence anything said by him: a reply by someone so low in esteem is not highly regarded, even if it is intrinsically worthwhile. In the third place, the form of humour, the structure of the joke, has a closure that marks a boundary round it: the joke is what it is, complete and unassailable, protected from criticism by the hermetic seal of its involution. The relationship between 'paling' and 'dirty dog' in Churchill's reply is such that the unit of meaning it composes is turned in on itself; the meaning given by 'paling' echoes backwards across the space of the words, reconstituting them in a new form of obviousness that is all the greater for the proairetic curiosity that the sentence arouses before its completion (and, no doubt, for the emotional charge of the circumstances). There is no reason to suppose that is true of all jokes, but it is likely that the discursive structure of the joke in general makes it particularly apt for this rhetorical purpose, for all jokes must arouse the proairetic tension of awaiting the punch-line, which then retroacts on the earlier moments.

So it is that humour is well suited to the purpose of inflicting spiritual suffering. Our final example is without any doubt an example of inflicting spiritual suffering; whether it is a joke is more open to question. It is the central scene in *Sophie's Choice* (Styron, 1979); the scene is also in the film version, with various changes which are – with one exception – unimportant for our purposes.

The narrative of *Sophie's Choice* moves towards the scene in Auschwitz which contains the event in question, her choice, which in turn casts light on the central questions of the novel; in other words, it is central in the sense that everything leads up to it. Sophie, a Catholic Pole, is sent to Auschwitz for being in possession of food that she is not entitled to under Nazi rules; her two young children are sent with her. On arrival she tries to finesse her way out of the fate she knows awaits her by pleading with the SS officer in charge of the arrival. At the arrival point an initial selection is made between those prisoners capable of working and those who are not; those incapable are sent straight to the gas chamber. Sophie's plea is based on the fact that she is not Jewish, but a Polish Catholic. The SS officer, who is hopelessly drunk, uses Sophie's assertion that she believes in Christ to improvise a sadistic trick: he quotes Christ's words 'Suffer little children to come unto me' and says he will take one of her two children for the gas chamber; she can keep the other one – a 'privilege' to which her Polish race entitles her. She must choose which one to keep.

The consummate cruelty of this infliction is central to the economy of the novel, and the narrator reflects on its meaning: he concludes that the SS officer is different in kind from the majority of his fellows who are no more than brutal automata; such refinement in cruelty sets him apart as a man who has a knowledge of evil, and therefore a knowledge of good; he is, in short, a religious man who has despaired of doing good and therefore chooses the most sinful act he can imagine (1979: 643–7). But the narrator also refers to another side to the SS officer's act, which is represented only in a fragmentary form: this act has something in common with a joke. Sophie arrives at Auschwitz on April Fool's Day (this detail is inexplicably omitted in the film), which is stressed several times (for example, at pp. 504–5). The SS officer is described as 'a maverick, a sport' who imagines an 'ingenious deed' (1979: 643). At the point when Sophie tells the narrator that it was a beautiful spring day when she arrived at Auschwitz, he reflects that this was the moment at which he first understood the meaning of the Absurd, in all its horror (1979: 618).

Of course, there is no way in which interpreting the SS officer's action as a joke corresponds to the structure of the novel, where the act is presented entirely from Sophie's and the narrator's point of view, in all its horror, and as something that exceeds comprehension. And yet, in a sense, it is a joke, or at least has something in common with a joke. If we can see the act from the point of view of the SS officer, we can see that its ingenious incongruity, deviating the meaning of Christ's words in this way, so neatly turning the tables on Sophie's rhetorical strategem, corresponds to something in the structure of humour as outlined here. It has the mixture of plausibility and implausibility, the incongruity, the sense-in-nonsense, of the joke: Christ's words are indeed accurately reproduced, so the situation has an element of plausibility, but their meaning is so fundamentally traduced that his 'interpretation' of their meaning is also utterly implausible. If this interpretation of the SS officer's act seems unlikely, it may be compared with this: in July, 1992, as I wrote this chapter, it was revealed in a British Government report that nurses at a high-security mental hospital in this country had been brutalising patients by beating them and playing sadistic jokes on them. This comment by Melanie Phillips appeared in the *Guardian* newspaper on 7 August:

> The nursing staff, or a large section of it, ran a brutal regime in which they tormented patients not just by physical ill-treatment . . . but by psychological abuse which they regarded as a joke. After all, if you are terrifying someone by a severed pig's head, or by sending them a snake in a package, or by using them as a human ash-tray by dropping cigarette ash inside the waistband of their trousers, it's all tremendously funny if you start from the premise that these patients are a kind of sub-human species, an assumption which appears to have been implicit in the behaviour of these nurses.

Of course, where the degree of evil is concerned, this behaviour is relatively benign compared with what the SS officer does; yet – assuming that the reports of the British nurses are accurate, and that these acts were indeed jokes in their eyes – it is difficult to avoid the conclusion that here sadism and humour were compatible. What is common between the two sets of events is the assumption of sub-humanity on the part of the victims.

It may be said that it is ethically impossible for us to accept that the SS officer's act is a joke. This may well be so, but it seems scarcely relevant, in the sense that anyone likely to be affected by such considerations is highly unlikely to be tempted to find it a joke in the first place, and those who might accept it as a joke are unlikely to have any respect for ethics. Moreover, the ethical question is to one side of the question being asked here, which is this: did the SS officer think it was a joke? Does he need permission to make it a joke? This question is in a sense impossible to answer, since the SS officer is a character in a novel, and in the novel there is no indication – beyond the fragmentary and indirect ones referred to already – of a humorous dimension to the incident; the only indication of a reaction by a fellow SS in the novel is that the officer's assistant is stunned with incredulity (1979: 643). Thus in this

171

sense, the novel does not portray the incident as a joke. But it is not difficult to imagine a scenario in reality in which other SS personnel would have found this funny. There are examples in the literature about the death camps that recount events which were similar in nature (for example, witnesses' accounts at the trial of Klaus Barbie included in the TV documentary made by Ophuls), where it is clear that the perpetrators were entertaining themselves.

A second way in which it is possible to say that this act cannot be considered a joke, even from the point of view of the SS officer himself, could be derived from a psychoanalytic account. Esmein (1991) has suggested that all humour takes place in a realm which is ontologically distinct from the real, in the realm of representation. The distinction representation/real would be the same as the distinction sign/real, where the sign is defined as something that 'stands in for' something else; signs are of course real objects, with a phonic or graphic physical existence, but they are objects that have a special ontology derived from their intentionality. Representations would share in this status in the sense that a representation is always a 'representation of' whatever it is a representation of. As a result, the fundamental criterion of whether something can be considered humorous or not is to be found here: if the would-be joke is in the realm of representation, it may be held to be a joke, but if it is in the realm of the real, it cannot. Clearly the SS officer's act cannot be considered to be in the realm of representation, therefore it cannot be a joke, not even from his own point of view. More exactly, it is only possible for him to consider this as a joke on the condition of denying that it has any reality; that is to say, he must insist to himself that his act is only a representation, not an act with real consequences, therefore he must in a sense not see Sophie as a sentient being at all. But such a negation must follow a previous, suppressed recognition of the reality and truth of what is being denied: it can only be denied insofar as it has already been admitted. This is the Freudian sense of negation: the more true something is, the more it is rejected as a version of the world. Thus the SS officer's act becomes more akin to a psychoanalytic symptom than to a joke.

Clearly this analysis of the event has much to recommend it: it conforms to a common-sense recognition that however much the SS officer's act may resemble the structure of a joke, it cannot actually be one; it also satisfies a certain ethical sense that we cannot allow this to be a joke. And yet. . . . Everything turns on the distinction representation/reality, and the argument that jokes can only occur in the realm of representation. What happens in the instance of Churchill's put-down of the Labour MP? In a sense this is a representation: it is only words. But no one should doubt that these words have a direct effect on the real: the humiliation of Mr Paling is absolutely real, as is the rhetorical/political impact upon the House of Commons. At the same time there seems no doubt at all that this is a joke, albeit a biting one. At one level, this is the banal recognition that representations do indeed have impact upon the real, but more profoundly, it questions the distinction representation/

real, in the sense of denying that there are two distinct ontologies. If linguistic pragmatics – or enunciative linguistics – have taught us nothing else they must have taught us that all signs depend upon their inscription in the real in order to have meaning. It is true that in the Lacanian sense the distinction between representation and reality is located somewhat differently, since for Lacan the real is that which resists symbolisation; in other words, anything that can be symbolised escapes from the realm of the real insofar as it enters into symbolisation. If we take the terms in this sense, then it is perhaps true that what is happening between the SS officer and Sophie escapes symbolisation: there is nothing in our culture which allows for the symbolisation of this act, and it occurs entirely in the realm of the real. But it seems to me that this is equally true of the witty put-down Churchill aimed at Paling. Moreover, if we think of the activities commonly described in anthropology under the heading of 'joking activities' it seems clear that they too involve all sorts of things which have a status which is difficult to reconcile with a strict division between representation and reality. Commonly they involve transgressive activities of gross horseplay – throwing cow-dung at your cousins, lying down in the open grave of your dead joking partner at the funeral and refusing to move until payment has been made, etc. (see Douglas, 1968: 363). Perhaps in a sense these things are representations of the world: anthropologists often interpret such activities as a form of cosmological thought (e.g. Rigby, 1968). But it is clear that they are also events which take place in the real, and insofar as they are held to be jokes or something akin to jokes it is on the basis of the social relationships that underpin them: to put this with a more philosophical stress, it is the reality of the social relationships that is responsible for the activities in question having the status that they do.

These are murky waters. Few people in our society – it is to be hoped – would actually find the SS officer's cruelty to Sophie funny, but this does not change the theoretical issue concerning permission to joke – the victim's consent is not necessary. As to the more general issue of the relationship between reality and symbolisation, this can only hope to be resolved by reference to a theory of the relationship between knowledge and the social structure which far exceeds the bounds of an essay on humour, even though it is true that such an essay inevitably raises these matters.

CONCLUSION TO PART IV

It has become a commonplace of social scientific thought about humour that nothing in the world is naturally funny, that the acceptance of anything as funny is a process of negotiation. In one respect, this principle seems erroneous, because it would confront us with a logical difficulty: if no phenomenon external to the subject had any property that marked it as funny,

173

or potentially funny, then negotiations about what to find funny would take place literally at random, apropos anything. We may conclude that phenomena must be marked as potentially funny in order to avoid this, and thus negotiations about the funniness or otherwise of given phenomena are conducted on grounds determined by some feature of the circumstances in question; in short by the structure of humour. Thus humour is subject to the universal law of communication: all messages must be encoded and decoded, and between the encoding and the decoding come various variables which potentially produce lack of fit between the two.

Lack of fit might take many forms. In Part II I suggested that certain jokes about sex might be enjoyed on the basis of very different subject positions: two people might laugh at the same joke for utterly different reasons – and given the ephemeral nature of much humour this might never become obvious. In any event, if Freud is right we never know why we laugh. The form of lack of fit that has been the focus of Part IV is where humour fails to amuse: here the deviation between encoding and decoding is at a maximum.

The importance of this divergence is that it proposes a modification to previous theories of humour: what occurs at the limits of humour must be built into the theory in some form. Previously, either theories of humour assumed its success, or they assumed that it had no intrinsic structure and was established only in a process of negotiation. The assumption of success allows an overwhelming concentration upon structure, but falls foul of the commonsensical observation that much humour fails. The assumption of no structure falls foul of a logical objection. The analysis of the limits of humour suggests that it does indeed have a structure, but that the significance of that structure is negotiable according to certain principles: comprehensibility, performative adequacy and inoffensiveness.

Beyond these considerations, the question of the failure of humour raises the question of aesthetic judgment, in the sense that to speak of failure demands that we consider the grounds of an act of judgment of quality. We may see failure as (sometimes) a question of comprehension, which by-passes the question of judgment, but even here we have seen that comprehension is not purely cognitive. If I fail to understand a philosophical argument, it can be explained, and the belatedness of my understanding will not reduce its effectiveness, but a joke explained is a joke ruined, and therefore the reception of a joke is not purely cognitive, as we have seen. The role of pleasure in joke reception, which is especially visible in joke failure, focuses our attention upon the judgment of quality implicit in this act. This is the subject matter of the Conclusion.

CONCLUSION

In the Introduction we saw the argument that what people laugh at is much the same throughout history, and the countervailing argument: the joke about the Emperor Vespasian's meanness made sense across two millennia, but the occasion of its delivery did not. This is a nutshell version of a widespread current debate: are the meanings of artefacts only specifiable within the cultures that produce them, or do they refer to some wider context? In particular, we must now focus on a narrower version of this debate: are there some artefacts – or classes of artefacts – which are objectively and eternally more beautiful, of greater aesthetic worth, than others? This is important here because it is one of the foundations of the distinction between 'humour' and 'comedy'.

It is not difficult to demonstrate that artefacts change their meaning as they move between cultures. Many objects that are now to be found in museums in the Western world were originally of ritual, magic or religious significance for the peoples who produced them; placing them in a museum has given them the new meaning of curios, or objects of scientific investigation. Particularly striking is the treatment of dead bodies. Remains of native American and Australian dead have been shown in various museums in Britain and the United States, and their descendants have pointed out the inhumanity of such treatment, arguing that it is an unacceptable remnant of colonialism; in some recent instances the remains have been returned for reburial. European nations have been prepared to treat their own ancestors in the same way. In Denmark the chemical characteristics of peat bogs have preserved some corpses dating from the Iron and Bronze Ages. Such corpses have been disinterred from at least the eighteenth century onwards during peat digging. At that time, the corpses were reburied with Christian rites, but from the late nineteenth century onwards they were taken away for scientific examination and in our century the possibility of chemical preservation in the open air has led to their exhibition in museums (Glob, 1971). Without entering into controversy about the humanity or otherwise of these decisions, nor about the meaning of the original burials, it is clear that their status as human remains has been changed: they have

175

become objects of curiosity. Or – we could say – the 'objects' in question have changed their meaning.

The same would be true of Greek drama. We saw in Part I how the Greek theatre in its earliest manifestations was intimately linked with both the Dionysiac religion and civic democracy. When these plays are performed nowadays they are inevitably devoid of these meanings since both Dionysus and Athenian civic democracy are long since departed. No doubt they also have a different meaning in modern Greek performances in the ancient theatres to the meaning they have in London or New York, where they are not part of national heritage (nor a tourist spectacle). By the same token long-tern comic stereotypes no doubt change their meaning: the 'affable rogue' so commonly found in modern sitcom derives from the ingenious slaves of classical antiquity (Menander and Plautus), but in the absence of slavery the type has a different meaning, deriving from the contradiction of respectability, not a topic of concern in a slave-owning society.

There is little point in multiplying examples, since the principle is clear and well known. It is the wider implications of what is involved that are now our focus. It must be obvious that this book has pursued a line of enquiry which favours a relativist account – the attention given to the separation of farce and comedy in Part III alone would establish that. Are there any features of humour and comedy which would suggest that the relativistic account should be rejected? Clearly an account which suggested that humour always performed the same psychological or social function would do so, as would any account that demonstrated a universal semiotic structure. But it seems unlikely that any functionalist account can survive critical examination – even the most sophisticated (Freud's) has a lacuna, as we have seen. Equally, supposedly universal semiotic structures must operate within socially located mechanisms ('occasions)', which have cue properties responsible for the allocation of meaning to semiotic units. This suggests the conclusion tentatively offered in Part III: that European history is incompatible with a theory of any comic universal.

Thus at least where humour and comedy are concerned the relativist case seems strong. But beyond the issue of whether artefacts change their meanings through time, there remains the question of aesthetic discrimination: despite the changing meanings – or perhaps because of them – it may be the case that there are certain works which are more worthy of our admiration, across a long period of history, than others. In our instance, the works which provoke laughter and which have entered the literary canon under the heading 'comedy' may belong to a radically separate category of artefact to the everyday phenomena, and more 'popular' works, usually categorised as 'humour' or 'farce'. This is the burden of the argument to be found in Suzanne Langer's influential *Feeling and Form* (1953).

For Langer – following Cornford's (1914) analysis of the origins of Athenian Old Comedy – the essence of comedy is the assertion of man's unsuppressible 'life force' or vitality, and the feature of comic narrative that distinguishes it from its opposite, tragic narrative, is that in comedy the threats to the hero's happiness which derive from the external world are never internalised, whereas in tragedy they are and as a result give rise to the tragic agon, the fundamental self-questioning characteristic of this genre. One might contrast two literary examples of unhappiness to make the point: first, the way in which David Copperfield reacts to the mistake he makes in marrying Dora – whose incapacity as a house-keeper, one suspects, is the real cause of her untimely demise – a mistake which certainly causes real unhappiness but which does not lead him to any fundamental reorganisation of his innermost self; second, the implosion of Othello's psyche that follows on his discovery of how he has been deceived. For Langer, such a distinction is the mark of the difference between comedy and tragedy. It follows from this that for her there is no intrinsic relationship between comedy and humour: everyday humour is the product of stimuli that only work if we are in the mood for them, whereas in comedy humour is carefully articulated onto the structure of the narrative, which is responsible for the meaning the humorous moments have. Certainly some comedy is funny, but much of it is not; for example, she is able to argue that most French classical tragedy is really comedy, even though notably unhumorous in tone.

Such a theory seems well suited to canonical literature, where it is often the case that there is not much relationship between the desire to amuse (in the humorous sense) and the basic forms of comic narrative. However, the assertion of no intrinsic link between comedy and funniness has an unexpected side-effect: this theory can say nothing about what the form of such a relationship is where it occurs – precisely because of the insistence that there is no necessary general relationship between the two – except insofar as it relies on an entirely common-sense theory of humour to say that a joke is appropriate on such-and-such an occasion. What is needed at this point, and cannot be supplied, is some statement about *why* a joke is appropriate at this point, which in its turn entails a theory of the structure of the joke, since we clearly need to know what a joke is before we can say why it is appropriate at such-and-such a moment. Common sense may appear to be adequate here, but in reality it is not because of the fundamental principle that the intention to joke is not enough for a joke to occur: it must also be understood and permitted, otherwise it may well fall flat or be regarded as childish or offensive. The sociological and psychological differences that underpin this principle render common sense nugatory: just as one man's meat is another man's poison, so one man's joke is another man's offensiveness or bored incomprehension. Crucially, a joke may not even be recognised as such; different jokes, or different types of joke (i.e. jokes with different themes) are appropriate for different sets of circumstances. That is to say, the reasons why such-and-such a joke element may be inserted into a 'comic' text (in Langer's sense of the term) and the impact this placing has for its intended audience may be non-recuperable without a sense of the structure of humour under those circumstances. The well-known uncertainties about which bits of Shakespeare's comedies are or were intended to be funny is a clear illustration of this principle; for instance, Mercutio, dying, says 'Tomorrow you shall find me a grave man': is this meant to be funny? Moreover, we must observe that even if there are many examples in canonical literature of comedy which is not funny (and clearly not intended as such, as in the instance of much French classical tragedy), there are also many indeed where funniness is extremely important in the structure of the narrative – nowhere, perhaps, more so than in the example which originally gave rise to the theory of unsuppressible vitality, Athenian Old Comedy and especially Aristophanes.

Langer's theory is intended to distinguish canonical form from mere entertainment, but is not very sucessful for reasons that refer us to the relativist form of analysis. At the heart of this criticism lies the notion of pleasure, for if there is any universal core to humour it is surely here. In farce and popular everyday humour, it may be argued, everything is subordinate to the production of pleasure, whereas in canonical comedy, such pleasure is subordinate to other dimensions of the text. The centrality of humour to our debates is easily demonstrated: for Freud, it is pleasure that enables the joke to do its ecological work; for anthropologists, it is questionable whether 'joking relationships' should be seen as primarily a matter of joking pleasure or aggressive pleasure – perhaps they should be thought of as 'insulting relationships'; if we knew what type of pleasure was involved we would be able to settle the dispute. Similarly, when we ask how we recognise that a joke is such, pleasure is one of the key mechanisms. We recognise a joke on several grounds: conventional signs, the relationship between occasion and transgression, and crucially the pleasure associated with a particular semiotic mechanism.

Here we are at the heart of our enquiry. We started with the question of meaning and its location in culture, and came to the scarcely startling conclusion that humorous meaning (among others) is localised. But one of the purposes of the canon as traditionally conceived is to avoid this situation, to set up a set of texts whose meanings transcend historical and social change because they connect with universal concerns. This is not to deny that readings of these texts may change through time – the historical record is indeed clear that they do so – but it asserts that such localised rereadings are undertaken within a consensual framework about some of the meanings of such texts, and especially about their worth. Now the element of pleasure is central to these distinctions, for pleasure is both central to aesthetic discrimination, and distinct from it, for the purpose of aesthetic discrimination is to distinguish between worthy and unworthy pleasures.

Traditionally, in Western Europe and the USA, this form of judgment has been taken to found the more general judgment that there are cultural forms which are more central to the order of civilisation than others, in other words to justify the existence of a canon. Familiarising oneself with this canon is considered to be one form of the pursuit of excellence, and the objective worth of the canon is taken as grounds for its central role in the education system and for state underwriting of relevant activities through grants to artists, theatres, etc.

Certainly this is not the only conclusion to which the exercise of discrimination leads. All aesthetic response involves the act of discrimination, regardless of whether the work in question is of the type likely to be accepted into a canon and appear on education syllabuses. As is a commonplace in reader-response criticism, all response is inextricably evaluation as well as meaning-assignation (Striedter, 1989: 102, 160, 183). At least, this is so in societies which separate the arts and entertainment from other categories of social action, such as religion, myth, ritual, work, etc.; whether aesthetic response involves discrimination under such circumstances is open to question. In our own time it is clear that popular music audiences exercise very fine discrimination in their choice of styles, as well as their evaluation of individual artists and performances (Frith, 1991). Any conversation with music fans turns on acts of discrimination: who is the best drummer in a particular style, which of such-and-such an artist's records is the best, etc. Even the much-maligned Music Chart is not only a commercial device to guide producers and retailers in their marketing strategies: it is also (despite some manipulation by commercial interests) the trace of myriad individual acts of taste and discrimination. It is well known that commercial attempts to manipulate 'mass taste', or cash in on known features of it, regularly fail (Fiske, 1991). That the same is true of television audiences can easily be established through introspection, and is also revealed in the (admittedly crude) appreciation index which forms part of all modern commercial audience research. Moreover, until relatively recently, the distinct separation between canonical and non-canonical works was far from firmly established. For instance, nineteenth-century concert programmes commonly mixed works of what we would regard as 'canonical' music with the 'lightest' of popular song-writing. Museums commonly mixed what we would now think of as 'serious' art with elements of circus entertainment – Romantic painting alongside bearded ladies and mutant animals. Theatres played Shakespeare alongside gymnasts and contortionists – until the 1880s American theatres regularly featured Shakespearian clowns, who recited the bards' lines in full clowns' regalia (Frith, 1991; di Maggio, 1986: 195). This 'generic promiscuity', far from suggesting lack of aesthetic discrimination, implies that it was exercised within a cultural framework where it roamed over a much wider body of work than subsequently.

But if all aesthetic response is in a sense an act of discrimination, perhaps not all such discriminations result in a hierarchy of works. In a sense, of course, any act of discrimination involves erecting a hierarchy: 'this is what I like, therefore it is better than that, which I don't like'. When a large number of people agree on a discrimination, popular success is the result, and at least for some time there is a stable hierarchy within the art-form in question, reflected in star incomes, star treatment by the media (celebrity interviews etc.), ready availability of the works in question through distribution systems, sympathetic – even sycophantic – reviews and a regular output of new but usually similar works; these interact to reinforce the already existing discrimination, playing the role of relays and incitements within the circuit of meaning-assignation and value judgment. Any hierarchy of discrimination which is to remain stable must have some institutional base: here it is the mass media. Any discrimination which does have an institutional base can also serve as a token of social inclusion and exclusion, where groups grant or refuse admission on the grounds of shared taste; this is a well-documented phenomenon, but it is sometimes insufficiently stressed that shared taste necessarily involves shared discrimination, not only in the sense of excluding a certain range of artefacts as beyond the pale, because stylistically utterly different, but also in the sense of accepting that within the shared style there is a hierarchy of quality. However, social groups themselves are distinguished not only by their shared and differentiated tastes, but by their distribution in terms of power as well (at least in a stratified society), and this is crucial to the way in which different classes of discrimination occupy different places within the social structure. Simply and dogmatically put, the set of discriminations which have resulted in the canon of 'civilised culture' has an institutional base which is wider and more stable than the set of discriminations which are permanently at work within any culture, and may be readily seen at work in popular culture: the institutional base of the canon is the taste of the dominant class promoted by the State, especially in the form of the education system – hence the now protracted arguments in both the UK and the USA about the role of the literary canon in school and university syllabuses.[1] As we have seen in the case of humour and manners, the type of text or artefact which has become a candidate for the canon is also likely to have been approved as the taste of a particular social group, a group which over the years has acquired a close hold on the mechanisms of power (cf. Bourdieu, 1979).

What arguments are there in favour of this hierarchy of discriminations, in favour of the canon and the place that it currently occupies in our culture? Clearly, the nodal point in all such arguments is the assertion that canonical works objectively do have greater aesthetic value than the other works often dismissively categorised as 'kitsch'. In a nutshell, some discriminations are more discriminating than others, or so it is said. This argument always falls foul of the counter-argument that such works are often ineffective in communication, i.e. many people simply do not like them. In reply, defendants of the canon point out two things: first, that if people are educated to respond effectively to great art, they do like it; second, that greatness is a feature of the work independent of its actual reception.

One of the most sophisticated attempts to go beyond this impasse of argument and counter-argument is to be found in Striedter (1989), surveying the relationship between reception theory and aesthetic evaluation. It has to be recognised that a work of art is only ever potentially such until it is 'realised' in the act of reception. As Sartre said of literature, in this respect no different from the other arts:

> To summon it up, a real act is needed, that is called reading, and it only exists for as long as this reading lasts. Beyond that, there is nothing but black marks on paper. Now the writer cannot read what he writes. . . . While reading, you foresee, you wait. You foresee the end of the sentence, the next sentence. You wait for them to confirm or invalidate these predictions; reading consists of a host of hypotheses. . . . Readers are always ahead of the sentence they are reading, in an only probable future. . . . Now the operation of writing includes a quasi-reading that makes real reading impossible. As words form themselves under the pen, the author no doubt sees them, but he does not see them like the reader because he knows them before writing them. . . . The operation of writing implies that of reading as its dialectical correlative and these two connected actions demand two distinct agents. It is the combined effort of the author and the reader which will summon up this concrete and imaginary object. . . . There is no art except for and through others.
>
> (1948: 52–5)

Sartre deduces the necessity of a recipient of narrative from fundamental features of the act of writing. As Striedter shows, it is possible to combine the centrality of reception ('concretisation', as it is usually called in reception aesthetics) with the simultaneous assertion that objective aesthetic value exists. To this end he distinguishes three types of aesthetic value:

1 actual or immediate, realised in any given concretisation;
2 general or universal, i.e. the capacity that literary works have to receive multiple concretisations under different cultural conditions;
3 evolutionary, which refers to the form of innovation the work produces at the moment of its first appearance.

'Actual' aesthetic value is related to the non-aesthetic, functional values of the receiving community (this is in fact the condition of interpretability of the work), but it casts them in a new light because of the way in which the semiotic structure of art reorients the individual values (signifieds) in relation to each other; this gives an anthropological function to art, which is a permanent feature of the human world; the function is to promote awareness of our 'polyfunctionality' as opposed to our workaday 'mono-functionality'.

Thus the focus on the historical conditions of reception is insufficent. Its necessary complement is a theory of evaluation centred on the relationship between the aesthetic object and the receiver. On the one hand this leads to a theory of canonisation: works which are capable of multiple and discrepant concretisations tend to be canonised, whereas those which are entirely in accordance with the values of the initial receiving community are mere 'kitsch' (1989: 193–205, 241). Alternatively, it can be argued that works which reorganise our 'horizon of expectations' about what constitutes valid art are most likely to be canonised (Jauss, quoted Wolff, 1983: 34–6). On the other hand we are led to recognise that all aesthetic objects perform an aesthetic function, which is part of the general process whereby we use values as part of the process of orienting action in everyday life: 'actual aesthetic value' consists of the capacity to 'actualise and challenge the receiver's perception and evaluation of reality through the perception and evaluation of the artifact as an aesthetic object' (Striedter, 1989: 239).

What is central from our point of view is that ultimately the defence of discrimination rests on a function that 'art' – as opposed to kitsch – is said to perform. Indeed, in general, canonical culture must always ultimately be defended in terms of some social function or other that it performs. No doubt this is a paradoxical assertion because it is well known that some of the best-known defences of discrimination are that no functional defence is needed; indeed, the most famous of all – in Kant's *Critique of Judgment* (1952) – defines aesthetic discrimination in terms of its radical separation from any such function, by its disinterest. We can unravel the paradox by reviewing the 'functionalist' defences, then the anti-functionalist tradition.

Throughout the nineteenth century there developed what has been called the 'sociological aesthetic', a body of thought which understood – and ultimately sought to justify – the arts by seeing a social function in, or for, them. For example for the Saint-Simonian tradition of social engineering the arts played the role of showing how planned change could make the world a better place; for the tradition stemming from Fourier and Proudhon, the basic human desire for beauty should be tied to the development of collective morality; for Comte, art cultivated the sense of perfection, which would feed into political programmes for planned change. For Ruskin, the appreciation of beauty was a moral force, and an environment which did not meet its demands was incompatible with decency in the population (Needham, 1926).

Aligned against this tradition were those thinkers who insisted that the search for and appreciation of beauty were inherent in humanity, and therefore did not need any social justification. However, for such thinkers – Lamennais or Carlyle, for example – the thirst for beauty was part of the wider process of self-perfection, understood in a fundamentally Christian manner. Put at is crudest, the eighteenth century conceived society as a good place provided all men strove for self-perfection, individually; in the nineteenth century, it came to be realised that this process of self-perfection needed an institutional base of some sort – the Church or the State, or some mixture of the two, which would create the conditions for 'cultivation', or culture (Williams, 1958: esp. 29–30, 76–7, 93; Needham, 1926: ch. 2). Thus even in thinkers apparently opposed to the notion of a social justification of art we find a move towards seeing a social function for it. Insofar as there were two traditions, they became thoroughly synthesised in the second half of the century; the best known version, no doubt, is in Matthew Arnold. Arnold's famous dictum to the effect that culture is the pursuit of all that is best continues with the emphasis on improvement: cultivation of the 'best-self' will produce social order, but only through the State: 'He who gave our nature to be perfected by our virtue willed also the necessary means of its perfection: He willed therefore the State' (quoted Williams, 1958: 129). Now it must be noted that such ideas do not invalidate the insistence, fundamental to aesthetic theory, that there are features of form which transcend history, social determination of every kind, relativistic judgment and the use of the arts for social purposes, for the nineteenth-century argument about culture presupposes that art has some features which make it suitable for the purposes to which it is to be put. Moreover, even if we could show that particular aesthetic judgments were largely motivated by some group interest or other – as Bourdieu claims to do – this would still not invalidate traditional canonical claims about the objectivity of beauty, it would only ascribe blame for their social abuse. As Wolff says 'exposing the genesis and ideological operation of traditional aesthetics does not in itself invalidate it' (1983: 37).

In short, the realm of the aesthetic can still be seen as a transcendental absolute while asserting (1) that art has some social function or other; (2) that self-perfection occurs in the form of the State; and (3) that such statements are a disguise for group self-interest. To pursue this argument any further we must reconsider the grounds of the absolutist claims made by aesthetics. We will follow Kant's version.

In the *Critique of Judgment* Kant is concerned to reconcile the observable fact that tastes differ considerably from individual to individual and from group to group, with his desire to demonstrate that universal standards of beauty do exist.[2] The mechanism by which this occurs also plays a role in Kant's philosophy of subjectivity in general, a question to which we shall return. Kant distinguishes between pleasure in 'the agreeable' and pleasure in beauty. The former is indeed sociologically and psychologically variable, and for Kant there is no reason why it should not be. Pleasure in beauty is distinguished from the agreeable by its internal structure. The agreeable gives pleasure because there is some concordance between the object and a need or a desire felt by the subject; that is to say, something about the nature of the object, as it is functionally apprehended by the perceiving subject, fits in with what we want out of it; the key to this fit is what we conceive the object to be, i.e. the concept which we have in our minds and which enables us to recognise the object as belonging to such-and-such a category of objects. Aesthetic pleasure, the recognition of beauty, however, functions in a fundamentally different manner. When we respond to an object in terms of its beauty we are responding to a dimension of its being which does not correspond to any concept we may have of the object or of its function in the world; the beauty of the object, in short, does not correspond to any desire we have for the object, as a functional entity, nor to any concept of the object we may have which would assign it to a category. If the object, for example, is a vase, its beauty is independent of its 'vase-ness' – i.e. the attributes that make it a vase – and of any function that vases in general might fulfil. What occurs when we respond to an object in this way, Kant argues, is that the various 'faculties' of the mind (as he calls them), in other words the different types of activity that the mind is capable of undertaking, are brought into an unexpected harmony with each other.[3] Specifically, he thinks that our mind apprehends the outside world through two distinct processes, imagination and understanding. By imagination he means approximately the body of perceptions, which he thinks is held together by concepts; that is to say, perception functions via recognition of objects, and this concordance is essential if the mind is to function. In aesthetic response, he thinks, the response to an object above and beyond any conceptually based recognition brings about an especially fruitful harmony of the imagination and the understanding, in such a way that they and the object itself become fused together in a single mental entity.

It is in the sense defined by this analysis that Kant refers to aesthetic delight as 'disinterested'. For him 'interest' is defined by the relationship between particular faculties of the mind and their objects in the outside world, especially the delight we take in the agreeable, deriving from desire for it. It is because it is disinterested in Kant's meaning of the term that aesthetic delight can lay claim to universality. This is because the mental process involved in making the judgment of beauty is a universal process in the sense that all human minds are constituted in the same way, and thus anyone can share in the delight aroused by the form of the object, whereas this is not true of pleasure taken in the agreeable because it is subject to all sorts of determinations that are psychologically and sociologically specific. We are justified in claiming that any judgment of the beauty of an object should be regarded as universally binding, says Kant, because such a judgment is exemplary: it exemplifies a 'universal rule incapable of formulation', and therefore must be assented to by all (Kant, quoted Crowther, 1989: 61). It must be assented to by all because it is an example of a universal rule, but also precisely because it is incapable of formulation, i.e. it cannot be reduced to any set of concepts; it is only manifest to us in the feeling of pleasure that it evokes. Although the process involved can be analysed – as Kant has done – it is not directly accessible to consciousness, and is only present to consciousness in the form of this pleasure.[4]

In short, for Kant there is a mental process unique to the judgment that an object is beautiful, and this uniqueness grounds the claim of its universality. Central to his argument is the independence of the pleasure of beauty from any conceptual determination, because this frees the judgment of taste from any contamination by culture in the sociological sense. Thus Kant's argument – taken at face value – is not affected by sociological criticisms to the effect that there is no such thing as a disinterested judgment: such criticisms miss the point because of the way in which Kant defines interest, and such is the defence of traditional aesthetics to be found in Kant, and frequently advanced. However, this argument does indeed depend upon taking Kant's argument at face value, and while the conclusion of an essay on humour and comedy is probably no place to go into detail, a brief indication of the problems involved will enable us to place what is at issue here and to round off our discussion of the relationship between comedy and humour.

In the recent past there has been a divergence between Anglo-Saxon readings of Kant's aesthetics and French deconstructionist readings. In the Anglo-Saxon version, Kant's aesthetic thought can be read in isolation from the rest of his philosophy, in the sense that although one clearly needs some reference to it to understand what Kant is saying, the adequacy or otherwise of Kant's argument here can be established fairly unproblematically by reference to the real-world object of his analysis, namely aesthetic pleasure in beauty; specifically, the distinction in Kant between an aesthetics of the beautiful and an aesthetics of the sublime is systematically downgraded in importance – in this reading the sublime is little more than a historical curio (Guyer and Cohen, 1982: 2, 4). In the French reading, on the other hand, the relationship between Kant's aesthetic theory and the rest of his philosophy is crucial, for they argue that Kant's aesthetics only make sense in relationship to his general theory of knowledge and the will; the category of the sublime is absolutely central, because Kant's aesthetics do not make sense unless you include this category (Derrida, 1978; Lyotard, 1991). At the heart of this debate is the nature of human subjectivity, and the role of the aesthetic in it. For the Anglo-Saxons, it seems as though the discussion of aesthetics can be pursued without any reference to this subject, whereas for the deconstructionists the analysis of the aesthetic reveals something essential about human subjectivity. Kant's analysis of disinterest implies a subjectivity which is detached from all empirical existence, because any such existence would inevitably contaminate aesthetic delight with interest (in Kant's sense of the term); in Derrida's words: 'it is an in- or an-existant subjectivity that rises up on the crypt[5] of the empirical subject and all its world'. This aesthetic pleasure thus has no empirical location, and therefore it casts a doubt over what kind of self it is that is experiencing the pleasure in question. It is an affect which is subjective, but is oriented entirely towards an outside, since it has no location. It is a pure 'auto-affection', i.e. a state of the soul which has a self, but which is also a pure 'hetero-affection', i.e. is entirely elsewhere:

> the structure of the auto-affection is such that it takes the form of a pure objectivity of which it *must* be said 'it *is* beautiful. ... *The totally-other*

makes me take the form of pure pleasure while depriving me of both concept and enjoyment.

(1978: 54–5; emphases in original)

Such an entity is a 'being-of-reason', i.e. an entity which can have no empirical existence, which exists only as an ideal construct. Examples of other such beings would be 'triangle' (since all existing triangles have features which distinguish them from the mathematical definition of a triangle), or 'proletariat' in the Marxist sense of the word, since all actual working classes are only partial exemplifications of this construct. But such idealities are nonetheless real in that they act as motives and yardsticks against which to judge actualities.

Where Kant's aesthetics are concerned, the deconstructionists' reading insists that the universality of beauty is never an actual empirical agreement of taste, but a version of an as yet unrealised – and perhaps unrealisable – community, the location of all those dimensions of human possibility that might occur and recognition of which implies that history has never run its course.

Such a conception of beauty is apparently a long way from the location of humour and comedy within culture. Yet there is a link. For Kant, as we have seen, the rule of taste cannot be formulated because it is only given to us in the form of pleasure. Similarly, according to Freud, we cannot know what we are laughing at because the pleasure derives its efficacy from the drives of the unconscious. We should remember that it was the analysis of the relationship between the pleasures of humour and the structure of narrative that turned us in the direction of the debate we have been following. No doubt there are many implications to be drawn from this parallel, of which one will suffice: the Chinese wall – or perhaps Berlin Wall – between canonical culture and popular pleasures may not be as leak-proof as is often thought. The other implications I shall return to in another book.

NOTES

INTRODUCTION

1 I regret not being familiar with John Morreall's *Taking Laughter Seriously* (1983) when I originally invented this phrase, as the title of a chapter in my *The Logic of the Absurd* (1987).

2 CLOWNS AND RELIGION

1 As recognised by the aristocratic Olivia in Shakespeare's *Twelfth Night*: 'There is no slander in an allowed fool' (Act I, Scene 5).
2 For an overview of current anthropological research on the subject, see Apte (1985: ch. 5); the geographical spread of this phenomenon is examined in Steward (1931). There is a brief, informal summary of this material in Towson (1976: ch. 1).
3 Early travellers' records of Amerindian civilisations are often quoted in anthropological literature; see, for example, Ray (1945: 92, 101). Apte comments briefly on possible motives for academic interest in these aspects of Amerindian ceremonial (1985: 152f.).
4 This is one of the most frequently reported aspects of Amerindian clowning: see Parsons and Beales (1934); Steward (1931); Towson (1976: ch. 1).
5 Apte (1985: ch. 5). Curiously, Apte pays no attention to the theoretical problem posed by the dividing line between the humorous and non-humorous activities of the clowns.
6 This account is based largely on the following sources: Bieber (1961); Cornford (1914); Nicoll (1931); James (1961); Easterling and Knox (1985: ch. 12); Guthrie (1950); Winkler and Zeitlin (1990); Henderson (1991); Giangrande (1963); Ghiron-Bistagne (1976).

3 MEDIEVAL COMEDY: FOOLS AND FOLLY

1 See Chambers (1909: vol. I, 386ff.); Doran (1858); Billington (1984: ch. 3); Swain (1932: ch. 4).
2 This paragraph is based on Billington (1984: ch. 2) and Swain (1932: chs 1–3).
3 Details of the Feast are extensively given in Chambers (1909: vol. I, ch. 13). It was also known as the Feast of Asses, the Feast of the Sub-Deacons and the Feast of the Staff, from one of the symbols used in it. It seems to have been more widespread and deeply rooted in France than in other European countries, but was

certainly widely practised elsewhere. It is also discussed in Petit de Julleville (1968), and is the subject of detailed monographs, notably Lucotte du Tilliot (1751).

4 The fullest description of the Mère Folle is in Lucotte du Tilliot (1751); see also Petit de Julleville (1968: chs 6 and 7) and Chambers (1909: ch. 16). On the *sociétés joyeuses* in general see Petit de Julleville (1968: chs 5–7); Swain (1931: ch. 5); Aubailly (1975: 54ff.).

4 FUNCTION AND FUNCTIONALISM

1 For a modern reflection on humour in broadly the same vein as the medieval Christian arguments, see Karassev (1990).

2 To make the point understandable, we might crudely contrast this situation with a society which placed most importance upon trust in customary tradition and religious faith, and where intelligence in the modern abstract form would not be centrally valued; here we would not expect jokes about stupidity to be a commonplace feature of culture. Davies is apparently following Max Weber's thesis about modernity, where it is understood on the basis of a contrast with 'traditional' society: here modernity is based in goal-defined rationality and bureaucracy, whereas traditional society is defined by acceptance of charisma and magic.

5 GENDER AND HUMOUR

1 This model of humour – a surprising mixture of the implausible and the plausible – is discussed at greater length in my *The Logic of the Absurd* (1987) and below (Part III).

6 FREUD

1 References are to the *Standard Edition*, unless otherwise stated. Some reference to other works by Freud is necessary to understand his theory of jokes, but no attempt will be made to give any overall account of Freud's system.

2 We shall see in Part III that the 'mixture of sense and nonsense' is in fact the location of major contemporary theories of jokes and humour.

3 My discussion of thought as disguise is indebted to Weber (1982) and to Lyotard (1971: 239–70). There is an irony in Weber's mistranslation that both Freudians and deconstructionists should be the first to appreciate: Freudians because it is clearly a slip of the pen, with all the usual connotations of wishful thinking; deconstructionists because it has happened at such a central stage in the argument.

4 Thus, in semiotic terms, the signifier is producing an effect at the level of the signified; this would therefore be an example of the 'productivity of the signifier'.

5 We shall see in Part III that there is a historical dimension to this debate, since it is well known that verbal echoes of this variety had a higher epistemological status at earlier periods of European history, as they were held to indicate correspondences in the Great Chain of Being.

7 INCONGRUITY

1 Many writers have developed a model of humour using incongruity as the basis; readers must judge for themselves which are the most adequate. Well-known ones

are Koestler's theory of 'bisociation' (Koestler, 1964); Schaeffer (1981); Raskin (1985). Similar anaylses are to found in Mulkay (1988) and Freud (1960) where he speaks of jokes being a mixture of 'sense and nonsense'. In general, the difficulty most commonly found in such theories is that they are either under- or over-predictive: i.e. either they describe phenomena which intuitively are not funny (such as metaphor), as well as ones which are, and fail to distinguish between them, or else they exclude phenomena which intuition shows us are funny. See Suls (1983: 52–4) for a brief summary of some of these problems from a psychological perspective, Schaeffer (1981: 18–25) and Palmer (1987: 36–7, 60–74) for more extended discussions, especially of the relationship between jokes and metaphor.

2 See also my *The Logic of the Absurd* (1987: 52ff.) for further discussion of graffiti and similar phenomena.

9 HUMOUR AND NARRATIVE STRUCTURE

1 I have already discussed this at greater length in my *The Logic of the Absurd* (1987: 101ff.).

2 There is a fuller discussion of this example in my *The Logic of the Absurd* (1987: 107–11, and further examples at 116–33).

3 See below, Conclusion, for a more detailed summary. This topic clearly has a historical dimension, as Part I of this study has indicated; see below, Chapter 10, for some further discussion of developments during the Renaissance period.

4 Space does not allow a development of this idea, which is taken from Lyotard (1971).

5 For a discussion of character as a narratological concept, see Palmer (1991: 46–7, 61–2); Chatman (1978: 108–32); Martin (1986: 119–21).

6 See Kerbrat-Orecchioni (1980). In my *The Logic of the Absurd* (1987) I discussed two parallel scenes based on similar ironies – the 'Friends, Romans, countrymen' scene in *Julius Caesar*, and a scene in Racine's *Britannicus*. I attempted to show that purely semantic mechanisms in the two plays were capable of distinguishing between comic and tragic irony. I now think that this was an oversimplification, as the discussion here shows.

10 COMEDY, FARCE AND NEO-CLASSICISM

1 This distinction is not entirely satisfactory because it does not make allowances for a form such as TV sitcom, which is at least in part realistic, unlike farce in its traditional sense, but where everything is clearly subordinate to laughter pro-duction. Nonetheless, the distinction is adequate for the current argument.

12 COMPREHENSION AND HUMOUR

1 I regret not being familiar with the following article until this book was in proof stage: J. Fontanille, 'Le Cynisme: du sensible au risible', *Homoresques* 4, 1993, 9–26. Fontanille presents cynicism in Ancient Greek philosophy as the pro-gramme of an entire way of life, in which humour is an integral element of praxis, an 'operator' of effects which are part of the programme. Cynicism consists of the rejection of all values and the attempt to inculcate this rejection in others in the name of a radical realism (or nominalism) and individualism, where only the individual entity has any relaity, and all concepts and values would be illusory. This

involves a rejection of any demands by the collectivity, from which the cynic utterly excludes himself.

In this programme laughter has an integral role. Cynical laughter is the exact opposite of *bonhomie*, of collective good humour: it is always derision, a laughter of exclusion, including covering oneself with ridicule to further one's own exclusion. Its role is threefold. First, it is to desensitise the listener to his values by ridiculing them. Second, since all concepts and all values are rejected, rational argument is impossible, and jests, puns, ridicule, nonsense, etc., destabilise attempts at rationality (cf. Aristotle's comments on the rhetorical power of jokes: p. 94 above). Third, the constant preference for witty, destructive sallies rather than argument implies utter disregard for the sensitivities of others, thus marking and encouraging exclusion.

Clearly, the structure of humour has an elective affinity with such a programme for life. Better, one structure of humour, for cynical humour – as Fontanille analyses it – is characterised by certain features:

1 the aggressive assertion of superiority;
2 the careful choice of butts of humour as an act of aggression against the audience;
3 rejection of permission as a precondition of laughter.

Clearly humour can be constructed in this way and can deliver what the cynics wanted of it; but we still need to ask how it is that humour is capable of this: what features of the semiotic and pragmatic structure of humour make it capable? Nonetheless, what Fontanille's argument shows is that statements about humour's capacity to include and exclude should never, ultimately, be taken in isolation from the analysis of particular enunciative circumstances. In anticipation of later arguments, we should also note that cynical humour is to be carefully differentiated from sadistic humour – see pp. 170–3 below.

CONCLUSION

1 As a random example, the howl of outrage in the London *Evening Standard* (4.2.92) provoked by the discovery that in some English universities Shakespeare is no longer a compulsory author in English Literature degrees.
2 Here I am following Guyer (1982: 24–32).
3 Here I am following Crowther (1989: 44–60).
4 This formulation is designed to avoid taking sides in a controversy over the details of Kant's argument. It is controversial whether Kant says that the universality of the judgment of taste (i.e. of beauty) lies in the feelings inspired by the object alone, or in their communicability to others. For the two sides of this argument, see Guyer (1982), Crowther (1989: 61–4).
5 Derrida's word is *crypte*, which has the same two meanings in both French and English: as well as the architectural sense, here implying death, it also means a small secretory gland, implying that subjectivity 'secretes', i.e. locates, itself here; that is, the crypt is where subjectivity both sets itself up and fails to survive.

BIBLIOGRAPHY

Agee, J. (1963) 'Comedy's Greatest Era' in *Agee on Film*, vol. I, London: Peter Owen.

Ahl, F. (1988) 'Ars est Caelare Artem (Art in Puns and Anagrams Engraved)' in J. Culler (ed.) *On Puns*, Oxford: Basil Blackwell.

Apte, M.L. (1985) *Humor and Laughter, an Anthropological Approach*, Ithaca, NY: Cornell University Press.

Apter, M.J. (1982a) *The Experience of Motivation*, London: Academic Press.

Apter, M.J. (1982b) 'Metaphor as Synergy' in D.S. Miall (ed.) *Metaphor: Problems and Perspectives*, Brighton: Harvester.

Apter, M.J. (n.d.) 'Fawlty Towers: a Reversal Theory Analysis of a Popular Television Comedy Series', unpublished manuscript.

Apter, M.J. and Smith, J. (1977) 'The Theory of Humorous Reversals' in A.J. Chapman and H.C. Foot (eds) *It's a Funny Thing, Humour*, New York: Pergamon.

Aristotle (1973) *Rhétorique*, trans. M. Dufour and A. Wartelle, Paris: Les Belles Lettres.

Aubailly, J-C. (1975) *Le Théâtre médiéval profane et comique*, Paris: Larousse.

Austen, J. (1965) *Persuasion*, London: Penguin.

Bakhtin, M. (1970) *L'Oeuvre de François Rabelais*, Paris: Gallimard.

Banks, M. and Swift, A. (1987) *The Joke's on Us*, London: Pandora.

Barasch, F.K. (1971) *The Grotesque: A Study in Meanings*, The Hague: Mouton.

Barber, F. (1959) *Shakespeare's Festive Comedy*, Princeton, NJ: Princeton University Press.

Barley, N. (1983) *The Innocent Anthropologist*, London: Penguin.

Barley, N. (1987) Personal communication.

Baudin, H. (1990) 'Pour une axiomatique de l'Humour', *Cahiers de Recherche CORHUM* 1: 1–10.

Baudin, H. (1991) Personal communication.

Beare, W. (1955) *The Roman Stage*, London: Methuen.

Bennett, G. (ed.) (1991) *Spoken in Jest*, Sheffield: Academic Press.

Bennett, T. (1979) *Formalism and Marxism*, London: Methuen.

Bertrand, D. (1991) 'Dire le Rire à l'age classique: le travail de l'histoire', *Cahiers de Recherche CORHUM* 2: 69–85.

Bieber, M. (1961) *The History of the Greek and Roman Theater*, Princeton, NJ: Princeton University Press.

Billington, S. (1979) '"Suffer Fools Gladly": The Fool in Medieval England and the Play *Mankind*' in P.V.A. Williams (ed.) *The Fool and the Trickster*, London: Brewer.

Billington, S. (1984) *The Social History of the Fool*, Brighton: Harvester.

Bouhours (1687) *La Manière de bien penser dans les ouvrages d'esprit*, Paris: Mabre-Cramoisy.

Bourdieu, P. (1979) *La Distinction*, Paris: Editions de Minuit.

Bradney, P. (1957) 'The Joking Relationship in Industry', *Human Relations* 10: 179–87.

Brant, C.S. (1948) 'On Joking Relationships', *American Anthropologist* 50: 160–2.

Burke, P. (1978) *Popular Culture in Early Modern Europe*, New York: Harper.

Cantor, J. (1976) 'What is Funny to Whom?', *Journal of Communication* 26: 164–72.

Carrington Lancaster, H. (1929) *French Dramatic Literature in the Seventeenth Century*, Baltimore, MD: Johns Hopkins University Press.

Castell, P.J. and Goldstein, J.H. (1977) 'Social Occasions for Joking' in A.J. Chapman and H.C. Foot (eds) *It's a Funny Thing, Humour*, New York: Pergamon.

Castellani, V. (1988) 'Plautus Versus *Komoidia*: Popular Farce at Rome', *Themes in Drama 10: Farce*, Cambridge: Cambridge University Press, 53–82.

Castiglione, B. (1967) *The Book of the Courtier*, London: Penguin.

Chambers, E.K. (1909) *The Medieval Stage*, 2 vols, Oxford: Clarendon.

Chanfrault, B. (1990) 'Les stéréotypes de la France Profonde dans l'Almanach Vermot', *Cahiers de Recherche CORHUM* 1: 11–24.

Chapelain, J. (1936) *Opuscules critiques*, ed. A. Hunter, Paris: Droz.

Chapman, A.J. and Foot, H.C. (eds) (1977) *It's a Funny Thing, Humour*, New York: Pergamon.

Chapman, A.J. and Gadfield, N.J. (1976) 'Is Sexual Humor Sexist?', *Journal of Communication* 26: 141–53.

Charles, L.H. (1945) 'The Clown's Function', *Journal of American Folklore* 58: 25–34.

Chatman, S. (1978) *Story and Discourse*, Ithaca, NY: Cornell University Press.

Christensen, J.B. (1963) 'Utani: Joking, Sexual License and Social Obligations among the Luguru', *American Anthropologist* 65: 1314–27.

Cohen, J. (1970) 'Théorie de la figure', *Communications* 16: 3–25.

Cohen, T. (1979) 'Metaphor and the Cultivation of Intimacy' in S. Sacks (ed.) *On Metaphor*, Chicago: University of Chicago Press.

Cook, J. (ed.) (1982) *Sitcom Dossier*, London: British Film Institute.

Cornford, F.M. (1914) *The Origins of Attic Comedy*, London: Edward Arnold.

Coser, R.L. (1959) 'Some Social Functions of Laughter', *Human Relations* 12: 171–81.

Coser, R.L. (1960) 'Laughter among Colleagues', *Psychiatry* 23: 81–95.

Crowther, P. (1989) *The Kantian Sublime*, Oxford: Oxford Unversity Press.

Culler, J. (ed) (1988) *On Puns*, Oxford: Basil Blackwell.

Cunningham, K. and Lorenzo, A. (1991) '"He Just Fell Over and Died!", Navajo Humour, Navajo Hozho' in G. Bennett (ed.) *Spoken in Jest*, Sheffield: Academic Press.

Davies, C. (1982) 'Ethnic Jokes, Moral Values and Social Boundaries', *British Journal of Sociology* 33: 383–403.

Derrida, J. (1978) *La Vérité en peinture*, Paris: Flammarion.

Dickens, C. (1968) *Martin Chuzzlewit*, London: Penguin.

Dickens, C. (1973) *Barnaby Rudge*, London: Penguin.

di Maggio, P. (1986) 'Cultural Entrepreneurship in Nineteenth-Century Boston' in R. Collins *et al.* (eds) *Media, Culture and Society: A Critical Reader*, London: Sage.

Dobrov, G. (1988) 'The Dawn of Farce: Aristophanes' in *Themes in Drama 10: Farce*, Cambridge: Cambridge University Press, 15–33.

Doran, J. (1858) *History of Court Fools*, London: Eyre Methuen.

Dotoli, G. (1987) *Littérature et société en France au XVIIe siècle*, Bari-Paris: Schena-Nizet.

Douglas, M. (1968) 'The Social Control of Cognition: Some Factors in Joke Recognition', *Man* (new series) 3: 361–76.

Duckworth, G.E. (1952) *The Nature of Roman Comedy*, Princeton, NJ: Princeton University Press.

Easterling, P.E. and Knox, B.M.W. (eds) (1985) *Cambridge History of Classical Literature*, vol. 1, *Greek Literature*, Cambridge: Cambridge University Press.

Eaton, M. (1981) 'Laughter in the Dark', *Screen* 22: 21–8.

Eggan, F. (ed.) (1937) *The Social Anthropology of the North American Tribes*, Chicago: University of Chicago Press.

Ekmann, B. (1981) 'Wieso und zu welchem Ende wir lachen', *Text und Kontext* 9: 7–46.

Elias, N. (1978) *The Civilising Process*, vol.1, *History of Manners*, Oxford: Blackwell.

Ellis, A. (1956) *The Penny Universities*, London: Secker and Warburg.

Ellis, J. (1975) 'Made in Ealing', *Screen* 16: 78–127.

Emerson, J.P. (1969) 'Negotiating the Serious Import of Humor', *Sociometry* 32: 169–81.

Esmein, B. (1991) Personal Communication.

Evans, I. (1976) *A Short History of English Literature*, London: Penguin.

Faivre, B. (1988) 'La Piété et la Fête' and 'La Profession de Comédie' in J. de Jomoron (ed.) *Le Théâtre en France, I. Du Moyen Age â 1789*, Paris: Colin.

Fine, G.A. (1976) 'Obscene Joking across Cultures', *Journal of Communication* 26: 134–40.

Fine, G.A. (1983) 'Sociological Approaches to the Study of Humor' in P. McGhee and J.H. Goldstein (eds) *Handbook of Humor Research*, vol. I, *Basic Issues*, New York: Springer Verlag, 159–81.

Fiske, J. (1991) 'Popular Discrimination' in J. Naremore and P. Brantlinger (eds) *Modernity and Mass Culture*, Bloomington, IN: Indiana University Press.

Foucault, M. (1961) *Histoire de la folie à l'âge classique*, Paris: Union Générale d'Editions, 10/18.

Foucault, M. (1966) *Les Mots et les choses*, Paris: Gallimard.

Foucault, M. (1970) *The Order of Things*, London: Tavistock.

France, P. (1972) *Rhetoric and Truth in France: Descartes to Diderot*, Oxford: Oxford University Press.

France, P. (1992) *Politeness and its Discontents*, Cambridge: Cambridge University Press.

Freud, S. (1925) *Der Witz und seine Beziehung zum Unbewussten* in *Gesammelte Schriften* 9, 1–269, Leipzig/Vienna/Zurich: Internationaler Psychoanalytischer Verlag.

Freud, S. (1928) 'Humour', *Imago* 14; trans. J Strachey, *Standard Edition of the Complete Psychological Works of Sigmund Freud*, vol. 20, London: Hogarth Press.

Freud, S. (1930) *Le Mot d'esprit et ses rapports avec l'inconscient*, trans. M. Bonaparte and M. Nathan, Paris: Gallimard.

Freud, S. (1940) *Der Witz und seine Beziehung zum Unbewussten* in *Gesammelte Werke* 6, 1–285, London: Imago Publishing Co.

Freud, S. (1953) *The Interpretation of Dreams* in *Standard Edition of the Complete Psychological Works of Sigmund Freud*, vols 4–5, London: Hogarth Press.

Freud, S. (1958) *Der Witz und seine Beziehung zum Unbewussten*, Frankfurt am Main: Fischer.

Freud, S. (1960) *Jokes and their Relation to the Unconscious* in *Standard Edition of the Complete Psychological Works of Sigmund Freud*, vol. 8, London: Hogarth Press.

Freud, S. (1976) *Jokes and their Relation to the Unconscious*, London: Pelican.

Friedrich, R. (1983) 'Drama and Ritual' in *Themes in Drama 5: Drama and Ritual*, Cambridge: Cambridge University Press, 159–223.

Frith, S. (1991) 'The Good, the Bad and the Indifferent: Defending Popular Culture from the Populists', paper presented to the Danish Association for Mass Communication Research, November 1991.

Gadfield, N.J. (1977) 'Sex Differences in Humour Appreciation: a Question of Conformity?' in A.J. Chapman and H.C. Foot (eds) *It's a Funny Thing, Humour*, New York: Pergamon.

Genette, G. (1986) *Théorie des genres*, Paris: Editions du Seuil.

Ghiron-Bistagne, L. (1976) *Recherches sur les acteurs dans la Grèce antique*, Paris: Société d'Edition 'Les Belles Lettres'.

Giangrande, G. (1963) 'The Origin of Attic Comedy', *Eranos* 61: 1–24.

Glob, P.V. (1971) *The Bog People*, London: Paladin.

Goldhill, S. (1990) 'The Great Dionysia and Civic Ideology' in J.J. Winkler and F.I. Zeitlin (eds) *Nothing to Do With Dionysos?*, Princeton, NJ: Princeton University Press.

Goldstein, J.H. and McGhee, P.M. (eds) (1972) *The Psychology of Humor*, New York: Academic Press.

Goldstein, J.H. and McGhee, P.M. (eds) (1983) *Handbook of Humor Research*, vol. 1, New York: Springer.

Grant, M. (1964) *Roman Literature*, London: Penguin.

Groethuysen, B. (1927) *Origines de l'esprit bourgeois en France*, Paris: Gallimard.

Grote, D. (1983) *The End of Comedy*, Hamden, CT: Shoestring Press.

Gurewitch, M. (1975) *Comedy: the Irrational Vision*, Ithaca, NY: Cornell University Press.

Guthrie, W.K.C. (1950) *The Greeks and their Gods*, London: Methuen.

Guyer, P. (1982) 'Pleasure and Society in Kant's theory of Taste' in P. Guyer and T. Cohen (eds) *Essays in Kant's Aesthetics*, Chicago: University of Chicago Press.

Guyer, P. and Cohen, T. (1982) 'Introduction' in P. Guyer and T. Cohen (eds) *Essays in Kant's Aesthetics*, Chicago: University of Chicago Press.

Hammond, P.B. (1964) 'Mossi Joking', *Ethnology* 3: 259–67.

Handelman, D. and Kapferer, B. (1972) 'Forms of Joking Activity: A Comparative Approach', *American Anthropologist* 74: 484–517.

Henderson, J. (1990) 'The Demos and the Comic Competition' in J.J. Winkler and F.I. Zeitlin (eds) *Nothing to Do With Dionysos?*, Princeton, NJ: Princeton University Press.

Henderson, J. (1991) *The Maculate Muse: Obscene Language in Attic Comedy*, New Haven, CT: Yale University Press.

Hobbes, T. (1651) *Leviathan* (1968 edn) London: Penguin.

Hobbes, T. (1860a) 'Letter to Davenant' in *Works in English*, ed. W. Molesworth, vol. 4, London: Bohn.

Hobbes, T. (1860b) 'Human Nature' in *Works in English*, ed. W. Molesworth, vol. 4, London: Bohn.

Horowitz, J. and Menache, S. (1992) 'Le rire au quotidien dans la société médiévale au miroir de la prédication', paper given at the Tenth International Conference on Humour, Paris, University of Paris VIII, July 1992.

Howell, W.S. (1961) *Logic and Rhetoric in England, 1500–1700*, New York: Russell and Russell.

Huyssen, A. (1988) *After the Great Divide*, London: Macmillan.

Ignatieff, M. (1991) *The Observer*, 1.12.91 and 8.12.91.

James, E.O. (1961) *Seasonal Feasts and Festivals*, London: Thames and Hudson.

Jefferson, G. (1979) 'A Technique for Inviting Laughter and its Subsequent Acceptance Declination' in G. Psathas (ed.) *Everyday Language*, Boston, MA: Irvington Publishers Inc.

Johnson, S. (1905) 'Life of Cowley' in *Lives of the Poets*, ed. G.B. Hill, vol. I (3rd edn), Oxford: Clarendon Press.

Jomaron, J. de (ed.) (1988) *Le Théâtre en France, I. Du Moyen Age à 1789*, Paris: Colin.

Jones, M. (1991) 'Marcolf the Trickster' in G. Bennett (ed.) *Spoken in Jest*, Sheffield: Academic Press.

Jones, R.F. (1953) *The Triumph of the English Language*, Stanford, CA: University of California Press.

Kant, I. (1952) *The Critique of Judgment*, Oxford: Oxford University Press.

Karassev, L. (1990) 'L'antithèse du rire', paper presented at the International Conference on Humour, Marie Curie Sklodowska University, Lublin, October 1990.

Kayser, W. (1963) *The Grotesque in Art and Literature*, trans. U. Weisstein, Bloomington, IN: Indiana University Press.

Kennedy, J.G. (1970) 'Bonds of Laughter among the Tarahumara Indians: Toward the Rethinking of Joking Relationship Theory' in W. Goldschmidt and H. Hoijer (eds) *The Social Anthropology of Latin America*, Los Angeles: Latin American Studies Center, University of California.

Kenney, E.J. and Clausen, W.V. (eds) (1982) *Cambridge History of Classical Literature*, vol. 2, *Roman Literature*, Cambridge: Cambridge University Press.

Kerbrat-Orecchioni, C. (1980) 'L'ironie comme trope', *Poétique* 11: 108–27.

Kerenyi, K. (1962) *Religion of the Greeks and Romans*, London: Thames and Hudson.

King, P.M. (1987) 'Spatial Semantics and the Medieval Theatre' in *Themes in Drama 9: Theatrical Space*, Cambridge: Cambridge University Press, 45–58.

Knight, G. (ed.) (1990) *Honourable Insults: A Century of Political Invective*, London: Robson Books.

Koestler, A. (1964) *The Act of Creation*, New York.

Konigson, E. (1979) 'Drama in France at the End of the Middle Ages' in *Themes in Drama 1*, Cambridge: Cambridge University Press, 23–36.

Labouret, H. (1929) 'La Parenté à plaisanteries en Afrique Occidentale', *Africa* 2: 244–54.

La Fave, L. (1972) 'Humor Judgments as a Function of Reference Groups and Identification Classes' in J.H. Goldstein and P.M. McGhee (eds) *The Psychology of Humor*, New York: Academic Press.

Lagrave, H. (1988) 'Privilèges et Libertés' in J. de Jomoron (ed.) *Le Théâtre en France, I. Du Moyen Age à 1789*, Paris: Colin.

Langer, S. (1953) *Feeling and Form*, London: Routledge.

Legman, G. (1968) *Rationale of the Dirty Joke*, New York: Grove Press.

Le Goff, J. (1989) 'Rire au Moyen Age', *Cahiers du Centre de Recherches Historiques*, EHESS, April 1989, 1–14.

Levine, J. (1961) 'Regression in Primitive Clowning', *Psychoanalytic Quarterly* 30: 72–83.

Levine, J. (1976) 'The Feminine Routine', *Journal of Communication* 26: 173–5.

Levine, J. and Abelson, R. (1959) 'Humor as a Disturbing Stimulus', *The Journal of General Psychology* 60: 191–200.

Longo, O. (1990) 'The Theater of the *Polis*' in J.J. Winkler and F.I. Zeitlin (eds) *Nothing to Do With Dionysos?*, Princeton, NJ: Princeton University Press.

Lucotte du Tilliot (1751) *Memoire pour servir à l'histoire de la Fête des Fous*, Lausanne and Geneva.

Lyotard, J-F. (1971) *Discours Figure*, Paris: Klincksieck.

Lyotard, J-F. (1991) *Leçons sur l'analytique du sublime de Kant*, Paris: Editions Galilée.

Magendie, M. (1925) *La Politesse Mondaine*, Paris: Alcan.

Makarius, L. (1970) 'Ritual Clowns and Symbolic Behaviour', *Diogenes* 69: 44–58.

Malcolmson, R.W. (1973) *Popular Recreations in English Society 1700–1850*, Cambridge: Cambridge University Press.

Mandrou, R. (1964) *De la culture populaire au 17e et 18e siècles*, Paris: Stock.

Martin, W. (1986) *Recent Theories of Narrative*, Ithaca, NY: Cornell University Press.

Miller, F.C. (1967) 'Humor in a Chippewa Tribal Council', *Ethnology* 6: 263–71.

Miller, J. (n.d.a) *Thinking Aloud*, Channel 4 UK TV discussion programme chaired by Michael Ignatieff.

Miller, J. (n.d.b) televised lecture on humour.

Molière (1934) *Les Précieuses ridicules* and *Tartuffe* in *Oeuvres Complètes*, Paris: Garnier.

Moriarty, M. (1988) *Taste and Ideology in Seventeenth-Century France*, Cambridge: Cambridge University Press.

Mornet, D. (1929) *Histoire de la Clarté Française*, Paris: Payot.

Morreall, J. (1983) *Taking Laughter Seriously*, New York: SUNY Press.

Mulkay, M. (1988) *On Humour*, Cambridge: Polity Press.

Needham, J. (1926) *Le Développement de l'esthétique sociologique*, Paris: Champion.

Nicoll, A. (1931) *Masks, Mimes and Miracles*, London: Harrap.

Obrdlik, A.J. (1941) 'Gallows Humour', *American Sociological Review* 47: 709–13.

Orwell, G. (1961) 'The Art of Donald MacGill' in *Collected Essays*, London: Heinemann.

Palmer, J.N.J. (1971) *Form and Meaning in the Early French Classical Theatre*, PhD thesis, University of Southampton.

Palmer, J.N.J. (1981) 'Merit and Destiny: Ideology and Narrative in French Classicism', in F. Barker *et al.* (eds) *1642: Literature and Power in the Seventeenth Century*, Colchester: Essex University Press.

Palmer, J.N.J. (1987) *The Logic of the Absurd: On Film and Television Comedy*, London: British Film Institute.

Palmer, J.N.J. (1991) *Potboilers: Methods, Concepts and Case Studies in Popular Fiction*, London: Routledge.

Parsons, E.C. and Beales, R.L. (1934) 'The Sacred Clowns of the Pueblo and Mayo-Yaqui Indians', *American Anthropologist* 36: 491–514.

Paulme, D. (1939) 'Parenté à plaisanteries et alliance par le sang en Afrique Occidentale', *Africa* 12: 433–44.

Pedler, F. (1940) 'Joking Relationships in East Africa', *Africa* 13: 170–3.

Pepys, S. (1919) *The Diary*, vol. 4, London: Bell.

Petit de Julleville, L. (1968) *Les Comédiens en France au Moyen Age*, Geneva: Slatkine Reprints; original edn 1885, Paris: Librairie Cerf.

Pooley, R. (1981) 'Anglicans, Puritans and Plain Style' in F. Barker *et al.* (eds) *1642: Literature and Power in the Seventeenth Century*, Colchester: Essex University Press.

Pope, A. (n.d.) *Works*, London: Warne.

Powell, C. (1983) Paper delivered at the British Sociological Association Working Group on Humour, Bradford, April 1983.

Rabelais, F. (1955) *Gargantua and Pantagruel*, London: Penguin.

Radcliffe-Brown, J. (1952) 'On Joking Relationships' and 'A Further Note on Joking Relationships' in *Structure and Function in Primitive Society*, London: Cohen and West.

Radin, P. (1976) *The Trickster*, New York: Schocken Books.

Raskin, V. (1985) *Semantic Mechanisms of Humor*, New York: Reidel/Kluwer.

Ray, V.F. (1945) 'The Contrary Behaviour Pattern in American Indian Ceremonialism', *South-Western Journal of Anthropology* 1: 75–113.

Reich, A. (1949) 'The Structure of the Grotesque-Comic Sublimation', *Bulletin of the Menninger Clinic* 13: 160–71.

Richards, T. and Aldgate, T. (1983) *The Best of British*, Oxford: Blackwell.

Ricoeur, P. (1979) 'The Metaphorical Process as Cognition, Imagination and Feeling' in S. Sacks (ed.) *On Metaphor*, Chicago: University of Chicago Press.

Rigby, C. (1968) 'Joking Relationships, Kin Categories and Clanship among the Gogo', *Africa* 38: 133–55.

Roth, P. (1973) *The Breast*, London: Cape.

Rothbart, M.K. (1977) 'Psychological Approaches to the Study of Humour' in A.J. Chapman and H.C. Foot (eds) *It's a Funny Thing, Humour*, New York: Pergamon.

Russell, W.M.S. (1991) '"A Funny Thing Happened ...": Humour in Greek and Roman Life, Literature and the Theatre' in G. Bennett (ed.) *Spoken in Jest*, Sheffield: Academic Press.

Sartre, J-P. (1948) *Qu'est-ce que la littérature?*, Paris: Gallimard.

Schaeffer, J-M. (1989) *Qu'est-ce qu'un genre littéraire?*, Paris: Editions du Seuil.

Schaeffer, N. (1981) *The Art of Laughter*, New York: Columbia University Press.

Sharman, A. (1969) 'Joking in Padhola', *Man* (new series) 4: 103–17.

Skvorecky, J. (1986) *The Engineer of Human Souls*, London: Picador.

Slater, N.W. (1987) 'Transformations of Space in New Comedy' in *Themes in Drama 9: Theatrical Space*, Cambridge: Cambridge University Press, 1–11.

Solis, C.V. (1992) 'On Situational Humor', paper given at the Tenth International Conference on Humour, Paris, University of Paris VIII, July 1992.

Spingarn, J.E. (ed.) (1908) *Critical Essays of the Seventeenth Century*, vol. 1, Oxford: Oxford University Press.

Sprat, T. (1667) *A History of the Royal Society*, ed. J.I. Cope and H. W. Jones, St Louis, MO: Washington University Press (repr. 1958).

Stallybrass, P. and White, A. (1986) *The Politics and Poetics of Transgression*, London: Methuen.

Steig, M. (1970) 'Defining the Grotesque: an Attempt at Synthesis', *Journal of Aesthetics and Art Criticism* 29: 253–60.

Steward, J. (1931) 'The Ceremonial Buffoon of the American Indian', *Papers of the Michigan Academy of Sciences, Arts and Letters* 14: 187–207.

Stora-Sandor, J. (1992) 'Humour et Crise d'Identité', *Humoresques* 4.

Striedter, J. (1989) *Literary Structure, Evolution and Value*, Cambridge, MA: Harvard University Press.

Styron, W. (1979) *Sophie's Choice*, London: Picador.

Suls, J. (1983) 'Cognitive Processes in Humor Appreciation' in P.E. McGhee and J.H. Goldstein (eds) *Handbook of Humor Research*, vol. I, Basic Issues, New York: Springer Verlag.

Swain, B. (1932) *Fools and Folly During the Middle Ages and Renaissance*, New York: Columbia University Press.

Sykes, A.J.M. (1966) 'The Joking Relationship in an Industrial Setting', *American Anthropologist* 68: 188–93.

Terry, R.L. and Estel, S.L. (1974) 'Exploration of Individual Differences in Preferences for Humor', *Psychological Reports* 3: 1031–7.

Thomas, K.V. (1977) 'The Place of Laughter in Tudor and Stuart England', *Times Literary Supplement* 3906: 77 (21.1.77).

Todorov, T. (1970) *Introduction à la littérature fantastique*, Paris: Editions du Seuil.

Todorov, T. (1976) 'La Rhétorique de Freud' and 'Freud sur L'enonciation' in *Théories du symbole*, Paris: Editions du Seuil.

Towson, R. (1976) *Clowns*, New York: Hawthorn Books.

Weber, S. (1982) *The Legend of Freud*, Minneapolis: Minnesota University Press.

Welsford, E. (1935) *The Fool*, New York.

Wiley, W.L. (1960) *The Early Public Theatre in France*, Cambridge, MA: Harvard University Press.

Willey, B. (1962) *The Seventeenth-Century Background*, London: Penguin.

Williams, R. (1958) *Culture and Society*, London: Penguin.

BIBLIOGRAPHY

Williams, R. (1965) *The Long Revolution*, London: Penguin.

Wilson, C.P. (1979) *Jokes: Form, Content, Use and Function*, London: Academic Press.

Winkler, J.J. (1990) 'The Ephebes' Song: *Tragoidia* and *Polis*' in J.J. Winkler and F.I. Zeitlin (eds) *Nothing to Do With Dionysos?*, Princeton, NJ: Princeton University Press.

Winkler, J.J. and Zeitlin, F.I. (eds) (1990) *Nothing to Do With Dionysos?*, Princeton, NJ: Princeton University Press.

Wolff, J. (1983) *Aesthetics and the Sociology of Art*, London: Allen and Unwin.

Wrightson, K. (1981) 'Alehouses, Order and Reformation in Rural England, 1590–1660' in E. and S. Yeo, *Popular Culture and Class Conflict, 1590–1914*, Brighton: Harvester.

Zillman, D. (1983) 'Disparagement Humor' in P.E. McGhee and J.H. Goldstein (eds) *Handbook of Humor Research*, vol. I, *Basic Issues*, New York: Springer Verlag.

Zillman, D. and Stocking, S.H. (1976) 'Putdown Humor', *Journal of Communication* 26: 154–63.

Zijderveldt, A.C. (1968) 'Jokes and their Relationship to Reality', *Social Research* 35: 286–311.

Ziv, A. (1992) Paper delivered at the Tenth International Conference on Humour, Paris, University of Paris VIII, July 1992.

INDEX